Betty Ald

The first-born daughter of the Pilgrims

Jane G. Austin

Alpha Editions

This edition published in 2024

ISBN : 9789367246351

Design and Setting By
Alpha Editions
www.alphaedis.com
Email - info@alphaedis.com

As per information held with us this book is in Public Domain.
This book is a reproduction of an important historical work. Alpha Editions uses the best technology to reproduce historical work in the same manner it was first published to preserve its original nature. Any marks or number seen are left intentionally to preserve its true form.

Contents

PREFACE. ....- 1 -

CHAPTER I. ....- 4 -

CHAPTER II. ....- 10 -

CHAPTER III. ....- 14 -

CHAPTER IV. ....- 19 -

CHAPTER V. ....- 29 -

CHAPTER VI. ....- 40 -

CHAPTER VII. ....- 48 -

CHAPTER VIII. ....- 52 -

CHAPTER IX. ....- 65 -

CHAPTER X. ....- 72 -

CHAPTER XI. ....- 78 -

CHAPTER XII. ....- 84 -

CHAPTER XIII. ....- 89 -

CHAPTER XIV. ....- 94 -

CHAPTER XV ....- 100 -

- CHAPTER XVI. .... - 109 -
- CHAPTER XVII. .... - 117 -
- CHAPTER XVIII. .... - 124 -
- CHAPTER XIX. .... - 129 -
- CHAPTER XX. .... - 134 -
- CHAPTER XXI. .... - 142 -
- CHAPTER XXII. .... - 151 -
- CHAPTER XXIII. .... - 158 -
- CHAPTER XXIV. .... - 163 -
- CHAPTER XXV. .... - 171 -
- CHAPTER XXVI. .... - 181 -
- CHAPTER XXVII. .... - 187 -
- CHAPTER XXVIII. .... - 194 -
- CHAPTER XXIX. .... - 201 -
- CHAPTER XXX. .... - 208 -
- CHAPTER XXXI. .... - 216 -
- CHAPTER XXXII. .... - 224 -

CHAPTER XXXIII...- 233 -

CHAPTER XXXIV. ....- 243 -

CHAPTER XXXV...- 248 -

CHAPTER XXXVI. ....- 254 -

CHAPTER XXXVII. ....- 259 -

PREFACE.

Everybody has sympathized with Mr. Dick who could not keep King Charles's head out of his memorial, and I hope everybody will sympathize with me who have been unable to keep Betty Alden in this her memorial so constantly as I wished and she deserved. But as the whole includes the less, her story will be found threaded through that of her people and her times in that modest subordination to which the lives of her sex were trained in that day. He who would read for himself the story of this noble woman, the first-born daughter of the Pilgrims, must seek it through ancient volumes and mouldering records, until at Little Compton in Rhode Island he finds upon her gravestone the last affectionate and honorable mention of Elizabeth, daughter of John and Priscilla Alden, and wife of William Pabodie. Or in lighter mood, he may consider the rugged rhyme tradition places in her mouth upon the occasion of the birth of her great great grandchild:—

"Rise daughter! To thy daughter run!

Thy daughter's daughter hath a son."

One word upon a subject which has of late been a good deal discussed, but by no means settled, and that is, the burial place of Myles Standish. In the absence of all proof in any such matter, tradition becomes important, and so far as I have been able to determine, the tradition that some of the earliest settlers were buried in the vicinity of a temporary meeting-house upon Harden Hill in Duxbury is more reliable than the tradition that Standish was laid in an old burying ground at Hall's Corner which probably was not set aside as a burial place in 1656, the date of his death.

It is matter of surprise and regret to most persons that the Pilgrims took so little pains to perpetuate the memory of their graves, and their doing so would have been a wonderful aid to those who would read the palimpsest of the past. But a little recollection diminishes the wonder, if not the regret. Practically, the Pilgrims had neither the money wherewith to import gravestones, nor the skill to fashion and sculpture them; ethically, their lives were fashioned after an ideal, and that ideal was Protestantism in its most primitive intention, a protest against Rome, her creeds and her usages; prayers for the dead were to them a horrible superstition; Purgatory a mere invention of the powers of hell; an appeal to saints, angels, or the spirits of the departed was a direct insult to the Divine Supremacy. The instant the soul left the body Protestantism decreed that it was not only useless but profane to follow it with prayers (much less masses), or with any other remembrance which might be construed as intruding upon "the counsels of the Almighty," so that while private grief was sternly rebuked as rebellion against the chastisements of a just and offended God, every form of funeral service, domestic or congregational, was set aside as superstitious and dangerous.

The only exceptions to this rule were the volleys of musketry fired over the graves of certain of the leaders, as Carver, Standish, Bradford, and a few others, but these stern military honors were unaccompanied by even the prayer of a chaplain.

It was perhaps not altogether from fear of the Indians that the fifty of the Mayflower Pilgrims who were left alive that first spring smoothed the graves of the fifty who were gone, and planted them to corn; possibly they also feared their own hearts, sorely tempted by nature to cherish and adorn those barren graves where so much love and hope lay buried; and any step in that direction was a step backward from that "city" they had crossed the seas to seek in the wilderness.

It is I think certain that not one of the original Pilgrim graves was marked by any sort of monument. The few we now delight to honor were identified by those of their children to whom the third generation erected tablets. A few persons, of loving and unbigoted hearts, begged to be buried beside their departed friends, and Standish in his last will allowed a sunset gleam of his tender nature to shine out when he asked to be laid as near as conveniently might be to his two dear daughters; but neither he nor any of the others who made this testamentary petition mentioned where the graves were, beside which they fain would lie, nor in any one instance have they been positively identified. That of Elder Brewster, concerning whose burial we have many particulars, is altogether unknown, except that it seems to have been made upon Burying Hill. Perhaps that of Standish is there also, for when he says,—"If I die at Duxburrow I should like," etc., he may mean that if he dies in Duxbury he would fain be carried to Plymouth, there to lie beside his daughters and very likely his two little sons as well.

But to me it seems a small matter, this question of the grave of Standish. He lived to be old and very infirm, and neither his old age, his infirmities, nor his final surrender to death are any part of his memory. For me, he stands forever as he stood in his glorious prime among the people he so unselfishly championed, a tower of strength, courage, and endurance, the shining survival of chivalry, the gallant paladin whose coat-armor gleams amid the throng of russet jerkins and mantles of hodden gray, like the dash of color with which Turner accents his wastes of sombre water and sky. So let him stand, so let us look upon him, and honor him and glory in him, nor seek to draw the veil with which Time mercifully hides the only defeat our hero ever knew, that last fatal battle when age, and "dolorous pain," and fell disease, conquered the invincible, and restored to earth all that was mortal of a magnificent immortality. We cannot erect a monument over that forgotten grave, but in some coming day let us hope that the descendants of the soldier Pilgrim will possess themselves of the little peninsula where the site of his home may still be traced, and there place some memorial stone to tell that on this fairest spot of fair Duxbury's shore lived and died the man who gave Duxbury her name, and bequeathed to us an inheritance far richer than that which was "surreptitiously detained" from him.

BOSTON, *October, 1891.*

CHAPTER I.

A WHISPER IN THE EAR.

"Tell him yourself, Pris."

"No, no, Bab, I know too much for that! These men love not to be taught by a woman, although, if all were known, full many a whisper in the bedchamber comes out next day at the council board, and one grave master says to another, 'Now look you, tell it not to the women lest they blab it!' never mistrusting in his owl-head that a woman set the whole matter afloat."

"Oh, Pris, you do love to jibe at the men. How did you ever persuade yourself to marry one of them?"

"Why, so that one of them might be guided into some sort of discretion. Doesn't John Alden show as a bright example to his fellows?"

"And all through his wife's training, eh, Pris?"

"Why, surely. Didst doubt such a patent fact, Mistress Standish?"

"But now, Pris, in sober sadness tell me what has given you such dark suspicions of these new-comers, and how do you venture to whisper 'treason' and 'traitor' about a man who has been anointed God's messenger, even though it has been in the papistical Church of England?"

"If the English bishops are such servants of antichrist as the governor and the Elder make them out, I should conceive that their anointing would be rather against a man's character than a warrant for it." And Priscilla Alden laughed saucily into the thoughtful face of her friend and neighbor, Barbara Standish, who, knitting busily at a little lamb's-wool stocking, shook her head as she replied,—

"Mr. Lyford is not a man to my taste, and I care not to hear him preach, but yet, we are told in Holy Writ not to speak evil of dignitaries, nor to rail against those set over us"—

"Then surely it is contrary to Holy Writ for this Master Lyford to speak evil of the governor and to rail against the captain, as he doth continually"—

"Who rails against the captain, Mistress Alden?" demanded a cheerful voice, as Myles Standish entered at the open door of his house, and, removing the broad-leafed hat picturesquely pulled over his brow, revealed temples worn bare of the rust-colored locks still clustering thickly upon the rest of his head, and matching in color the close, pointed beard and the heavy brows, beneath which the resolute and piercing eyes his enemies learned to dread in early days now shone with a genial smile.

"Who has been abusing the captain?" repeated he, as the women laughed in some confusion, looking at each other for an answer. Priscilla was the first to find it, and glancing frankly into the face of the man she might once have loved replied,—

"Why, 'tis I that am trying to stir Barbara into showing you what a nest of adders we are nourishing here in Plymouth, and moving you and the governor to set your heels upon them before it be too late."

As she spoke, the merry gleam died out of the captain's eyes, and grasping his beard in the left hand, as was his wont in perplexity, he said gravely,—

"These are large matters for a woman's handling, Priscilla, and it may chance that Barbara's silence is the better part of your valor. But still,—what do you mean?"

"I mean that Master Oldhame and Master Lyford as the head, and their followers and creatures as the tail, are maturing into a very pretty monster here in our midst, which if let alone will some fine morning swallow the colony for its breakfast, and if only it would be content with the men I would say grace for it, but, unfortunately, the women and children are the tender bits, and will serve as a relish to the coarser meat."

"Come, now, Priscilla, a truce to your quips and jibes, and tell me what there is to tell. I cry you pardon for noting your forwardness in what concerned you not"—

"Nay, Myles, you've said it now," interposed Barbara, with a little laugh, while Priscilla, gathering her work in her apron, and looking very pretty with her flaming cheeks and sparkling eyes, jumped up saying,—

"At all events, John Alden's dinner concerns both him and me, and I will go and make it ready; a nod is as good as a wink to a blind horse, and a penny pipe as well as a trumpet to warn a deaf man that the enemy is upon him. Put your nose in the air, Captain Standish, and march stoutly on into the pitfall dug for your feet."

"Come, come, Mistress Alden! These are no words for a gentlewoman," began the captain angrily, but on the threshold Priscilla turned, a saucy laugh flashing through the anger of her face, and reminding the captain in his own despite of a sudden sunbeam glinting across dark Manomet in the midst of a thunder-storm.

"Here's the governor coming up the hill, Myles," whispered she, "and you may finish the rest of your scolding to him. I'm frighted as much as is safe for me a'ready."

And light as a bird she ran down the hill just as Bradford reached the door and, glancing in, said in his sonorous and benevolent voice, "Good-morrow to you, Mistress Standish. I am sorry to have frighted away your merry gossip, but I am seeking the goodman— Ah, there you are, Captain! I would have a word with you at your leisure."

"Shall I run after Priscilla, Myles?" asked Barbara, cordially returning the governor's greeting.

"Nay, wife, we two will walk up to the Fort," replied Standish, and replacing his hat, he led the way up the hill to the Fort, where he ushered his friend into a little room contrived in the southeastern angle for his private use: his office, his study, his den, or his growlery by turns, for here was his little stock of books, his writing-table and official records; here his pipes and tobacco; a stand of private arms crowned by Gideon; the colony's telescope fashioned by Galileo; and here a deep leathern chair with a bench nigh at hand, where through many a silent hour the captain sat, and amid the smoke-wreaths of his pipe mused upon things that had been, things that might have been, and things that never could be, never could have been.

"Have a stool by the porthole, Will; 'tis something warm for September," said he, as he closed the door.

"Ay, but you always have a good air at this east window, and a fair view as well," returned the governor, seating himself.

"The view of the Charity is but a fleeting one, since she sails in the morning," remarked Standish dryly.

"Yes, she does," assented Bradford, with an air of embarrassment not lost upon the captain, who smiled ever so little, and lighted his pipe, saying between the puffs,—

"'Tis safe enough to smoke in this den of mine, Will, and your tobacco is a wonderful counselor."

"Say you so, Myles? Then pass over your pouch, for I am in sore need of counsel and sought it of you."

"Such as I have is at your command, Governor. What is the matter?"

"Well, 'tis hard to put it in any dignified or magisterial phrase, Myles, since, truth to tell, it comes of the distaff side of the house"—

"Ay, ay, I can believe it! Has Priscilla Alden been whispering with your wife?"

"Nay, not that I know of; in truth, 'tis somewhat idler than even that foundation, for Mistress Alden is one of our own, but this—well, to tell the story in manful sincerity, my wife informs me that Dame Lyford, who is as you know in childbed, and much beholden for care and comfort to both your wife and mine, as well as to Priscilla Alden, last night fell a-crying, and said she was a miserable wretch to receive nourishment and tendance at their hands when her husband was practicing with Oldhame and others for our destruction. In the beginning, Alice set this all down as the querulous maundering of a sick woman; but when the other persisted, and spoke of treasonable letters that her husband had writ, and read out to Oldhame in her very presence, Dame Bradford began to pay some heed, and ask questions, until by the time the woman's strength was overborne and she could say no more, the skeleton of a plot lay bare, which should it be clothed upon with sinew, and flesh, and armor, and weapons, might slay us all both as a colony and as particular men."

"A dragon, Priscilla called it," interposed the captain.

"Priscilla! Did Mistress Lyford say as much to her as to my wife?" asked the governor, a little piqued.

"Nay, I know not, for I was, according to my wont, too outspoken to listen as I should."

"Well, but explain, I beg of you."

"All is, that Priscilla began some sort of warning anent this very matter, and I angered her with some jibe at women meddling in matters too mighty for them, so that I know not what she might have had to tell."

The Governor of Plymouth smiled in a subtle fashion peculiar to men whose vision extends beyond their own time. "Women," said he slowly, as he pressed the tobacco into his pipe,—"women, Myles, are like the bit of lighted tinder I will lay upon this inert mass of dried weed. The tinder is so trivial, so slight a thing, so difficult to handle, so easily destroyed,—and yet, brother man, how without it should we derive the solace and counsel of our pipes?"

Glancing at each other, the soldier and the statesman laughed somewhat shamefacedly, and Myles said,—

"Ay, 'tis the pith of Æsop's fable of the Lion and the Mouse."

"Well, yes, although that is a thought too arrogant, perhaps; and yet Master Lion is ofttimes a stupid fellow, though he is styled king of beasts."

"And what is the net just now, my Lord Lion?" demanded Standish, who could not quite relish Bradford's philosophy. The governor roused himself at the question, and laying aside his meditative mood replied,—

"We both know, Captain, that all who are with us are not of us, and we have not forgot what false reports those disaffected fellows carried home in the Anne, nor the mutterings and plottings we have heard and suspected since."

"Shorten John Oldhame by the head and you will kill the whole mutiny."

"That sounds very simple, but is hardly a feasible course, Captain, especially as we have no proof in the matter, and it is upon this very question of proof that I came to consult you."

"And I just shut off the only source of proof I am like to get."

"Nay, it is not likely that Mistress Alden knows more than my wife has already repeated to me of what Dame Lyford can reveal, but our good friend Master Pierce came to my house to-day about some matters I am sending to my wife's sister, Mary Carpenter, and all by chance mentioned that he had in trust a parcel of letters writ by Lyford, with one or two by Oldhame, and that both men had charged him to secrecy in the business. Now, Standish, those letters contain the moral of the whole matter."

"To be sure; it is like drawing a double tooth to see them sail out of the harbor."

"Captain, it is my duty as the chief officer of this colony to learn the contents of these missives."

"Yes, but how? The traitors will not betray themselves."

"I must privately open and read their letters,—it is my duty."

"No, no, Will; no, no! I can't give in to that; I can't help you there, man! To open and read another man's letter, and on the sly, is all one with hearkening at a keyhole, or telling a lie, or turning your back on an enemy without a blow. You can't do that, Will, let the cause be what it may."

And as the captain's astonished gaze fixed itself upon his friend's face, Bradford colored deeply, yet made reply in a voice both resolute and self-respecting,—

"I feel as you do, Standish, and as any honorable man must; but this is a matter involving more than mine own honor or pleasure. If these men are persuading our associates in England to withdraw from their agreement, and refuse to send us further supplies, or to find a market for our commodities, and so help out our own struggles for subsistence, we and all these weaklings dependent upon us are lost. You know yourself how hardly we came through the famine of last year, and although by the mercy of God we now may hope to provide our own food, what can we do for clothes, for tools, for even the means of communication with our old home, if the Adventurers throw us over, or if they demand immediate repayment of the moneys advanced? In every way, and for all sakes, it is imperative that we prevent an evil and false report going home to those upon whose help we still must rely for the planting of our colony."

"To be sure it is the usage of war to intercept the enemy's dispatches," mused Standish, tugging at his russet beard and scowling heavily.

"To be sure it is," returned Bradford eagerly. "And although these men are not avowed enemies, we can see that they are not friends. Do but mark how thick they are with Billington, and Hicks, and all the other malcontents. Oldhame's house is a regular Cave of Adullam."

"Well, Will, tell me what I am to do or to say in the matter. You know that I am ready for any duty, however odious."

"I fain would have you go aboard the Charity with me to inspect her carriages."

"Is there any chance of a fight?"

"No, no. I shall not go aboard until the last moment, when all but Winslow have left."

"Winslow's errand home is to see the Adventurers?"

"As the colony's agent, yes."

"And he knows your intent?"

"Not yet. I have spoken of it to no man until I had your mind upon it, Standish. To-night I shall summon the Assistants to my house, and lay the matter before them, but I felt moved to speak of it first to you in private."

"Lest I should blaze out before them all, where you could not argue the matter coolly with me, eh?"

Bradford smiled as he knocked the ashes out of his pipe and rose to go.

"I could not do with your disapproval, old friend," said he.

CHAPTER II

A SHARP PAIR OF SCISSORS.

Two men stood upon Cole's Hill, half sheltering themselves behind the ragged growth of scrub oaks and poplars sprung from those graves of the first winter, sown by the survivors to wheat lest the savages should perceive that half the company were dead. That pathetic crop of grain had perished on the ground and never been renewed; but Nature, tender mother, soon replaced it with a robe of her own symbolism, green as her favorite clothing ever is, and embroidered with the starry flowers of the succory, blue as heaven.

From the grave of John Carver and Katharine his wife had sprung a graceful clump of birches, and it was behind these that the two men finally took up their post of observation. One of them was John Lyford, a smooth and white faced man, whose semi-clerical garb only accented his cunning eyes and sensual mouth. A double renegade this, for, flying to the New World to escape the punishment of his sins in England, he proffered himself to the Pilgrims as a convert to their creed, renouncing with oaths and tears his Episcopal ordination, although assured by those liberal-minded men that such recantation was not required or desired; then, having joined the Church of the Separation entirely of his own free will, he turned viperwise upon the hand that fed him, and began plotting against the peace, nay the very life, of his generous hosts, and leading away those weak and disaffected souls to be found in every community.

John Oldhame, his companion, was a very different sort of person. Big, loud-voiced, and dogmatic, he was the sailor who would see the ship driven to destruction on the rocks unless he could be captain and give orders to every one else.

The motives of these two conspirators were as diverse as their antecedents, although both came out under the auspices of the London Adventurers, of whom a word must be said. These gentlemen, knowing a good deal less of New England than we do of the sources of the Nile, had *adventured* certain moneys in fitting out the Pilgrims, and in sustaining them until they should be able to repay the sums thus advanced "with interest thereto." When the Mayflower made her first return, leaving fifty of the Pilgrims in their graves and the other fifty just struggling back to life and feebly beginning their plantation and house building, the Adventurers were exceedingly wroth that she did not come freighted with lumber, furs, and especially salted fish enough to nearly pay for her voyage. Their bitter reproaches written to

Carver were answered with manly dignity by Bradford, but a really cordial feeling was never reëstablished, and when the Pilgrims requested that either Robinson or some other minister should be sent out to them, the Adventurers imposed Lyford upon them, some of them giving him secret instructions to act as a spy in their behalf.

John Oldhame, a man of means and position, came out upon a different footing, paying his own expenses, and being, as the Pilgrims phrased it, "on his own particular" instead of "on the general" or joint stock account. But events soon made it plain that a very good understanding existed between Oldhame and the Adventurers, and that if he should be enabled to detect his hosts in defrauding the Adventurers, whose greedy maws never were fully satisfied, they would transfer their protection and countenance to him, sustaining him as a rival or even supplanter of the interests of the men they had undertaken to befriend.

The Pilgrims had the faults of their virtues in very marked degree, and carried patience, meekness, long-suffering, and credulity to a point most irritating to their historians and very subversive of their worldly interests. Doubtless, however, they found their account in the final reckoning, and one must try to be patient with their goodness. All which means that if this growing treason in their midst was at all suspected it was not noticed, and both Oldhame and Lyford were admitted to the full privileges of townsmen, including a seat at the Council and full knowledge of the colony's concerns. Lyford, in virtue of the ordination, so scornfully abjured by himself, was requested to act as minister in association with Elder Brewster, although some quiet doubts still prevented his admission to the position of pastor.

With this necessary explanation of the position of affairs we return to the hiding-place behind the birches, whence the conspirators watched a boat manned by four sailors which lay uneasily tossing on the flood tide, rubbing its nose against the Rock, while, in the offing, a ship ready for sea lay awaiting it.

"Bradford is certainly going aboard the Charity. They're waiting for him, and there he comes down The Street," growled Oldhame at length.

"Perhaps only to see Winslow off. He, he! the Adventurers will show Master Envoy Winslow but a sour face when they've read our letters," sniggered Lyford.

"I wish he might be clapt up in jail for the rest of his life, confound him!"

"There's Standish along of Bradford! Think he's going aboard, too?" And Lyford's face showed such craven terror that Oldhame laughed aloud.

"Afraid of Captain Shrimp, as Tom Morton calls him?" demanded he. "I've put a spoke in *his* wheel, at any rate. You writ down what I advised about another commander, didn't you?"

"Ay. To send him over at all odds, and to arrest this fellow for high treason."

"Ah! He's not going aboard after all," ejaculated Oldhame venomously. "Feels he must stay ashore and watch you and me and Hicks and Billington and some of the rest. Set him up for a sneaking, prying little watch-dog! But let him undertake to order me about as he did t'other day, and I'll cram his square teeth down his bull's throat for him, damn him!"

"He, he, he! There's no love lost between you and Captain Standish, is there, Master Oldhame? There, they're off,—Winslow and Bradford only; and Captain Shrimp returns up the hill with the rest. I sore mistrust me the governor has got scent of those letters, Oldhame."

"Pho, pho, man! Don't be so timorous. Pierce won't give up the letters, and if he did, Bradford would think twice before opening them. Let him dare put a finger to one of mine, and I'll bring the whole house about his ears! I'd like to catch him at it. I'd—why, I'd give him a taste of my fists,—one for himself, and one to pass on to his neighbor, and after that"—

"M-o-o-o!" broke in a voice close behind, and, with a start, the conspirators faced round to meet "the great red cow," recently arrived in the Charity, and, with her, the comely but scoffing face of Priscilla Alden.

"I cry your pardon, gentlemen, if I have disturbed a secret conclave, but as my babes have a share of this cow's milk, I like her not to feed among the graves. All sorts of unclean creatures lurk here, and I fear lest the poor beast find contamination."

"A saucy wench, and one that would well grace the ducking-stool," growled Oldhame as Priscilla drove her cow away; while Lyford, remembering that she had that morning brought his wife a delicate breakfast, laughed uneasily and made no reply.

The governor's boat meanwhile, merrily driven by the "white-ash breeze" of four stalwart oars, had reached the ship's side, signaling, as she passed, the colony's pinnace, which, under easy sail, lay off and on the anchorage of the Charity.

"Good-morrow, Governor. You are welcome aboard, Master Winslow," cried the hearty voice of William Pierce, master of the Charity, and friend of the Pilgrims, as the passengers came aboard; and then, as if their errand were one needing no explanation, he led the way at once to his own cabin, fastened the door, and from a small locker at the foot of the bed-place took a packet of letters enveloped in oilskin. Laying these upon the little table and still resting his hand upon them, the honest mariner looked steadily in the faces of his visitors.

"Master Bradford, you are the governor of this colony and its chief authority. Do you, in the presence of Master Edward Winslow, your agent to the home government and one of your principal assistants, demand the surrender of these letters confided to my care by persons under your government?"

"I do, Master Pierce," replied Bradford distinctly, "and I call Edward Winslow to witness that the responsibility is mine and that of my Board of Assistants, and that you are guiltless in the matter. Nevertheless, I will not pretend that Master Oldhame and his party are directly under my government, since they came to Plymouth on their own account, and are not ranked as of the general company, but rather on their own particular."

"Still they are bound by the laws we all have subscribed to for our mutual safety and advantage," suggested Winslow, and would have said more had not Pierce bluffly interposed,—

"Well, well, all these niceties are out of my line. Some colonists have confided certain letters to me; the governor of the colony makes requisition upon me before a competent witness for these letters, suspecting treason therein; I surrender them to his keeping, and there ends my responsibility. And now I will go and make sail upon my ship. Governor, your pinnace shall be summoned whenever you give the signal." And Captain Pierce turned toward the companion-way, but presently returned, a genial smile replacing the slight annoyance darkening his face, and going to the "ditty bag" suspended near the porthole, he fumbled for a moment, then threw what he had found upon the table, adding merrily, "And if you want to make a neat job of it, Bradford, here's a sharp little pair of scissors. We sailors hate to see a trick of work bungled, if it's nothing better than ferreting out treason."

And with a smart westerly breeze the Charity set her nose toward England, and plunged bravely out into the Atlantic. Before she sighted the scene of the Pilgrim Mothers' first washing-day, however, she lay to, while the governor's pinnace was brought alongside, and he and Winslow came on deck and stood for a moment hand in hand.

"God be with you, brother," said Bradford in a voice of restrained emotion. "Remember that until you return we are as a man half whose limbs are palsied; nay, Carver in that prophetic moment called you our brain. Remember it, Winslow."

CHAPTER III.

TREASON.

"Master Oldhame, you are set upon the watch to-night, and will report after the evening gun at the Fort."

"The devil you say, Giles Hopkins! And who gave you leave to order your betters about?"

"Captain Standish names the watch, and I as ancient-bearer am under his orders and carry his messages."

"You may be under Satan's orders or under a monkey's orders for aught I care, Giles, my boy, but if you dare come nigh me with any more of Captain Shrimp's orders I'll wring your neck for you, master bantam cockerel, mark you that."

"I will report to the captain," calmly replied Hopkins, who, despite his father's restless example, was fast becoming one of the colony's most valued young citizens.

A profane exclamation was Oldhame's only reply, but as the ensign strode away he turned his head and called into the house at whose door he sat,—

"Lyford! Lyford! Here's some merry-making afoot! Captain Shrimp has summoned me to stand on watch to-night, and I have sent him and his errand-boy to the devil. Aha! here he comes himself with fury stiffening every hair of his red beard and snapping out of his eyes. Stand behind the door and hearken"—

"Good-even, Master Oldhame," struck in the firm and repressed tones of a voice at sound of which Lyford cringed closer in his corner, and Oldhame blustered uneasily,—

"Good-even, Myles Standish."

"It is your turn in regular rotation, Master Oldhame, to stand sentry-watch to-night as you have done before, and as every man in the colony is called upon to do. Will you kindly report at the Fort after gun-fire this evening?"

"No, I won't, Captain Shrimp."

"You refuse to obey the law of the colony?"

"I refuse to be said by you, you beggarly little rascal."

"Then I shall arrest you as a traitor, and if I had my will, I'd have you out and shoot you at sunrise."

"Oh, you would, would you, you wretched baseborn—

"Have a care, man, have a care. Stop while you may!" And the captain's voice deepened to a growl, and his eyes, wide open, yet contracted in the pupil to a point of fire, fixed themselves like weapons upon those of the mutineer, who, maddened by their menace, sprung to his feet knife in hand, and aimed a blow at the captain's face that might have forever quenched the light of those magnetic eyes, had it not been caught on the hilt of Gideon, the good sword that in these days hung ever at his master's side, although he seldom needed to quit his scabbard.

"Villain, you've broken my wrist!" yelled Oldhame, dropping his knife, upon which Standish planted his foot.

"To me! To me, men! Help! Murder! To me, Oldhames!" again shouted the traitor, but although a score or so of the townsmen gathered at the cry, not one made any demonstration or reply, while Standish, setting his lips and drawing two or three heavy breaths, hardly cast a glance at the crowd, but laying a hand upon Gideon's hilt coldly demanded,—

"John Oldhame, do you refuse to stand your watch to-night?"

A volley of abuse from Oldhame was interrupted by a messenger from Bradford, who, saluting the captain, reported,—

"The governor sends to know the cause of the tumult, and desires Captain Standish to arrest any disorderly persons refusing to submit to authority."

"My respects to the governor, and I am about to do so," replied Standish in the hard and cold tone which at once repressed and betrayed his passion.

"John Oldhame, I arrest you in the name of the law! Alden, Howland, Browne, I summon you to my aid! Convey this man to the Fort and lock him in the strong-room. Do him no bodily harm unless he resist, but secure him without delay."

Then ensued such a scene as Plymouth had as yet never seen, for with one or two exceptions the men who shared the struggles and perils of the colony's first days had become too closely welded together, and were too self-respecting, to rebel against the authority they had themselves elected.

But no sooner were the goodly foundations of the new home laid and cemented in the blood of those who dared all for Freedom's sake, than the anarchist arrived to throw down what was already wrought, and erect his own den upon the ruins.

Oldhame, maddened both at his defeat and the failure of those who had listened to his treason to make an open revolt in his favor, lost all control both of words and actions, and so ramped and raved, so cursed and vituperated, so kicked and smote and struggled, that it was not without a most unseemly contest that he was finally secured and dragged up the Burying Hill to the Fort, where in the corner opposite to the captain's den was a strong-room, small, but as yet quite sufficient for the colony's need of a prison.

A few hours of silence and solitude wrought a change, however, and John Alden, who held the position of prison-warden, came down the hill toward sunset with a request from the prisoner that he might see Master Lyford.

"The wolf would fain take counsel with the fox," remarked Priscilla when her husband told her his errand. "And our over-amiable sheep-dogs will never say nay to such a modest request."

"Pity but they made thee governor, Pris," suggested John with a bovine smile intended to be sarcastical.

"Ay," coolly replied his wife. "'Twould save some trouble. 'Tis a roundabout way we women have to manage now."

"Eh? what do all those fine words mean when they're put straight, wife?"

"They mean that you'd better do your errand to the governor before sunset, and then come home to eat my bannocks while they're fresh."

"You're right, Pris, and I'm gone."

But the bannocks were not to be eaten for another hour or so, during which time Master Lyford was closeted with his associate in the strong-room, and Alden kept ward without.

That evening the ex-minister sought the governor's presence, and with many protestations of regret at the late unfortunate misunderstanding, as he phrased it, offered Oldhame's submission and willingness to comply with the military requirements of the government, adding craftily,—

"If our worthy governor were also our captain there could never be any of these troubles."

"That would be to burn down the house because the chimney smokes now and again," replied Bradford good-humoredly. "It is largely due to Captain Standish's courage and skill, not to mention his loyalty, his steadfastness, and his wisdom, that this colony is other than a handful of ashes and a field of graves. When you new-comers have learned to know him, you will value our captain as we do."

The next morning Master Oldhame was released, and the next night stood his watch, nor, jealously as he watched and listened for them, was there a look or a tone from the captain or any of his adherents to remind the conquered rebel of his discomfiture, or the triumph of authority.

The next Sunday, or as it was universally called, the Lord's Day, the plot laid in the strong-room of the Fort developed most unexpectedly.

When at ten o'clock Bartholomew Allerton, now promoted to the post of band-master to the colony's army, beat the "assembly" in the Town Square as a summons to the church-goers to meet and form in their usual procession up the hill, he was confronted by Peter Oldhame, a lad somewhat younger than himself, who swung a cow bell almost in the drummer's face, shouting,—

"To church! To church! Englishmen hearken to the English Church! To church! To church!"

Bradford, who was just coming out of his house with Alice and Christian Penn, her buxom handmaiden, following meekly behind, stopped and looked sternly at the intruder until he, turning his back, walked down Leyden Street toward the old Common House, disused now except for storage.

"Shall I arrest the varlet, and clap him up in the strong-room?" asked Bart Allerton eagerly, as he swung the drum-gear off his shoulder.

"Nay, my son; it is the Lord's Day and we will not farther disturb its peace. This rebel has ceased his summons and you may do so also, lest worse come of it."

"Does your honor see Master Lyford in gown and bands coming out of Master Oldhame's house?"

"Nay, Bart, I see him not, for I look not at him. Now no more, good youth, but fall into rank with your fellows."

And fifty men or more, each armed and ready for battle either with men or the Ghostly Enemy who inspires men, moved in solemn procession of threes up Burying Hill to the Fort, the rear closed by the governor in his robe of office, with the Elder in his gown at his right hand, and the captain in full uniform at his left.

Not a word was exchanged between the leaders upon the events of the morning, but it was no news to any of them, when the long service was over and in the seclusion of home the women's tongues were let loose, to hear that Lyford, in spite of his abject repudiation of his Episcopal ordination, and membership with the Separatist Church, had gathered a congregation, read the English Service, preached a vituperative sermon against the leaders of the colony, and administered the Communion.

Such open bravado and schism as this could not be allowed to continue, for although the Pilgrims never persecuted any man for honest difference of religious belief, and were on very cordial terms with many members of the English Church, whom their pastor Robinson received to Communion and fellowship, it was hardly to be expected that they would permit a double apostate like Lyford to gather a body of malcontents in their midst, and hold services avowedly antagonistic to the church of the Pilgrims.

Nobody, therefore, was surprised when, on the Monday following this Sunday, the governor's message went forth summoning all the men of the colony, whether church-members, citizens, or only temporary residents, to assemble at the Fort at nine of the clock on Tuesday morning in a Court of the People, the colony not yet having outgrown this, the ideal mode of popular government.

CHAPTER IV.

THOU ART THE MAN!

Again Bartholomew Allerton, with much pride in the performance, beat out the "assembly" in the Town Square, and at the sound some fourscore men gathered from the houses, the shore, or those impaled garden plots surrounding each house, where already patient toil had produced in the wilderness very sweet reminiscences of English cottage-gardens.

The weather was wild, and ominous with the promise of one of those fierce storms of wind and rain, pretty sure to visit the coast in March and September, and still called by Plymouth folk the line storm, or the equinoctial, in calm contempt of modern meteorological theories. They also call a thunder-shower, however slight, a "tempest," and who is to object? Not I.

"Master Lyford's friends are gathering in force," remarked Standish, as he stood at the door of his house just below the Fort on Burying Hill.

"His friends!" repeated Alden, who, living in the house between that of the governor and the captain, was often to be found in company of the latter. "I did not think he had friends enough in Plymouth to be called a force."

"Not in Plymouth, nor yet in heaven, but somewhere between the two. The armies of the Prince of the Power of the Air."

And Standish, smiling grimly, pointed to the troops of clouds scurrying up over Manomet, and Watson's Hill, and all along the eastern and southern horizon; serried ranks, and scattered outposts, and flying vedettes, which, now by a flank movement, and now by an onward rush, seemed taking possession of all the blue battlefield above, blotting out the azure, and audaciously attacking the great sun himself.

"'Tis the equinoctial," stammered John Alden, perplexed.

"The wind, the great wind Euroclydon," replied Standish, who loved the sonorous and martial sound of old Bible English, and read it alternately with his Cæsar.

"Are you ready, Captain? You remember our arrangements?" asked Bradford, his fine face a little more pallid, a little more nervous than its wont, as he stopped on his way up the hill with the Elder and Doctor Fuller, who was vehemently saying,—

"Oh, he'll clear himself, Elder, he'll clear himself; an unsuspicious man like Brother Lyford may be led into unadvised action from the very best and soundest of motives."

"Then he must be restrained, for the safety of other people as well as for his own," replied the Elder coldly. "If one of your fever patients took a fancy in his delirium to set the house afire, I don't suppose you would leave him unchecked in his action, however blameless you might hold himself."

"No, no;—and yet—and yet"—muttered the doctor, whose common sense found itself sadly at war with a whimsical fancy he had conceived for Lyford, who was to be sure a university-bred man, and an accomplished botanist, thus affording to the alumnus of Peter-house, Cambridge, opportunity, which he did not often enjoy, for conversation on his favorite topics.

His annoyance found, however, no farther expression until, entering the Fort, he pettishly exclaimed, "Well, if we are to find an honest man we shall need Diogenes' lantern, or at any rate a twopenny dip or so."

"'Tis the gathering storm," replied Bradford in a depressed voice, as he stood upon the threshold of the low-ceiled chamber, lighted only by narrow slits intended more for defense than comfort. The bare benches were already occupied by some eighty or ninety men, their pointed hats, sombre doublets, and burnished "pieces" showing grotesquely through the gloom which seemed to solidify the shadows and exaggerate the lights, while an occasional flash of lightning added the last effect to the picture.

A restless movement, a sense rather than a sound of expectancy, a feeling of controversy, of doubt, of possible resistance, was in the air, and Bradford's sensitive organization responded at once to the thrill.

"Pray for us mightily to-day, Elder, pray for unworthy me," whispered he, as the two ascended the platform at the head of the hall, where stood the governor's armchair with seats at either hand for his five assistants, and benches for such persons as should be invited to occupy them.

To this appeal the Elder responded only by a searching glance from eyes of cold and wintry gray, and, passing on, he took his place at the governor's right hand, while Allerton and Doctor Fuller seated themselves at the left. Winslow's place was left vacant, and Standish, instead of assuming his, stood near the door, fully armed and equipped, watching Master Oldhame, who, with Lyford and several of their insolent followers, came strolling up the hill, laughing loudly, and displaying an exaggerated carelessness of demeanor.

As they entered, Standish, quietly placing himself between the two principals and their following, waved the latter to seats at the rear of the hall, and, courteously addressing the former, said,—

"The governor and council crave your presence upon the platform, gentlemen."

"And why so much ceremony to-day, Captain Standish?" demanded Oldhame in a blustering attempt to imitate the suavity of the soldier. "We have had the privilege and the honor, if there be any, of sitting upon yon platform more than once already, and need not to be marshaled thither to-day more than on other days."

"Ay, but to-day the governor designs to pay you some special attention, and your seats are not as before," replied Standish grimly, and, without waiting for reply, strode on up the hall followed by the mutineers, who, in spite of their best efforts at audacity, presented an aspect of mingled apprehension and wrath, ill becoming the leaders of a righteous revolution.

The elevated seats were, indeed, a little differently arranged from usual. The five official chairs stood in their customary position, but no other seat remained except one bench placed near the edge of the platform, and at such an angle that the occupants faced both the governor and the mass of the people. To this bench Standish silently but peremptorily waved the two men, who both felt and appeared more like prisoners than guests. Hesitating a moment, Oldhame led the way up the steps, and before seating himself would have pushed back the bench so as to place it at right angles to the front edge of the platform, but found it secured to the flooring. With an angry scowl he was about to speak, but Bradford, raising a hand with quiet dignity, said,—

"Let be, if it please you, Master Oldhame. This Court of the People is convened to inquire into certain matters concerning you, and it is best that you should be placed in the front of the assembly that all men may both see and hear your innocence, if haply you can prove it."

"Innocence, Master Governor! Innocence of what?" demanded Oldhame truculently, while Lyford's face suddenly lost its color, and moistening his lips with his tongue, he cast such crafty and alarmed looks around the assembly that Giles Hopkins whispered to Philip De la Noye,—

"Mind you that rat we found in the trap t'other day? I wish I had my little dog here to worry him."

"You shall be both heard and answered anon, friend," replied Bradford patiently. "First, however, we will ask the Elder to lead us in prayer for guidance and for wisdom."

Fervently and strongly did the Elder respond to this summons, nor did he at all forget the whispered petition Bradford had made in the moment of his weakness; and once again the prayer of faith became effectual, even in the moment of its utterance, so that when William Bradford said Amen it was in more calmness, more conscious strength, and more security of divine guidance, than he had been able to feel for days.

Standing before his people in all the simple dignity of his character and his position, he addressed them as friends, as associates, as freemen, taking for granted that each was as eager as himself to retain in all its completeness the great treasure of freedom and of self-government they had attained. "For," said he, turning his eyes for a moment upon the traitors, and then reverting to his friends, "both ye and all the world know we came hither to enjoy the liberty of our conscience and the free use of God's ordinances, and for that end have ventured our lives, and passed through much hardship hitherto; and we and our friends have borne the charge of these beginnings, which has not been small"—

"Spare us the preamble, I beseech you, Master Governor, and come to the root of the matter. Who has disturbed this somewhat sour-faced liberty and peace ye came here to seek?"

The insolence of the tone as well as of the words stirred even Bradford's chastened temper, and turning upon the traitor he angrily exclaimed,—

"Who?—who but you, John Oldhame, you and your followers! As Nathan said to David, so say I now to you, Thou art the man!"

The stinging contempt of the tone pierced like an arrow, and fairly stammering with rage the rebel sprang to his feet and made for the governor, but Standish quietly interposed with voice and presence,—

"Best be seated, Master Oldhame! The matter has not yet come to a passage at arms. Sit down man, sit down!"

"Yes, Master Oldhame," added the governor, resuming his usual self-restraint and manner of voice, "this is matter for sober discussion and not for heated wrangling." Then turning to the people he continued calmly:

"It is well known not only to these but to you all, that when the Charity arrived here some weeks gone by she brought letters from the gentlemen Adventurers, upon whom we depend for aid and comfort, demanding account of certain ill stories that had traveled home by the Anne, partly on the tongues of those who, daunted by the hardness of the life here, went back as soon as they might, and partly in letters writ by those Laodiceans who remained with us but are not of us. These tales were for the most part idle, such as that we have no grass for cattle; no wholesome water; that salt will not cure fish here; that neither fish nor wild fowl are to be found, and alas, alas! that moskeetos are to be found both in our fields and housen, which, indeed, is a plaint we may not deny.

"With these were weightier matters, to which I, with the help of the Assistants, made answer as seemed good to us, as that we have neither Sacrament in use, to which we answer, How can we have when to our great grief our pastor, Master Robinson, is withholden from coming to us, and no worthy minister is sent to supply his place? Next, that we have great diversity of religious belief, and this is a thing never heard of till last Lord's Day. But passing sundry other matters not best to enter upon now, we spoke to the lighter question, saying that although we do not contend that the water of our springs is as delightsome as the beer and wine these grumblers so sorely missed, it is as good, nay, I will say it is better, water than any other in the world, so far as I know of mine own experience. As for the lack of grass, we replied, Would we had one beast for every hundred that the grass would fatten. As for the lack of fish and fowl, and the story that salt would not cure fish caught in these waters, we did but ask, What is it brings so many sail to these parts year by year, and how do they carry home their fish, if they may not be cured?

"That fish may not be salted here is as true as that no ale or beer can be kept from souring in London. That we have thieves among us of late is sadly true, but if none were bred in England none would come hither, and as all men know, those who are caught have smarted well for their offense, and shall do so still more if they mend not their manners.

"But as for the moskeetos, we said, They were matter of such sadness and weight that we counseled such as cannot endure moskeeto bites to stay at home, at least until they are moskeeto proof, for surely they are all unfit for beginning new plantations, and must leave these emprises to hardier men.

"Glad am I to offer you matter of mirth and cheerfulness in the beginning, brethren, for now comes a tale of more serious import.

"Knowing that they who could write thus to our friends were still among us, it was but reasonable that we who stand as fathers to the colony should seek out who they were, and stop the mischief before it grew to larger dimensions. We have sought, and grieved am I to say we have found, these enemies where last we should have looked for them.

"Master John Oldhame, taking passage on the Anne with his family and his following, came among us as a stranger, asking at the first no more than permission to settle so near that in case of attack from Indians he might shelter under our wing, and profit by our countenance. We heartily bade him come and live in our village, helped him to build housen for himself and his people, portioned him a plot of land, aided him in every way that he desired, and gave him a voice in our assemblies.

"As for Master Lyford, he was, as you know, sent over at the company's charges, him and his large family, Master Winslow who was then in England having been wrought upon by the Adventurers to accept him as a minister of the gospel, and fit to become our pastor. Arrived here, he received a house, a double portion of food and stores, a man to serve him at our charge, and all such honor and observance as we knew how to bestow, although we determined to tarry for a season before accepting him as our minister in full. But now, how have these two carried themselves among us? Have they repaid love with love, and good with good? or has it not rather been after the fashion of the hedgehog in the fable, which the coney in a bitter cold day invited to shelter in her burrow, which at first was meek and gentle enow, but anon when he was comforted and warm, thrust out his prickles and so vext the poor coney that in the end it was she who was thrust out into the cold."

A low murmur of appreciation followed the parable, and Oldhame once more sprang to his feet, while Standish attentively followed every movement.

"So far as I can gather any serious meaning from the buffoonery Master Bradford intends for wit," began he, "I take it that he accuseth me and this godly minister of treason to this colony, where as he meanly reminds us we have received certain benefits, for the which I am quite ready to pay"—

"Shame! Shame!"

"Shame as much as you will, Alden and Soule, Bartlett and Prence! I've marked you, my springalds, but what I've to say is that the inditing is false and altogether malicious. Neither Lyford nor I have writ any such letters, or sent any such message now or ever. Say you not so, Master Lyford?"

"Oh verily, verily, good gentlemen all, no such thought has ever"—

"There, that will do, man. And now we call upon you, Master Governor, for any warrant you may have for this insult, and if you have none, we demand an ample apology."

"You positively deny writing any letters of complaint concerning us?" asked Bradford deliberately.

"We do."

"Master Allerton, be pleased to bring forth the papers you hold in charge."

Allerton, his crafty face illuminated with a smile of unusual satisfaction, brought forward a small table, and placed upon it some twenty or thirty letters, carefully arranged and docketed, in his neat and scholarly script. Laying his hand upon the papers, Bradford looked at the traitors with an austere sadness significant of his just yet gentle nature; then, turning to the people, he related how by the advice of his council he had seized these letters, already on their way to England, and with Winslow's help copied the most of them, retaining, however, some of the originals with which to confront the writers in case of denial.

But as the governor in his calm and judicial voice made this announcement, glancing as he spoke at the documents spread out upon the little table, Oldhame, furious at the humiliating discovery of his lie, started again to his feet, foaming out all sorts of threats and defiance, and threatening indefinite but terrible vengeance. Finally turning to the benches with a gesture almost magnificent in its reckless abandon, he cried,—

"My masters, where are your hearts! Now is the time to show yourselves men! How oft have you groaned in my ears under the tyranny of these oppressors, and now is your time to fling off the yoke! Stand to your arms, brethren! Make a move, and I am with you!"

As he recognized the intent of this seditious appeal, Standish sprang forward, his hand upon his sword's hilt, but Bradford, without rising, made a slight repressive gesture, and ran his eye quickly over the ranks of faces confronting him, marking the expression on each.

A few, notably Billington's, Hicks's, Hopkins's, and some of the newcomers', wore an anxious, a sheepish, or a frightened air, combined in two or three cases with truculence, and in others with doubt, but the great body of the freemen met the eye of their governor with cordial sympathy and reassurance, and although no man stirred, several handled their weapons and looked around them with an eagerness boding ill for the traitors should they proceed to extremity.

Oldhame also reviewed the fourscore faces arrayed before him, and was quick to perceive and accept his defeat.

"Ye coward dogs! Crouch under your master's lash till it cut your hearts out! What is it to me or mine!"

The bitter words ground between his teeth reached no ears but those of Lyford, upon whom, as he sank cowering back upon the bench, Bradford next turned his eyes demanding,—

"What is *your* opinion, Master Lyford, upon this question of opening another's letters?"

The ex-minister started as if stung by the lash of a whip, passed his hand across his trembling lips, and stammered,—

"I—I—I meant no harm. I"—

"Master Lyford answers the accusation of his own conscience rather than my question," said Bradford serenely, as the quavering voice trailed away into silence. "The matter in his mind is this: When our brother, Edward Winslow, was about sailing out of England in the Charity, bringing with him this man who had been pushed upon him as a worthy substitute for our own revered pastor, he writ with his own hand to Master Robinson an account of the matter, with sundry other things touching the spiritual and temporal concerns of the company. This letter he sealed, addressed, and left lying in his state cabin, along with sundry others, some of his own inditing, and some intrusted to him by friends, to convey hither. One of these was from a well-known English gentleman to Elder Brewster, and bore both names upon the cover.

"Master Winslow's affairs calling him back to London before the sailing of the vessel, he left all these letters in his writing-case under charge of Master Lyford, who used the same cabin. But no sooner was Winslow's back turned than Master Lyford, opening the chest with keys of his own, read the letters, and made copies of the two mentioned, telling under his own hand how he obtained them. These copies he brought hither, and now is sending them back into England by the Charity, and small charity of the godly sort doth he show in his comments inclosed with the copies to one of our most powerful and unloving opponents among the Adventurers.

"And why hath he done this? Not to fulfill a heavy and painful duty, and to protect a people and an emprise laid upon him by Almighty God, even as the children of Israel were laid upon the shoulders of Moses until he all but sank beneath the weight! No, Master Lyford can plead no such necessity for the opening and reading of letters writ and sealed by one who trusted him, but rather his motive seems to have been the desire of doing despite to his benefactors, and of working mischief and destruction to them who have never done him other than kindness, trusting and befriending him as one of themselves.

"And now, Master Allerton, I will ask you to read out these letters, and any who will may draw near and look at the originals signed both by John Oldhame and John Lyford."

The letters were read, and as page after page of Lyford's malignant treachery, and Oldhame's fierce vituperation was turned, murmurs of indignation, ominous mutterings, with here and there a groan or a faint hiss arose from the benches, especially when the freemen heard it recommended that the Adventurers should, as soon as possible, send a body of men "to over-sway those here;" that they should at all risks prevent Pastor Robinson's coming, and should, if possible, depose Winslow from his position as agent. Again a subdued commotion was excited by the advice to send over a certain captain, who had apparently been previously mentioned, with the promise that he should at once be chosen military leader, "for this Captaine Standish looks like a silly boy, and is in utter contempt."

In hearing this philippic many an eye was turned upon its subject, but he, standing at ease with one hand upon Gideon's hilt, only gathered his beard in the other fist and smiled good-humoredly. He at least was "moskeeto-proof."

"And now, men," demanded the governor, turning to the people, "what have you to say? Let any one who would make a proposal as to our dealing with these two speak his mind freely."

But before any other could reply to this demand, Lyford, breaking away from Oldhame's fierce restraint, fell upon his knees, bursting into tears and sobs, wringing his hands, and cringing to the floor, while he howled out all sorts of self-accusations, calling himself a miserable sinner, "unsavorie salt," Judas, and many other opprobrious epithets, doubting, as he professed, if God would ever pardon him, and in any case despairing of the forgiveness of his benefactors and hosts, for he had so wronged them as to pass all forgiveness. Finally, he confessed in the most abject terms that "all he had writ against them was false and naught, both for matter and manner," and professed himself willing and anxious to retract everything in the presence of God, angels, and men.

But the scene was soon cut short, for the self-respecting men who listened to this abjection found it too great a humiliation of the divine image in man, and while the culprit still sobbed and whined at his feet, the governor, briefly ordering him to rise and be silent, turned to the people and repeated his demand for their suffrages.

A brief discussion ensued, chiefly among the elders, the younger men signifying their assent or dissent by a word or two, and Bradford, listening to all, watching the expression of all, and gathering the sense of the assembly as much by intuition as from spoken words, at last announced that the Court of the People found these two men guilty of the offenses with which they stood charged, and were decided to banish them from the settlement as dangerous to its safety. A murmur of assent ratified this decision, and the details arranged by the governor and council were unanimously accepted. Oldhame was to depart at once, while his family had permission to remain until he could find a comfortable home for them, and then rejoin him without his coming to fetch them.

As for Lyford, his retraction and professions of contrition had their effect, especially with the doctor, whose earnest appeals for indulgence finally procured permission for the penitent to remain in the village for six months on probation, his sentence then either to be acted upon or, in case his repentance should prove sincere, to possibly be altogether remitted.

The two culprits received their sentence very differently, yet very characteristically. Oldhame, breathing fire and fury, departed from the Fort at once in a blue flame of profanity and vituperation, and before night set sail for Nantasket to join the Gorges men settled in that neighborhood.

But the meaner traitor could hardly be persuaded to stand upon his feet, preferring to grovel at those of his judges, who for the most part received his demonstrations very coldly, Bradford suggesting, as he twisted away the hand Lyford was moistly kissing,—

"There's a homely old proverb, master, which you might do well to recall: 'Actions speak louder than words.'"

"And still another," broke in John Alden, "says that 'Promises butter no parsnips.'"

Thus ended the first trial for treason in America, and so was decided the most important cause ever brought before the Court of the People, a tribunal soon to be replaced by the trial by jury.

CHAPTER V.

HOW MISTRESS ALICE BRADFORD INTRODUCED HER SISTER PRISCILLA CARPENTER TO PLYMOUTH SOCIETY.

"Goodman, I've heavy news for you; so set your mind to bear it as best you may."

"Nay, goodwife, your winsome face is no herald of bad news, and certes, I'll not cross the bridge until it comes in sight."

"Well, then, since words won't daunt you, here's a fact, sir! We are to have a merry-making, and gather all the young folk of the village, and Master Bradford will have to lay off the governor's mantle of thought and worry, that he may be jocund with the rest."

"Nay, then, Alice, 'tis indeed heavy news!" And the governor pulled a long face, and looked mock-miserable with all his might. "And is it a dispensation not to be gainsaid? Is there good cause that we should submit ourselves to an affliction that might, as it would seem, be spared?"

"Well, dear, you know that my sister Pris has come"—

"Do you tell me so! Now *there* is news in very deed! And how did Mistress Priscilla Carpenter reach these parts?"

"Now, Will! if you torment me so, I'll e'en call in Priscilla Alden to take my part. *She'll* give you quip for crank, I'll warrant me."

"Nay, nay, wife, I'll be meek and good as your cosset lamb, so you'll keep me under your own hand. Come now, let us meet this enemy face to face. What is it all?"

Alice, who, tender soul that she was, loved not even playful and mock contention, sighed a little, and folding her hands in her lap gently said,—

"It is all just as thou pleasest, Will, but my thought was to call together all the young people and make a little feast to bring those acquainted with Pris, who, poor maid, has found it a trifle dull and straitened here, after leaving her merry young friends in England."

"Ever thinking of giving pleasure to others even at cost of much toil to thyself, sweetheart!" And the governor, placing a hand under his wife's round chin, raised her face and kissed it tenderly again and again, until the soft pink flushed to the roots of the fair hair.

"Do as thou wilt, darling, in this and everything, and call upon me for what thy men and maids cannot accomplish."

"Nay, I've help enough. Christian Penn is equal to two women, and sister Pris herself is very notable. Then Priscilla Alden will kindly put her hand to some of the dainty dishes, and she is a wonder at cooking, as you know."

"Yes, she proved it in—early days," interrupted Bradford, the smile fading off his face. "Had it not been for her skill in putting a savory touch to the coarsest food, I believe some of our sick folk would have died,—I am sure Dame Brewster would."

"Oh, you poor souls! How you suffered, and I there in England eating and drinking of the best, and—oh, Will, you should have married good dear Priscilla to reward her care of what I held so carelessly."

"Wonderful logic, madam! I should, to reward Mistress Molines for her care, have married her, when she loved another man, and I another woman, which latter was to thus be punished for carelessness in a matter she knew naught about!"

And with a tender little laugh, the governor pressed another kiss upon his wife's smooth cheek, before he went out to his fields, while she flew at once to her kitchen and set the domestic engine throbbing at double-quick time. Then she stepped up the hill to John Alden's house, and found Priscilla, her morning work already done, washing and dressing her little Betty, while John and Jo watched the operation with unflagging interest.

"Come and help you, Alice? I shall be gay and glad to do it, dear, just as soon as Betty is in her cradle, and I have told Mary-à-Becket what to do about the noon-meat. John, you and Jo run up the hill to the captain's, and ask Mistress Standish if Alick and Myles may come down and play with you in front of the governor's house so I may keep an eye on you."

"Two fine boys, those of Barbara's," said the governor's wife, and then affectionately, "yet no finer than your sturdy little knaves."

"Oh, ours are well enough for little yeomen, but the captain says his Alick is heir to a great estate, and is a gentleman born!" And the two young women laughed good-naturedly, while Priscilla laid her baby in the cradle, and Alice turned toward the door saying, "Well, I must be at home to mind the maids."

"And I'll be there anon. I trust you've good store of milk and cream. We did well enow without it for four years, but now we've had it for a while, one might as well be dead as lack it."

"I've plenty, and butter beside, both Dutch and fresh," replied Alice from outside the door, and in another ten minutes the wide kitchen recently added to William Bradford's house on the corner of Leyden Street and the King's Highway, now called Main Street, hummed again with the merry sounds of youthful voices, of the whisking of eggs, and grinding of spices, and stirring of golden compounds in wooden bowls, and chopping suet, and stoning raisins, and slicing citron, and the clatter of pewter dishes, which, by the way, with wooden ware were nearly all the "pottery" the Pilgrims possessed, hypothetical teapots and china cups to the contrary; for, since we all know that tea and coffee were never heard of in England until about the year 1666, and the former herb was sold for many years after at from ten to fifteen dollars per pound (Pepys in 1671 mentions it as a strange and barbaric beverage just introduced), it is improbable that either tea, teapot, or teacups ever reached America until after Mary Allerton, the last survivor of the Mayflower, rested upon Burying Hill.

All that day and part of the next the battle raged in the Bradford kitchen, for delicate appetites were in those times rather a defect than a grace, and hospitality largely consisted in first providing great quantities and many varieties of food, and then over-pressing the guests to partake of it. An "afternoon tea" with diaphanous bread and butter, wafer cakes, and Cambridge salts, as the only solid refreshment, would have seemed to Alice Bradford and her guests either a comic pretense or a niggardly insult, and very different was the feast to which as many as could sat down at a very early hour of the evening of the second day.

The company was large, for in the good Old Colony fashion it included both married and single persons, and would, if possible, have made no distinctions of age or position, but this catholicity had in the growth of the colony become impossible, and Mistress Bradford's invitations were, with much searching of spirit and desire to avoid offense, confined principally to young persons, married and unmarried, likely to become associates of her sister Priscilla, a fair-haired, sweet-lipped, and daintily colored lass, reproducing Dame Alice's own early charms.

"The Brewster girls must come, although I cannot yet be reconciled to Fear's having married Isaac Allerton, and calling herself mother to Bart, and Mary and Remember—great grown girls!" exclaimed the hostess in consultation with her husband, and he pleasantly replied,—

"Oh, well, dame, we must not hope to guide all the world by our own wisdom; and certes, if Fear's marriage is a little incongruous, her sister

Patience is well and fitly mated with Thomas Prence. It does one good to see such a comely and contented pair of wedded sweethearts."

"True enough, Will, and your thought is a rebuke to mine."

"Nay, wife, 'tis you that teach me to be charitable."

And the two, come together to reap in the glorious St. Martin's summer of their days the harvest sown amid the chill tears of spring, looked in each other's eyes with a smile of deep content. The woman was the first to set self aside, and cried,—

"Come, come, Sir Governor! To business! Mistress Allerton, and her *daughters*, Mary and Remember, Bartholomew, and the Prences, Constance Hopkins with Nicholas Snow, whom she will marry, the Aldens, the captain and his wife"—

"He is hardly to be ranked with the young folk, is he?"

"No, dear, no more than Master Allerton, or, for that matter, the governor and his old wife; but there, there, no more waste of time, sir! Who else is to come, and who to be left at home?"

"Nay, wife, I'm out of my depth already and will e'en get back to firm land, which means I leave all to your discretion. Call Barbara and Priscilla Alden to council, and let me know in time to put on my new green doublet and hose, for I suppose I am to don them."

"Indeed you are, and your ruffles and your silk stockings that I brought over. I will not let you live altogether in hodden gray, since even the Elder goes soberly fine on holidays."

"Well, well, I leave it all to you, and must betake myself to the woods. Good-by for a little."

"Good-by, dear."

And as the governor with an axe on his shoulder strode away down Market Street and across the brook to Watson's Hill, Dame Alice, a kerchief over her head, once more ran up the hill to Priscilla Alden's.

As the great gun upon the hill boomed out the sunset hour, and Captain Standish himself carefully covered it from the dews of night, Alice Bradford stood in the great lower room of her house and looked about her. All was done that could be done to put the place in festal array, and although the fair dame sighed a little at the remembrance of her stately home in Duke's Place, London, with its tapestries and carvings and carpets and pictures, she bravely put aside the regret, and affectionately smoothed and patted the fine damask "cubboard cloth" covering the lower shelf of the sideboard, or, as she called it, the "buffet," at one side of the room, and placed and replaced the precious properties set out thereon:—

A silver wine cup, a porringer that had been her mother's, nine silver teaspoons, and, crown of all, four genuine Venetian wine-glasses, tall and twisted of stem, gold-threaded and translucent of bowl, fragile and dainty of shape, and yet, like their as dainty owner, brave to make the pilgrimage from the home of luxury and art to the wilderness, where a shelter from the weather and a scant supply of the coarsest food was all to be hoped for.

But Dame Bradford, fingering her Venice glasses, and softly smiling at the touch, murmured to herself and to them, "'Tis our exceeding gain."

"What, Elsie, not dressed!" cried Priscilla Carpenter's blithe voice, as that young lady, running down the stairs leading to her little loft chamber, presented herself to her sister's inspection with a smile of conscious deserving.

"My word, Pris, but you are fine!" exclaimed Dame Alice, examining with an air of unwilling admiration the young girl's gay apparel and ornaments. It was indeed a pretty dress, consisting of a petticoat of cramoisie satin, quilted in an elaborate pattern of flowers, leaves, and birds; an open skirt of brocade turned back from the front, and caught high upon the hips with great bunches of cramoisie ribbons; a "waistcoat" of the satin, and a little open jacket of the brocade. Around the soft white throat of the wearer was loosely knotted a satin cravat of the same dull red tint with the skirt, edged with a deep lace, upon which Alice Bradford at once laid a practiced finger.

"Pris, that *jabot* is of Venise point! Where did you get it?"

"Ah! That was a present from"—

"Well, from whom?"

"Nay, never look so cross on't, my lady sister! Might not I have a sweetheart as well as you?"

"Priscilla, I'm glad you're here rather than with those gay friends of yours in London. I suppose Lady Judith Carr or her daughters gave you these clothes, did they not?"

"Well, I earned them hard enough putting up with all my lady's humors and the girls' jealous fancies," pouted Pris. "I was glad enough when you and brother Will wrote and offered me a home,—not but what Lady Judith was good to me and called me her daughter; but, Elsie, 'twas not they who gave me the laced cravat, 'twas—'twas"—

"Well, out with it, little sister! Who was it, if not our mother's old friend?"

"Why, Elsie, 'twas a noble gentleman that I met with them down at Bath, and—sister—he is coming over here to marry me right soon."

"Nay, then, but that's news indeed! And what may be his name, pet?"

"Sir Christopher Gardiner, and he's a Knight of the Holy Sepulchre."

And Pris, fondling the lace of her cravat, smiled proudly into her sister's astonished face; but before either could speak, Barbara Standish and Priscilla Alden appeared at the open door, the latter exclaiming in her blithe voice,—

"What, Alice, still in your workaday kirtle! Barbara and I came thus betimes to see if aught remained that we might do before the folk gather."

"Thank you, both; I—I—nay, then, I'm a little put about, dear friends; I hardly know,—well, well! Priscilla Carpenter, come you into my bedroom and help me do on my clothes, and if you two will look about and see what is ready and what is lacking, I shall be more than grateful. Come, Pris!"

"Something has chanced more than we know about!" suggested Priscilla Alden, as the bedroom door closed behind the sisters.

"Likely. But 'tis their affair and not ours," replied Barbara quietly. "Now let us see. Would you set open the case holding the twelve ivory-handled knives?"

"Yes, they're a rarity, and some of the folk may not have seen them. Alice says that in London they put a knife to every man's trencher now, and nobody uses his own sheath-knife as has been the wont."

"You tell me so! Well, one knife's enough for Myles and me, yes, and the boys to boot. But then I cut the meat in morsels, and spread the bread with butter, or ever it goes on the table."

"Of course; so we all do, I suppose. Well there, all is ready now, and here come the folk; there's Patty Brewster, or Patience Prence as she must now be called, and along with her Fear Allerton and Remember and Mary,—her daughters indeed! Marry come up! *I* might have had Isaac Allerton for myself, but"—

"And there is Constance Hopkins, and Nicholas Snow," interrupted Barbara, who was a deadly foe to gossip, "and John and Elizabeth Howland; then there's Stephen Dean with Betsey Ring, and Edward Bangs and Lyddy Hicks, and Mary Warren and Robert Bartlett, three pair of sweethearts together, and here they all are at the door."

But as the more lively Priscilla ran to open it, the governor's hearty voice was heard without, crying,—

"Welcome! Welcome, friends! I was called out for a moment, but have come home just in the nick of time and brought the captain with me."

"Now I do hope Myles has put on his ruff, and his other doublet that I laid out," murmured Barbara in Priscilla's ear. "When the governor and he get together, the world's well lost for both of them."

"Nay, he's all right, and a right proper man, as he always was," returned Priscilla, with a quick glance at the square figure and commanding head of the Captain of Plymouth, as he entered the room and smiled in courtly fashion at Dame Bradford's greeting.

"And here's your John, a head and shoulders above all the rest," added Barbara good-naturedly, as Alden, the Saxon giant, strode into the room and looked fondly across it at his wife.

Another half hour and all were gathered about the three long tables improvised from boards and barrels, but all covered with the fine napery brought from Holland by Alice Bradford, who had the true housewife's love of elegant damask, and during Edward Southworth's life was able to indulge it, laying up such store of table damask, of fine Holland "pillowbers"[1] and "cubboard cloths," towels of Holland, of dowlas, and of lockorum, and sheets of various qualities from "fine Holland" to tow (the latter probably spun and woven at home), that the inventory of her personal estate is as good reading to her descendants as a cookery book to a hungry man.

Plenty of trenchers both of pewter and wood lined the table, and by each lay a napkin and a spoon, but neither knives nor forks, the latter implement not having yet been invented, except in the shape of a powerful trident to lift the boiled beef from the kettle, while table knives, as Priscilla Alden had intimated, were still regarded as curious implements of extreme luxury. A knife of a different order, sometimes a clasp-knife, sometimes a sheath-knife, or even a dagger, was generally carried by each man, and used upon certain *pièces de resistance*, such as boar's head, a roasted peacock, a shape of brawn, a powdered and cloved and browned ham, or such other triumphs of the culinary art as must be served whole.

Such dishes were carried around the table, and every guest, taking hold of the morsel he coveted with his napkin, sliced it off with his own knife, displaying the elegance of his table manners by the skill with which he did it. But as saffron was a favorite condiment of the day, and pearline was not yet invented, one sighs in contemplating the condition of these napkins, and ceases to wonder at the store of them laid up by thrifty housekeepers.

Ordinarily, however, the meat was divided into morsels before appearing on the table, and thus was easily managed with the spoon,—*or* with the fingers.

Between each two plates stood a pewter or wooden basin of clam chowder, prepared by Priscilla Alden, who was held in Plymouth to possess a magic touch for this and several other dishes.

From these each guest transferred a portion to his own plate, except when two supped merrily from the same bowl in token of friendly intimacy. This first course finished and the bowls removed, all eyes turned upon the governor, who rose in his place at the head of the principal table, where were gathered the more important guests, and, looking affectionately up and down the board, said,—

"Friends, it hardly needs that I should say that you are welcome, for I see none that are ever less than welcome beneath this roof; but I well may thank you for the cheer your friendly faces bring to my heart to-night, and I well may pray you, of your goodness, to bestow upon my young sister here the same hearty kindness you have ever shown to me and mine." A murmur of eager assent went round the board, and the governor smiled cordially, as he grasped in both hands the great two-handled loving-cup standing before him,—a grand cup, a noble cup, of the measure of two quarts, of purest silver, beautifully fashioned, and richly carved, as tradition said, by the hand of Benvenuto Cellini himself; so precious a property that Katharine White, daughter of an English bishop, was proud to bring it as almost her sole dowry to John Carver, her husband. With him it came to the New World, and was used at the Feast of Treaty between the colonists and Massasoit, chief of the native owners of the soil. Katharine Carver, dying broken hearted six weeks after her husband, bequeathed the cup to William Bradford, his successor in the arduous post of Governor of the Colony, and from him it passed down into that Hades of lost and all but forgotten treasures, which may, for aught we know, become the recreation-ground for the spirits of antiquarians.

Filled to the brim with generous Canary, a pure and fine wine in those days, it crowned the table, and William Bradford, steadily raising it to his lips, smiled gravely upon his guests, adding to his little speech of welcome,—

"I pledge you my hearty good-will, friends!" then drank sincerely yet modestly, and giving one handle to Myles Standish, who sat at his left hand, he retained his hold at the other side while the captain drank, and in his turn gave one handle to Mistress Winslow, who came next, and so, all standing to honor the pledge of love and good-will, the cup passed round the board and came to Elder Brewster, at the governor's right hand; but he, having drank, looked around with his paternal smile and said,—

"There is yet enough in the loving-cup, friends, for each one to wet his lips, if nothing more, and I propose that we do so with our hearty welcome and best wishes to Mistress Priscilla Carpenter."

Once more the cup went gayly round, and reached the Elder so dry that he smiled, as he placed it to his lips, with a bow toward Pris savoring more of his early days in the court of Queen Bess than of New England's solitudes.

"And now to work, my friends, to work!" cried the governor. "I for one am famished, sith my dame was so busy at noontide with that wonderful structure yonder that she gave me naught but bread and cheese."

Everybody laughed, and Alice Bradford colored like a red, red rose, yet bravely answered,—

"The governor will have his jest, but I hope my raised pie will suffer roundly for its interference with his dinner."

"Faith, dame, but we'll all help to punish it," exclaimed Stephen Hopkins, gazing fondly at the elaborate mass of pastry representing, not inartistically, a castle with battlements and towers, and a floating banner of silk bearing an heraldic device. "Standish! we call upon you to lead us to the assault!"

"Nay, if Captain Standish is summoned to the field, my fortress surrenders without even a parley," said Alice Bradford, as she gracefully drew the little banner from its place, and, laying it aside, removed a tower, a bastion, and a section of the battlement from the doomed fortress, and, loading a plate with the spoils of its treasury, planted the banner upon the top, and sent it to the captain, who received it with a bow and a smile, but never a word.

"Speak up, man!" cried Hopkins boisterously. "Make a gallant speech in return for the courtesy of so fair a castellaine."

"Mistress Bradford needs no speech to assure her of my devoir," replied the captain simply, and the governor added,—

"Our captain speaks more by deeds than words, and Gideon is his most eloquent interpreter. You have not brought him to-day, Captain."

"No; Gideon sulks in these days of peace, and seldom stirs abroad."

"Long may he be idle!" exclaimed the Elder, and a gentle murmur around the board told that the women at least echoed the prayer.

But Hopkins, seated next to Mistress Bradford, and watching her distribution of the pie, cared naught for war or peace until he secured a trencher of its contents, and presently cried,—

"Now, by my faith, I did not know such a pye as this could be concocted out of Yorkshire! 'Tis perfect in all its parts: fowl, and game, and pork, and forcemeat, and yolks of eggs, and curious art of spicery, and melting bits of pastry within, and stout-built walls without; in fact, there is naught lacking to such a pye as my mother used to make before I had the wit to know such pyes sing not on every bush."

"You're Yorkshire, then, Master Hopkins?" asked John Howland, who with his young wife, once Elizabeth Tilley, sat opposite.

"Yes, I'm Yorkshire, root and branch, and you're Essex, and the captain and the governor Lancashire, but all shaken up in a bag now, and turned into New Englanders, and since the Yorkshire pye has come over along with us I'm content for one."

A general laugh indorsed this patriotic speech, but Myles Standish, toying with the silken banner of the now sacked and ruined fortress, said in Bradford's ear,—

"All very well for a man who has naught to lose in the old country. But for my part I mean to place at least my oldest son in the seat of his fathers."

The governor smiled, and then sighed. "Nor can I quite forget the lands of Austerfield held by Bradfords and Hansons for more than one century, and the path beside the Idle, where Brewster and I walked and talked in the days of my first awakening to the real things of life"—

"Real things of life, say you, Governor?" broke in Hopkins's strident voice; "well, if there is aught more real in its merit than this roasted suckling, I wish that I might meet with it."

And seizing with his napkin the hind leg of the little roasted pig presented to him by Christian Penn, the old campaigner deftly sliced it off with his sheath-knife and devoured it in the most inartificial manner possible.

It was probably about this epoch that our popular saying, "Fingers were made before forks," took shape and force.

To the chowder, and the "pye," and the roasted suckling succeeded a mighty dish of succotash, that compound of dried beans, hulled corn, salted beef, pork, and chicken which may be called the charter-dish of Plymouth; then came wild fowl dressed in various ways, a great bowl of "sallet," of Priscilla Alden's composition, and at last various sweet dishes, still served at the end of a meal, although soon after it was the mode to take them first.

"Oh, dear, when will the dignities stop eating and drinking and making compliments to each other?" murmured Priscilla Carpenter to Mary Warren at the side table where the girls and lads were grouped together, enjoying themselves as much as their elders, albeit in less ceremonious fashion.

"There! Your sister has laid down her napkin, and is gazing steadfastly at the governor, with 'Get up and say Grace' in her eye," replied Mary, nudging Jane Cooke to enforce silence; whereat that merry maid burst into a giggle, joined by Sarah and Elizabeth Warren, and Mary Allerton, and Betsey Ring, while Edward Bangs, and Robert Bartlett, and Sam Jenney, and Philip De la Noye, and Thomas Clarke, and John Cooke chuckled in sympathy, yet knew not what at.

A warning yet very gentle glance from Dame Bradford's eyes stifled the noise, and nearly did as much for its authors, who barely managed to preserve sobriety, while the governor returned thanks to the Giver of all good; so soon, however, as the elder party moved away, the painfully suppressed giggle burst into a storm of merriment, which as it subsided was renewed in fullest vigor by Sarah Warren's bewildered inquiry,—

"What *are* we all laughing at?"

"Never mind, we'll laugh first, and find the wherefore at our leisure," suggested Jane Cooke, and so the dear old foolish fun that seems to spring up in spontaneous growth where young folk are gathered together, and is sometimes scorned and sometimes coveted by their elders, went on, and, after the tables were cleared, took form in all sorts of old English games, not very intellectual, not even very refined, but as satisfactory to those who played as Buried Cities, and Twenty Questions, and Intellectual Salad, and capping Browning quotations are to the children of culture and æsthetics.

The elders, meanwhile, retiring to the smaller room at the other side of the front door, seated themselves to certain sober games of draughts, of backgammon, of loo, and beggar-my-neighbor, or picquet, while Elder Brewster challenged the governor to a game of chess which was not finished when, at ten o'clock, the company broke up, and with many a blithe good-night, and assurance of the pleasure they had enjoyed, betook themselves to their own homes.

Thus, then, was Priscilla Carpenter introduced into Plymouth society.

FOOTNOTE:

[1] Pillow-biers, now called pillow-cases.

CHAPTER VI.

A VIPER SCOTCHED, NOT KILLED.

"'Tis meat for my masters," muttered William Wright, plodding stubbornly up the hill toward the Fort; but as he passed John Alden's door the sturdy, middle-aged man paused to watch, with a smile of admiration rather strange to his commonplace visage, a game of romps between little Betty Alden and Priscilla Carpenter, and indeed it was a pretty sight. The maiden, her full yet lissome figure displayed in a short skirt of blue cloth and a kirtle of India chintz belted down by a little white apron, was teasing the child with a cluster of ripe blackberries held just beyond her reach, and, dancing hither and yon as Betty pursued, showed her pretty feet and ankles to perfection, while the exercise and fresh air had tinted her cheeks and brightened her eyes as cosmetics never could, and set a thousand little airy curls loose from the fair hair braided in a long plait down her back.

"You can't catch me, Betty! You can't have the plums till you catch me, and you can't—ah, now—catch if you can—catch if you can!"

But Betty, shrieking with laughter as she dived this way and that, suddenly grew so grave and frowned so terribly as she pointed her chubby finger and stammered, "Go 'way—s'ant look o' me—go 'way man!" that Priscilla turned sharply round, and catching the interloper in the very midst of a broad smile, she frowned, almost as terribly as Betty, and loftily inquired,—

"Am I in your path, Master Wright?"

"Nay, how could that be?" stammered Wright, utterly abashed before his two accusers. "I pray you excuse me, Mistress Prissie, but I—I was looking for the governor, and"—

"The governor?" interrupted Priscilla scornfully; "well, he's not in my pocket, is he in yours, Betty?"

And catching up the child, she was retreating into the house, when her admirer interposed with an air of dignity more becoming to his age and appearance than the confusion of a detected intruder upon a girl's pastime,—

"Nay, mistress, I need not drive you away; I am going to the Fort."

"Well, there is the governor coming down from the Fort so as to leave room for you," retorted Prissie, and setting the child inside the door, she fled down the hill as lightly as the wind that chased her.

"Good-morrow, Wright," cried Bradford cheerily, as the two men met.

"Good-morrow, Governor. May I have a word with you on business?"

"Surely. Come back to the Fort, where I have just left the captain. Ah, here he is now!"

And the three men were soon seated in the captain's little den, flooded with sunshine through its eastern window.

"I sail in the Little James to-day, sirs," began Wright abruptly; "and but now, not an hour agone, Master Lyford gave me this letter, praying me to hold it secret, and carry it to its address in London, and he would give me five shilling when I returned. Now, sirs, I am not a man to be hired for five shilling to do any man's dirty work, and I liked not Master Lyford's look or voice as he gave me his errand, nor have I forgot the matters concerning him and John Oldhame a while ago, and so—here 's the letter, Governor."

"Ha! 'Tis to the same address, Captain! Our well-known enemy and gainsayer among the Adventurers."

"Ay. The old proverb come true again of the dog that turns from good victual to vile," muttered Standish grimly. "And I suppose it is to be opened like the rest? Work I do not relish, Governor."

"Nor I. But Winslow and Allerton are both away, and you must come with me to the Elder. In his presence and yours I shall open and read this letter, as is my bounden duty."

And Bradford, leaning back in his chair, looked straight into the face of the captain, who, returning the gaze with one of his keen glances, nodded assent, saying in a surly voice,—

"You are the governor. It is for you to order and me to obey, but I like it not."

"As for you, Wright, you have done well and wisely in this matter. The James sails at three of the clock; come you to my house at two, and I will return you the letter with one of mine own."

"Will Priscilla Carpenter be in the room!" wondered William Wright, as he took his leave.

The letter examined by the triumvirate of governor, Elder, and captain proved that Lyford's penitence, if indeed it had ever existed, had spent its strength in protestation. The writer alluded to the letters the governor had allowed to go forward, either by original or copy, and declared that all they had stated was true, "only not the half," and that since their discovery he had been persecuted and browbeaten to the verge of existence, and all because he loved and clung to the Prayer Book and his Episcopal ordination. The letter closed with entreaties that a sufficient body of settlers, with military leaders, should at once be sent over to crush his present hosts and set him at liberty to follow his conscience.

"At least, we may at once grant our brother liberty to follow his conscience in matters spiritual," remarked the Elder with a grave smile, as he laid down the letter. "I think it will be best to summon a church meeting for next Lord's Day, and utterly dismiss Master Lyford from our fellowship and communion. It is no less than sacrilege for a man who can write after this fashion to sit down at the Lord's table with us, professing to be of us."

"You are right, Elder," replied Bradford sternly, "and I leave the spiritual matter to you; but it is my duty, and one not to be slighted, to drive this traitor out of our body politic. He must leave Plymouth at once. Say you not so, Captain Standish?"

"I say, bundle him into the Little James and send him back to England to his dear cronies there, or, better still, strip off his gown and bands and hang him as a traitor."

"To send him to England we have no warrant, nor would it be wise to invite English legislation in our particular affairs," retorted the governor; "and as for hanging him, it is a course open both to these same objections and to something more. No, we shall simply bid him leave the colony and not return hither on any pretense. The wife and children may remain until he has a home whither to carry them."

"A righteous judgment," pronounced the Elder, and as Standish growled assent, the matter was settled, and so promptly carried into effect that in less than forty-eight hours the renegade forever turned his back upon the place and the people who had trusted and honored him, and whom, had he been a faithful servant of his Master and the Church, he might undoubtedly have led to a renewed allegiance to the venerable Mother whose unwise severity rather than whose doctrine had driven them from the home of their ancestors.

"There goes a viper scotched, not killed, and we shall feel his sting yet," remarked Standish, as he with Peter Browne and John Alden stood on the brow of Cole's Hill, and watched Lyford's embarkation in a fishing-boat belonging to Nantucket, where Oldhame had pitched his tent for a while. Here also, or at neighboring Weymouth, Blackstone, Maverick, Walford, and a few other of the Gorges party had succeeded to the houses left empty by Weston's men after their deliverance by Myles Standish from Pecksuot, Wituwamat, and their horde. In course of time, Blackstone, carrying his clergyman's coat, removed to Boston Common, Walford to Charlestown, and Maverick to East Boston, each man representing the entire population of each place; but still some settlers remained on the old site, so that from the time of Weston's arrival in 1622, this neighborhood has been the home of white men.

"Scotched, not killed," repeated Standish, filling his pipe, as he sat and mused in the autumn sunshine outside of his cabin door, while Barbara in her noiseless but competent fashion got ready a savory supper within, and Alick, with a bow made for him by Hobomok, fired not unskillful arrows at a target set upon the hillside.

A week later the captain's words came true, for the same fishing boat that had carried away Lyford put into Plymouth Harbor on an ebb tide, and sent off her boat with four men, one of whom was soon recognized as Oldhame. As the banished man leaped upon the Rock, followed by his comrades, all strangers to Plymouth, some of the older townsmen met him, and one of them gravely inquired his business.

"Business quotha!" blustered Oldhame, who was evidently the worse for liquor. "My business is first to tweak Billy Bradford's nose, and then to kick Myles Standish into a rat-hole, and finally to burn down your wretched kennels, and root up this doghole of a place, where I and my friends have met such scurvy treatment."

"An' your errand is so large an one, you had better go and seek the governor and his assistants without delay," replied Francis Cooke, waving his hand up Leyden Street, and restraining by a look some of the younger men, who seemed disposed to dispute the landing.

"Why, so I will, Cooke; I'll go up and speak to your masters, but not my masters, mind you, good Cooke; good Cooke, ha, ha! Come, now, hop into my boat and I'll carry you home to be my cook, mine own good cook, Francis! Hop in, I say!"

And the roysterer, with a roar of drunken laughter, strode up the hill, the strangers, who looked both anxious and ashamed, following slowly after him.

In the Town Square the invaders encountered Bradford with Doctor Fuller and Stephen Hopkins, and Oldhame, pushing himself into the group, began a violent tirade upon the abuses and insults that he averred had been offered both him and Lyford, and was proceeding to the most scurrilous threats and vituperations, when the governor, beckoning Bart Allerton, who, with several other young men, was hanging around the group of elders, said calmly,—

"Bart, find Captain Standish, and bid him summon a couple of the train-band, and bring them hither."

"Oho! Captain Shrimp is to appear on the scene, is he? Well, I've come here to settle old scores with him as well as the rest! Go fetch him, Bart; trot, boy, trot!"

"It needs not to fetch him, Master Oldhame, since he is here at your service." Thus speaking, the captain, who had been hastening down the hill before he was summoned, strode into the circle, a grim smile upon his face and the red light of battle in his eye.

"Ha! my little bantam cock! are you there?" And the reckless fellow aimed a backhanded blow at the captain's face, which the latter easily evaded by a side-movement, and returned with a square blow from the shoulder, taking effect under Oldhame's jaw, and sending him staggering back into the arms of one of his new comrades.

"Enough, enough!" exclaimed Bradford, holding up his hand. "A street brawl is not befitting or seemly. Captain Standish, arrest this man, and put him in the strong-room until we consider what measure to deal out to him."

"The tide is gone, or we would carry him aboard and be off altogether," suggested one of the strangers.

"Possibly not," quietly returned the governor. "It might not seem right to so lightly dismiss such an offense. We would bear ourselves meekly with all men, but it is not meet that our townsfolk should see their leaders insulted and braved thus insolently with impunity."

"Captain Gorges would have run a man through for less," replied the other. "But Oldhame said the Plymouth men were crop-eared psalm-singers, who would not fight."

"If Plymouth men had not fought to some purpose on the spot where you have settled, you would have found but sorry housing there," retorted Standish savagely, as he led his captive away, securely bound, and Bradford in his usual calm tones explained,—

"After our captain had slain Pecksuot and Wituwamat and dispersed their following, he nailed a placard to the tree at the gate of the stockade, whereon he had hung one of the ringleaders, warning the savages that if they burned or destroyed the dwellings that remained, he would come back and serve them as he had their misleader; and this cartel, although they could not read it, so terrified their superstitious fancies that Captain Gorges found housen for his men, and a stoccado to protect them."

"Yes," replied the stranger, gazing curiously after Standish, "we found the bones of the hanged man lying in a heap under the tree, and the marks of a deadly fray in the house where Pecksuot fell."

"Ay, so. It was a sad necessity, and one almost as grievous to us as to the savages," returned Bradford. "Now, sirs, we have no quarrel with you, nor wish for any. Your skiff will not float until three hours after noon, and when she does we shall doubtless send away Master Oldhame in her; meantime, you are welcome to look about and see our town and Fort, and discourse with the people. Master Hopkins, will you see that these men have some dinner?"

"Such as 'tis, they're welcome to some of mine," promptly replied Hopkins, whose comfortable house stood on the corner of Leyden and Main streets just opposite the governor's, and whose garden stretched along to Middle Street, not yet laid out. The size and convenience of his house, and the bountiful and cheerful hospitality of his wife, who, with the aid of her daughters Constance, Damaris, and Deborah, administered the domestic affairs, combining English thrift and neatness with colonial abundance, gave Hopkins the frequent opportunity of entertaining visitors to Plymouth, while Bradford saw that he was no loser by such a course.

Meanwhile the governor and his council sat in conclave, secure that their decision would find favor with the people, or at any rate with that nucleus and backbone of the commonalty known as "the first-comers," meaning the passengers of the Mayflower, the Fortune, and the Anne, with her tender the Little James.

At noon the tide turned, and the town went to dinner. About half past two Bartholomew Allerton beat the "assembly" in the Town Square, and at the well-understood summons men, women, and children gathered in the square, or clustered in the open doorways, all filled with curiosity as to the mode of punishment about to be meted out to the returned exile, and yet none in the least doubt as to its justice. Even the men whom he had brought with him to be the witnesses of his triumph stood supinely to view his disgrace, muttering among themselves, and casting uneasy glances down the hill to where their shallop lay still aground at the foot of the Rock, while the larger boat hardly swung afloat on the breast of the young tide.

Three o'clock, and the governor, the Elder, and the captain came out of the house of the first, robed in their official garments, and stood upon a platform of squared logs erected at the intersection of the streets and mounted with two small cannon called pateteros. A blast from the trumpet, and the gate of the Fort upon the hill swung open, and out came a strange procession: first, Bart Allerton with his drum, and three other young fellows with wind instruments, who rendered a fair imitation of the Rogue's

March; then twenty picked men, mostly from among the first-comers, each carrying his snaphance reversed; then Master Oldhame, bareheaded and barefooted, and with his arms tied across his chest; and finally, Lieutenant John Alden, bearing a naked sword, followed by a guard of four men well armed.

Down the hill they came at a foot-pace, the bugles and trumpet shrilling out their contemptuous cadences, and Oldhame, his pride subdued and his pot-valiancy all evaporated, stepping delicately as Agog, for the pebbles hurt his bare feet, and perhaps feeling with Agog that the bitterness of death was at his lips.

Before the platform, where stood the magnates and the cannon, the procession paused, the music ceased, and upon the silence rose the governor's calm, strong voice.

"John Oldhame, you have come hither in defiance of the formal edict of this government banishing you from the colony; and you have come with violence and insult, refusing to accept warning, or to depart peaceably. We therefore have resolved that since you return dishonorably, you shall depart in dishonor, taking with you the warning for the future, that the barrels of our pieces are more deadly than their stocks. Go, and mend your manners!"

He waved his hand, and the bugles recommenced their blare, while the twenty men opened their ranks and ranged themselves in two lines some three feet apart, but not directly opposite each other.

"Go on, prisoner!" ordered Alden, touching Oldhame with the hilt of his sword. "Go, and mend your manners!" And as the cowed yet furious rebel stepped forward, the first man of the line struck upward with the stock of his reversed musket, saying,—

"Go, and mend your manners!" The next instant the same blow and the same words fell from the minuteman diagonally opposite, and so down the entire line, until as the twentieth blow and twenty-second adjuration to "Go, and mend your manners" fell upon the humiliated bully, he broke down utterly, and with a howl of mingled rage and pain bolted into the door of John Howland's house next below Stephen Hopkins's, but was met by Elizabeth, who with little John clinging to her skirts and Desire in her arms boldly faced the intruder for a moment, and then looking into his streaming face and hunted eyes cried pitifully,—

"Oh, poor soul!" and seizing the scissors at her girdle cut the band confining his arms, and catching up a tankard of ale set ready for her husband held it to his lips, muttering,—

"Mayhap 'tis treason, but there, poor creature, drink, and then slink away down the hill while— Why, what's to do now in the street?"

"Why don't you say, 'Go, and mend your manners!'" hoarsely asked Oldhame; but still he drank, and then, glancing over his hostess's shoulder as she stood in the doorway, he swore a great oath, and pushing her rudely aside dashed out and down the hill to his boat.

For, unseen by the townsmen, all of them absorbed in the punishment parade, the ship Jacob, Captain William Pierce, had sailed into harbor upon the flood-tide, dropped anchor beside the Nantucket fishing craft, and set ashore her master, with his distinguished passenger Edward Winslow, who had been to England to try to straighten the tangled relations between the Pilgrims and the Adventurers, already playing fast and loose with their promises.

Some good-natured raillery from Captain Pierce upon the negligent outlook kept by the colonists served to relieve the strain of the late occurrence, and as Winslow with a face full of portent followed the governor into his house, John Oldhame stepped aboard the fishing vessel, and sailed out of Plymouth Harbor in a condition of unwonted quiet and humiliation.

CHAPTER VII.

MORTON OF MERRY MOUNT.

"Well, Master Trumpeter, and what do you make of yon craft? Are the Don Spaniards coming to invade New Plymouth, or has the king sent to impress you as major-domo of the royal hand?"

"Good-morrow, Captain Standish. The governor lent me his perspective glass, and sent me up on the hill to spy out who was coming."

"And that's all right, Bart. No need to make excuse for doing the governor's bidding, my lad."

"I was thinking, Captain, you found it strange to see me on the Fort without notice to you"—

"And so came up to call you to account? No, my boy, I know who's to be trusted and who not, else had I served in vain through those long years in the Low Countries. Had it been Gyles Hopkins now, or Jack Billington— But there, what make you of the craft?"

"I think, sir, 'tis Master Maverick's boat from Noddle's Island, and there are four men in her whose faces I cannot yet make out."

"A friendly visit, belike. Stay you here, Bart, until you can determine the craft, and then carry the news to the governor. I am going down to the Rock on mine own occasions."

Bowling merrily along before an easterly breeze, the ketch soon rounded Beach Point, and dropped her anchor opposite the village, but in midstream, and so soon as the sails were snugged, and all made ready for some possible change of weather, the four visitors stepped into a skiff and were sculled ashore by a tall, fine-looking young fellow, whose bronzed face and lithe figure were well set off by the buckskin hunting-shirt and red cap worn with a jaunty air not inharmonious with the young man's roving black eyes and flashing smile.

"Master Maverick and his son, Master Blackstone from Shawmut, and Master Bursley and Master Jeffries from Wessagussett," reported Bart Allerton, hat in hand, at the governor's door, and Bradford, laying down his book, replied with a grave smile,—

"I will go to meet them."

Half an hour later the three elder visitors with the governor, the captain, Allerton, Doctor Fuller, and one or two more, were closeted in the new room recently added to the governor's house, and used by him as a council chamber and court room.

Moses Maverick, the handsome young boatman, had meanwhile somewhat pointedly sought out Bart Allerton, and almost invited himself to accompany him home.

"Go you into the front room and entertain him, Remember," directed the young step-mother with a mischievous smile. "I am too busy with little Isaac to leave him just now."

And Maverick received the apologies of his hostess with an air so strangely contented that Remember paused half way in making them, and faltered and blushed and laughed, very much as a modest but open-eyed girl would do to-day.

"I told you last Lady Day that I should soon be here again, Remember," murmured the youth rather irrelevantly.

"I know naught of Lady Days," retorted the Pilgrim maid with an effort at a saucy little laugh.

"'Tis because your father is a Separatist, but we Mavericks are sound Churchmen," replied the lover. "Some day, mayhap, you'll be better advised."

Let us discreetly leave them to themselves, and seek the council chamber where Blackstone is saying,—

"Yes, Governor Bradford, we have come to you for that aid and support against the common foe which all Christians have a right to demand of each other, no matter how the forms of their Christianity may disagree."

"The plea is one never disallowed by the men of Plymouth," returned Bradford in his sonorous voice. "But what would you have us to do?"

"Why, to capture this Morton by force of arms, since words have no effect, and ship him back to England, where they say there is a warrant out against him for murder of some man in the west country with whom he had business concerns."

"That were a high-handed proceeding, specially sith his settlement is not within the domain of Plymouth," suggested the Elder cautiously.

"True," broke in Bursley impetuously. "But as Master Blackstone has told you, Morton sells pieces and ammunition and rum to the savages without let or stint, and they, having naught else to do, practice at a mark all day long, and soon will prove better shots than any white man. Then, when some new Wituwamat or Pecksuot shall arise to stir them to revolt, where shall we be? You had not won so easy a triumph there where I live, Captain Standish, had your foes been armed with snaphances."

"Not so easy, perhaps, but to my mind more honorable," replied Standish coldly. "Howbeit, I do not approve of arming the Indians."

"Of course, Governor," resumed Blackstone, who had been the principal speaker, "the peril is not great for you who can count a hundred fighting men with Captain Standish to lead them; but none other of the settlements is of any force, although friend Maverick here has fortified his island, and may depend upon a dozen men or so of his household, and the Hilton brothers at Piscataqua and Cocheco are stout and well-armed fellows, and my neighbor Thomas Walford at Mishawum[2] has a palisado round his house, and his blacksmith's sledge with some other weapons inside. Then at Naumkeag[3] are Roger Conant, Peter Palfrey, and the rest, with your old friend Lyford as their parson, and Conant is a fighting man as well as a godly one. But I, as all men know, am a man of peace as befits a parson; and there is David Thompson's young widow and child abiding on the island bearing his name, with only a couple of men-servants to defend them. If all of us drew together in one hold we should not count half the force of Plymouth, but we do not wish so to abandon our plantations."

"Have you labored with Thomas Morton, showing him the wrong he does?" asked Elder Brewster coldly, and eying the Churchman with strong disfavor, for Blackstone, with questionable taste, had chosen to wear upon this expedition the long coat and shovel hat carefully brought by him from England as the uniform of his profession. Dressed in these canonicals, with the incongruous addition of "Geneva bands," Blackstone regularly read the Church of England service on Sundays at his house upon the Common, sometimes alone, and sometimes to a congregation composed of the Walfords from Charlestown, the Mavericks from Noddle's Island or East Boston, the settlers from Chelsea, and perhaps in fine weather the Grays from Hull, and some of the folk from Old Spain in Weymouth. For all these were adherents to the Church of England after a fashion, although by no means ardent religionists of any sort; and as such, held in considerable esteem the eccentric parson living in the solitude he loved among his apple-trees, and beside his clear spring, now merged in the Frog Pond of our Common. A lukewarm Churchman, he was friendly enough to the Separatists, and now replied to Brewster with a smile,—

"I have labored so vainly, Elder, that I fear even your authority would be of no avail. I opine that our friend Standish here is the only man whose eloquence Thomas Morton will heed in the smallest degree."

"And the chief men of all the settlements are agreed in making this request of Plymouth?" asked the governor.

"Not only the chief, but every man among them," answered Maverick. "And what is more to the purpose, each one of the settlements will bear its share in whatsoever charges the arrest and transportation may involve."

"That is well, but should be set down in writing with signatures and witnesses," suggested Allerton, to whom Maverick haughtily replied,—

"Oh, never fear, Master Allerton. The most of us are honest men and not traders."

"No offense, Master Maverick, no offense; but it is well that all things should be done decently and in order," returned the assistant smoothly, and the council soon after broke up with the understanding that Bradford, as the only recognized authority in New England, should write Morton a formal protest in the name of all the English settlers, reminding him that King James of happy memory had, as one of his latest acts, issued a royal proclamation forbidding the sale of fire-arms or spirits to the savages, and calling upon him as an English subject to obey this edict.

If this protest proved of none effect, the Governor of Plymouth pledged himself to suppress the rebel and his mischief with the high hand.

FOOTNOTES:

[2] Charlestown.

[3] Salem.

CHAPTER VIII.

STANDISH AT MERRY MOUNT.

Some two weeks had passed by since the visit of the committee of safety to Plymouth; long enough for Bradford, ever moderate, ever considerate, to write a letter of kindly expostulation to Morton, and to receive an insolent and defiant reply; and now in a pleasant June afternoon the Plymouth boat, commanded by Standish, and manned by eight picked followers, drew into Weymouth fore-river, where upon the water-course now known as Phillips Creek, Weston and his men, some six or seven years before, had founded their unlucky settlement.

The fate of this settlement we have seen, and also learned that the houses protected by Standish's warning to the savages had since become the dwelling-place of some of the followers of Ferdinando Gorges, that showy personage who, coming to the New World with the romantic idea of proclaiming himself its governor, found it so savage and forbidding of aspect that, after a few months spent mostly as a guest of Plymouth, he quietly returned to England, civilization, and a sovereignty on paper. The houses repaired or built by him still remained, however, and among the Gorges men who continued to live in them were the Mr. Jeffries and Mr. Bursley who accompanied Blackstone and Maverick to Plymouth.

A little below Phillips Creek, the Monatoquit River empties into the bay, and across the river lies a fair height, now included in the town of Quincy, but then known as Passonagessit, whence one might then, and still may, look east and north upon the lovely archipelago of Boston Harbor, or westward to the blue hills of Milton. On its eastern face this height of Passonagessit sloped gently to the sea, with good harborage for boats at its foot, promising facilities for fishing and for traffic with the northern Indians.

Upon this headland in the early summer of 1625 a wild and motley crowd of adventurers pitched their tents, and soon replaced the canvas with comfortable log-houses and a stockaded inclosure. The leader of this company was one Captain Wollaston, perhaps the same adventurer whom Captain John Smith of Pocahontas memory encountered, some fifteen years before, on the high seas, acting as lieutenant to one Captain Barry, an English pirate. With Wollaston were three or four partners, and a great crew of bound servants, men who had either pledged their own time, or been delivered into temporary slavery as punishment by English magistrates, and the purpose of the leaders was to found a settlement like that of Plymouth. The place was named Mount Wollaston by the white men, while the Indians continued to call it Passonagessit, just as they still speak of Weymouth as Wessagusset. One New England winter, however, cooled the courage of Captain Wollaston, as it had that of Robert Gorges, and in the spring of 1626 he took about half his bound men to Virginia, where he sold their services to the tobacco planters at such a profit, that he wrote back to Mr. Rasdall, his second in command, to bring down another gang as soon as possible, and to leave Mount Wollaston in charge of Lieutenant Fitcher, until he himself should return thither.

Rasdall obeyed, and in making his parting charges to Fitcher remarked,—

"All should go well, so that you keep Thomas Morton in check. Give him his head and he will run away with you and Wollaston."

Fitcher assented with a rueful countenance, for he knew himself to be but a timid rider, and the Morton a most unruly steed, and the event proved his fears well grounded, for Rasdall had not reached Virginia before Morton in the lieutenant's temporary absence called the eight remaining servants together, produced some bottles of rum, a net of lemons, and a bucket of sugar, to which he bade his guests heartily welcome, greeting each man jovially by name, and telling them that the time had come to throw off their chains, to assert their rights, and to reap for themselves the benefit of their hard work. He assured them that he, although a gentleman, a learned lawyer, and a man of means, felt himself no whit above them, and asked nothing better than to live with them in liberty, fraternity, and equality, finally proposing that they should seize upon "the plant" of Mount Wollaston, turn Lieutenant Fitcher out of doors, and establish a commonwealth of their own. No sooner said than done! The men whom Morton addressed were, in fact, the dregs of the company left behind by Wollaston as not worth trading off. Perhaps he never intended to come back to claim them; perhaps if indeed he had been a pirate he took Morton's action as nothing more than a reasonable proceeding; at any rate this disappearance of Captain Wollaston and Lieutenant Rasdall was final, and except that the neighborhood of Passonagessit is still called Wollaston Heights, the very name of this adventurer would probably have been forgotten.

It was at any rate disused, for so soon as Lieutenant Fitcher had been, as he reported to Bradford, "thrust out a dores," the name of the place was changed to Merry Mount, and the life of debauch and profligacy promised by Morton inaugurated; as a natural consequence, Merry Mount soon acquired so wide a fame for license and disorder that it became the resort of the lawless adventurers who haunted the coast in those days, sometimes calling themselves fishermen, sometimes privateers, and sometimes buccaneers, and the whole affair grew to be a scandal, not only to Godfearing Plymouth, but to those other settlements, of sober, law-abiding folk, scattered up and down the coast, especially when in the spring of 1627 Morton set up a Maypole at Merry Mount, and proclaimed a Saturnalia of a week.

Now a Maypole, and dancing around it crowned with flowers, is in our day a very pretty and pastoral affair, only open to the objections of cold, wet, and absurdity. But in old English times it was a very different matter, being in effect a remnant of heathenesse, and the profligate worship of the goddess Flora. William Bradford, writing an account of the attack upon Merry Mount, expresses himself thus:—

"They allso set up a Maypole, drinking and dancing aboute it many days togeather, inviting the Indean women for their consorts, dancing and frisking togeather like so many fairies (or furies, rather) and worse practices. As if they had anew revived and celebrated the feastes of the Roman goddes Flora, or the beastly practices of the madd Bacchinalians."

Although Plymouth and its neighbors were shocked at these practices, they would not probably have interfered, beyond a remonstrance, with the amusements of the Merry Mountaineers had the matter stopped there, but, as the delegates to Plymouth represented, the selling of fire-arms to the Indians, teaching them to shoot, and inflaming their murderous passions with alcohol, was a very different matter, a matter of public import, and one to be arrested by any means before it went farther.

So after this long digression, tiresome no doubt, but essential to understanding what follows, we come back to Myles Standish and his eight men, "first-comers" all of them, pulling up their boat upon the shore at Wessagusset, just as they had done five years before. As they turned toward the path leading to the stockade, a man came hurriedly down to meet them.

"Good-morrow, Master Bursley," cried the captain cheerfully. "We are on our way to Merry Mount, and called to tell you so."

But Bursley held up his hand with a warning gesture, and so soon as he was near enough hoarsely muttered in unconscious plagiarism,—

"The devil's broke loose."

"Say you so, Bill Bursley!" responded Standish, showing all his broad white teeth. "I did not know he'd ever been in the bilboes!"

"Morton's here at the house, full of liquor and swearing all sorts of wicked intent toward—well now, Captain, if you won't take it amiss, I'll tell you that he calls you Captain Shrimp!"

"Following Master Oldhame," replied Standish carelessly. "I must marvel at the lack of sound wit at Wessagusset when so small a jest has to serve so many men. But you say this roysterer is here in your house?"

"No, in Jeffries' house. He came this morning asking that we should return with him to Merry Mount and help him against the 'Plymouth insolents' as he called you."

"And what answer did he get, Master Bursley?"

"What but nay?" demanded Bursley with a glance of honest surprise. "Was not I one of those who came the other day to Plymouth begging Governor Bradford to take order with this rebel? But he has been drinking, and is in such a woundy bad humor that but now he drew a knife upon Jeffries, and may have slain him outright before this."

"Say you so! Then, let us hasten and bury him with all due honors!" exclaimed the captain, in whose nostrils the breath of battle was ever a pleasant savor. "Howland, Alden, Browne, all of you, my merry men! Leave the boat snug, and follow to the house, to chat with Master Morton who awaits us there."

And the captain sped joyously up the path, looking to the priming of his long pistols, and loosening Gideon in his scabbard as he went. A rod from the house, however, a bullet nearly found its billet in his brain, while on the threshold stood Morton, his face flushed, his gait unsteady, and a smoking pistol in his hand.

"Hola! Captain Shrimp, I warn you stand out of range of my pistol practice. You might get a hurt by chance!" cried he, raising another pistol, but before it could be aimed, or the captain take action, somebody within the house struck up the madman's arm, and as he turned savagely upon this new foe, Standish, whose muscles were strong and elastic as a panther's, sprang across the intervening space, and seizing his prisoner by the collar shouted,—

"Yield, Morton, or you're but a dead man!"

"One man may well yield to a mob," muttered Morton sullenly; and seeing that he was disarmed, Standish released his hold saying quietly,—

"Fair and softly, Master Morton! Governor Bradford sends me and these men, praying for your company at Plymouth, so soon as may be. If you will go quietly, well; but if you resist, you will go all the same; so choose you."

"The Governor of Plymouth does me too much honor to send so many of his servants with the major-domo at the head," replied Morton bitterly. "And sith as you say the invitation may not be refused, I'll e'en accept it, but would first return to Merry Mount to fetch some clothes and set my house in order."

"Your return to Merry Mount will be as the governor orders hereafter. I was bid to bring you to Plymouth without delay, and that I shall do."

"But not to-night, I trust, Captain Standish," interposed Jeffries. "A shrewd tempest is threatening, and by the time it is past, night will be upon us and no moon."

"With the shoals and sandbars of this coast thick as plums in a Christmas pudding," remarked Philip De la Noye, whereat Peter Browne growled, "Make it a Thanksgiving pudding, an it please you, Master Philip. We hold no Papist feasts here."

Stepping outside the door, Standish took a survey of the skies, the sea, and the forest, already waving its green boughs in welcome to the coming rain.

"Do you hear the 'calling of the sea,' Captain?" asked a Cornish man, placing his curved hand behind his ear, and bending it to catch the deep murmur and wail that float shoreward from the hollow of ocean when a thunder-storm is gathering in its unknown spaces.

"Yes," replied Standish in an unusually hushed voice, "we will stay awhile; perhaps the night, if our friends can keep us."

"Glad and gayly," said Jeffries, who, truth to tell, was a little afraid that the remaining garrison of Merry Mount might descend upon his house in the night to rescue their leader or avenge his loss.

"And we'll feast you on the pair of wild turkeys my boy shot to-day," cried Bursley. "Come, we'll make a night on't, sith there are not beds enough for all to lie down."

"With your leave, sirs, I will claim one of those beds and take my rest while I may," broke in Morton sourly. "I have no mind for reveling with tipstaves and jailers."

"Ne'ertheless you might keep a civil tongue in your head, Morton," angrily exclaimed Browne, but Standish interposed,—

"Tut, tut, man! Never jibe at a prisoner. A bruised creature ever solaces itself with its tongue, and so may a bruised man. Let him alone!"

"Thank you for nothing, Captain Shrimp!" snarled Morton; but Standish only nodded good-humoredly, and began looking about to see if the log hut could be made secure for the night. Finally, a small bedroom off the principal or living room was set aside for Morton, the window shutter nailed from the outside, and a man set to watch beside him, and be responsible for his safety.

The turkeys were soon plucked, dressed, and each hung by a string tied to one leg before a rousing fire, so oppressive for the June night, that Standish retreated to a shed at the back of the house, and stood watching the magnificent spectacle of the tempest now in full force. On one side lay the primeval forest, dense and gloomy with its evergreen growth, through whose serried ranks the mad wind ploughed like a charge of cavalry, rending the giants limb from limb, lashing the bowed heads of those who resisted, trampling down in its savage fury old and young, the sturdy veterans and the helpless saplings.

At the other hand lay the ocean, seen through a slant veil of hurtling rain, its waters flat and foaming like the head of a tigress that lays back her ears and gnashes her teeth as she crouches for her spring, and ever and anon, between the crashing peals of thunder and the splitting report of some lightning bolt riving the heart of oak or mast of pine, came the weird "calling of the sea," the voice of deep crying unto deep:—

"Watchman, what of the night? Watchman, what of the night? The watchman said, The morning cometh, and also the night: if ye will inquire, inquire ye!" "But hurt not the earth, neither the sea, nor the trees, till we shall have sealed the servants of our God!"

In face of this vast antiphony, Morton of Merry Mount and his concerns sank to insignificance; and so felt Myles Standish, who had all the love of nature inseparable from a great heart; but his had not been so great had it been capable of slighting the meanest duty, and his last act before midnight when he lay down for a few hours' repose was to see that his prisoner was both safe and comfortable, and that two reliable men were upon the watch. One of these was Richard Soule and the other John Alden, to whom the captain said,—

"Now mind you, Jack, it has been a hard day's work, and our friends' hospitality full liberal. Do you feel your head heavy? If so, say the word, and I'll watch myself and be none the worse for it on the morrow. Speak honest truth now, lad."

But Alden so indignantly protested that nothing could tempt him to sleep in such an emergency, and so affectionately besought his friend to take some rest, that the captain at length complied, much to the delight of Morton, who, feigning sleep, had listened to the conversation.

Twelve o'clock, and one, and two passed quietly, yet not unnoted, for Morton, among other claims to distinction, was the possessor of a "pocket-clock," the only one at Wessagusset that night, since even Standish did not aspire to such luxury, and was well content to divide his day by the sun and the dial, if it were clear, or by his instinct, if it were stormy, while the night was told by its stars, the deeper and lessening darkness, or the chill that always precedes the dawn. Half past two, and the prisoner turned himself silently upon his bed. At its foot sat John Alden, his snaphance between his knees, and his head fallen forward and sidewise till he seemed to be peering down its barrel; but alas, his stertorous breathing proclaimed that nature had succumbed to fatigue and the watchman was fast asleep.

A smile of elfish glee widened Morton's already wide and loose-lipped mouth and twinkled in his beady eyes, as without a sound, and with the cautious movements of a cat, he stole off the bed, seized his doublet which had been laid aside, and crept out of the bedroom into the kitchen where, with his head and shoulders sprawling over the table, and his piece lying upon it, Richard Soule lay sweetly dreaming of seizing the rebel by the hair of his head, and dragging him to the foot of a gallows high as Haman's. With the same malicious grin and the same cat-like movement Morton stole rapidly past this second Cerberus, pausing only to secure his snaphance. The outer door was made fast by an oaken bar dropped into iron staples, and this the runaway lightly lifted out and stood against the wall; but as he opened the door, the storm tore it from his hand, threw down the bar, extinguished the candles, and roused the sleepers.

Myles Standish, whose vigilant brain had warned him even through a heavy sleep that there was danger in the camp, was already afoot and groping for the ladder whereby to descend from his loft when the shriek of the wind and the bewildered outcries of the watch told him what had happened, and like a whirlwind he was down the steps, calling upon Alden and Soule, and loudly demanding news of their prisoner.

"He's gone! He's gone!" cried Soule, while Alden mutely bestirred himself with flint and steel to strike a light. When it was obtained, and disastrous certainty replaced the captain's worst suspicions, his anger knew no bounds, and the hot temper, generally controlled, for once burst its limits and poured out a short, sharp torrent of words that had better never have been spoken, until at last John Alden, slowly roused to a state of wrath very foreign to his nature, retorted,—

"The next time that Nell Billington is brought before the court as a scold, it might be well to present Myles Standish along with her. What say you, Dick?"

"Haw! Haw!" roared Soule, who, although a worthy citizen, was not a man of fine sensibilities. Standish glanced at him with angry contempt, and then fixed his eyes upon Alden with a look before which that honest fellow shrunk, and colored fiery red as he stammered,—

"I—I said amiss—nay, then,—forgive me, Captain."

"The captain can easily forgive what the friend will not soon forget, John," said Standish gravely, for indeed the brief treason of his ancient henchman had struck deep into the proud, loving heart of the soldier. "But," continued he in the same breath, "this is no time for private grievances—follow me!"

And opening the door he dashed out into the night, and down the path to the rude pier where his own boat and the two belonging to the settlement were made fast. As he approached, a figure slipped away, and was lost in the neighboring thicket; Myles could not see it, but surmised it, and quick as thought a rattling charge of buckshot followed the slight sound hardly to be distinguished amid the clashing of branches, the scream of the wind, and the sobbing blows of the surf upon the shore.

Morton, lying flat upon his face behind a big poplar, heard the shot fall around him, and knew that more would come; so, pursuing the tactics of his Indian allies, he wriggled backward, still clinging as closely as possible to mother earth, until, arrived at the roots of a giant oak, he drew himself upright behind it, and stood silent and waiting. The captain waited also, and in a moment came the green glare both men counted upon, and while Myles springing forward searched the thicket with another storm of shot and then with foot and sword, Morton, taking a rapid survey of the situation, selected his route, and sheltered by the crash of thunder which drowned all other sounds sprang from the oak to a clump of cedars higher up the hill, and so, guided by the lightning, and screened from the quick ear of his pursuer by the thunder, he gradually gained the trail made by the Indians between Wessagusset and the head waters of the tidal river Monatoquit; crossing this channel with infinite danger, the fugitive made his way down the other bank, and about daylight reached Merry Mount greatly to the astonishment of the only three of his comrades who remained at home, the rest of the garrison having gone under guidance of some of their Indian allies to trade for beaver in the interior.

Standish meanwhile, finding that the prisoner had made good his escape, returned to the house, and setting aside the condolences of his hosts and the shamefaced penitence of Richard Soule, for John Alden said never a word, he passed the remaining hours of darkness in examining his weapons, in pacing up and down his narrow quarters, gnawing his mustache, fondling the hilt of Gideon, and looking out of the door or the unglazed window-place. The hosts meantime bestirred themselves to prepare a savory meal of venison steaks, corn cakes, and mighty ale, to which, just as the first streaks of daylight appeared through the breaking clouds, the whole party sat down, the stern and silent captain among them, for angry and mortified though he was, the old soldier had served in too many rude campaigns not to secure his rations when and where they might be had. But the meal was very different from the jolly supper of the night before, and it was rather a relief when the captain rising briefly ordered,—

"Fall in, men! To the boat with you. Our thanks for your kind entertainment, Master Jeffries, and you, Master Bursley. We will let you know the ending of our enterprise so soon as may be."

And as the sun rose across the sea, whose blue expanse dimpled and laughed at thought of its wild frolic during his absence, the Plymouth boat, crossing the mouth of the Monatoquit and skirting its marshy basin, drew in to the landing place of Merry Mount, not without expectation of a volley from some ambush near at hand. None such came, however, and so soon as the boat was secured, the captain, deploying his men in open order that a shot might harm no more than one, led them up the gentle slope and halted in the shelter of a clump of cedars, whose survivor stands to-day lifeless and broken, but yet a witness to the mad revels of Merry Mount and their sombre ending. His men safe, Standish himself advanced to parley with the garrison. As he emerged from the shelter of the grove Alden silently stepped behind, and would have followed, but the captain, without looking round, coldly said,—

"Remain here, Lieutenant Alden, until you are ordered forward," and the young man slunk back just as a bullet whistled past the captain's ear. Pulling his handkerchief from his pocket Standish thrust his bayonet through the corner, and holding it above his head, advanced until Morton's voice shouted through a porthole beside the door,—

"Halt, there, Captain Shrimp! I'm on my own domain here, garrisoned, armed, victualed, and ready for a siege. What do you want, Shrimp?"

"I demand the body of Thomas Morton, and if the garrison of this place are wise, they will yield it up before it is taken by force of arms and their hold burned over their heads."

A little silence ensued, for the threat of fire was a formidable one, and Morton's three assistants had counted the enemy's force as it landed, and were now clamoring for surrender. But he, who at least was no coward, retorted upon them with a grotesque oath that alone, if need be, he would chase these psalm-singers into the ocean, and returning to the porthole shouted again,—

"Hola! Captain, Captain Shrimp"—

"I hold no parley with one so ignorant of the uses of war as to insult a flag of truce," interposed Standish, and Morton laughing boisterously rejoined,—

"I cry you mercy, noble sir, and will in future, that is to say, the near future, treat you with all the honor due to the Generalissimo of the Plymouth Army. And now deign, most puissant leader, to satisfy me as to the intent of the Governor of Plymouth should he gain possession of the body of Thomas Morton, that is to say of the living body, for should you see fit to carry him naught but a murdered carcass, well I wot he would hang it to the wall of his Fort upon the hill to keep company with the skull of Wituwamat. So again I demand—and I crave your pardon, most worshipful, if I am somewhat prolix; but indeed it is such a merry sight to watch your noble countenance waxing more and more rubicund and wrathful while I speak"—

"When I have counted ten I shall order the assault if I have no reasonable answer sooner," interrupted Standish briefly. "One, two"—

"Hold, hold, man! Why so violent and rash? Tell me in a word what will Bradford do with me an I yield?"

"Send you to England for trial."

"Trial on what count?" And as he asked the question Morton's voice took on a new tone, one of anxiety and even alarm, for conscience was clamoring that a dark story of robbery and murder might have followed him from the western shores of Old England to the eastern coast of New. But Standish's reply reassured him.

"For selling arms and ammunition to the Indians contrary to the king's proclamation."

"And what is a proclamation, Master General?" demanded the rebel truculently. "Mayhap you do not know that I, Thomas Morton, Gentleman, am a clerk learned in the law, a solicitor and barrister of Clifford's Inn, London, and I assure you that a royal proclamation is not law, and its breach entails no penalty. Do you comprehend this subtlety, mine ancient?

Suppose I *have* broken a proclamation of King James's, what penalty have I incurred, if not that of the law?"

"The penalty of those who disobey and insult a king, whatever that may be," sturdily replied Standish. "But all that"—

"Nay, nay; know you not, most valiant Generalissimo, that while a law entered upon the statute book of England remains in force until it is repealed, a royal proclamation dies with the monarch who utters it? King James's proclamation sleeps with him at Westminster, and I never have heard that King Charles has uttered any."

"Let it be so! I know naught and care less for these quips and quiddities of the law. The Standishes are not pettifoggers of Clifford's nor any other Inn. My errand is to fetch you to Plymouth, and there has been more than enough delay already. Will you surrender peaceably?"

"Surrender! Why look you here, man, or rather take my word for it sith you may not look. My table is spread with dishes of powder, and bowls of shot, and flagons of Dutch courage; we are a goodly garrison, and armed to the teeth; we are behind walls, and could, if we willed, pick you off man by man without giving you the chance of a return shot. In fact, it is only my tenderness of human life that holds me back from greeting you as you deserve"—

"Enough, enough! I will wait here no longer to be the butt of your ribaldry. Before you can patter a prayer we will smoke you out of your hole like rats."

And Myles was in fact retreating upon the body of his command when Morton hailed again,—

"Hold, hold, my valiant! I was about to say that I purpose surrender, both to save the effusion of human blood and to prevent damage to the house, which although no lordly castle serves our turn indifferently well as a shelter."

"You surrender, do you?"

"On conditions, Captain. The garrison shall retain its colors and arms, and march out with all the honors"—

"Pshaw, man! I know as well as you that four of your men are away, and that there can be no more than three with you. As for conditions, it is our part to dictate them, and I hereby offer your men their freedom if they abandon the evil practices learned of their betters. For yourself I promise naught but safe convoy to Plymouth."

"'Perdition seize thee, ruthless' Shrimp!" shouted Morton in a fury; "we will come out and drive you into the sea to feed the fishes."

"Ay, come out as fast as you may, or you'll be smoked out like so many wasps," retorted Standish, tearing away his flag of truce, and waving his sword as signal for the advance of his little troop, four of whom carried blazing torches. But Morton, although he had stimulated his courage a little too freely, had not quite lost sight of that discretion which is valor's better part, and absolutely sure that whatever Standish threatened he would fully perform, he resolved at all events to save his house; so seizing a handful of buckshot he crammed it into his already overloaded piece, called upon his men to follow, and flinging open the door rushed out shouting,—

"Death to Standish! Death! Death!" But the clumsy musket was too heavy for his inebriated grasp, and before he could bring it to an aim Standish sprang in, seized the barrel with one hand and Morton's collar with the other, at the same time so twisting his right foot between the rebel's legs as to bring him flat upon his back, while the blunderbuss harmlessly exploding supplied the din of battle.

"There, my lad, that's a Lancashire fall," cried Standish with an angry laugh. "They didn't teach you that in Clifford's Inn, did they now?"

"Oh, murder! murder! I'm but a dead man! Oh! Oh!" shrieked the voice of one of the besieged, and Standish turning sharply demanded,—

"Who gave the order to strike? Alden, how dare you attack without orders!"—

"I attacked nobody, Captain Standish," replied John Alden more nearly in the same tone than he had ever addressed his beloved commander. "I carried my sword in my hand thus, and was making in to the house when this drunken fool stumbled out and ran his nose against the point. He'll be none the worse for a little blood-letting."

"Two of my fellows were drunk, and one an arrant coward, or you had not made so easy a venture of your piracy," snarled Morton viciously, and one of the younger of the Plymouth men would have dealt him a blow with the flat of his sword, but Standish struck it up saying sternly,—

"Hands off, Philip De la Noye, or you'll feel the edge instead of the flat of my sword. Know you nothing, nothing at all of the usages of war that you would strike an unarmed prisoner!"

A few moments more and the whole affair was over. Morton's three men, foolish, worthless fellows, hardly dangerous even under his guidance, and perfectly harmless when deprived of it, were set at liberty with a stern warning from Standish that they were simply left at Merry Mount on probation, and that the smallest disobedience to the law prohibiting the sale of fire-arms, or instruction of the Indians in their use, would at once be known at Plymouth and most severely punished.

"As for your Maypole, and your Indian blowzabellas, and your dancing and mummery," concluded the captain, "I for one have naught to say, except that there must be some warlock-work in the matter to tempt even a squaw to frisk round a Maypole with such as you."

Morton, sullen, silent, and disarmed, was meantime led to the boat between Alden and Howland, the other men after, and last of all Standish muttering,—

"Better if there had been a garrison strong enough to hold the position. Then we might have burned the house and haply slain the traitor in hot blood."

CHAPTER IX.

THE KYLOE COW.

"Barbara! Wife!"

"I am here, Myles, straining the milk. I shall make some furmety for supper. Even Lora begins to beg for it, and the boys dote upon it, little knaves!"

"Let the furmety wait for a bit, and come out here to see old Manomet in the evening light. 'Tis a sight I never tire of."

"Ay, 'tis very fair," replied Barbara coldly, as she came and sat for a moment upon the bench at the cottage door, where Myles was wont to smoke his pipe, and muse upon many matters never brought to words.

A little lower down the hill Alick and his brother Myles were playing with John and Joseph Alden, while Betty, a stick in her hand, drove all four boys before her, she with mimic airs of anger and they of terror.

"Very fair!" echoed the captain irritably. "You know naught and care less for Nature, Bab. Your thought never gets beyond your furmety pot or Alick's breeches."

"And that's all the better for you and Alick, Myles," replied the wife in her usual placid tones; but then, with one of those sudden revulsions by which placid people occasionally surprise their friends, she drew in her breath with something between a sob and a groan and burst out:

"Oh, Myles! Myles! Nature do you call it, and I not love the face of Nature do you say! Nay, man, this is not Nature, these dark woods and barren sands and lonesome hills, with never a chimney in sight,—that's not the Nature I love and long for. My heart goes back to the pleasant fields and good old hills of Man. There are mountains grander by far than yon dark Manomet, as you call it, and yet pranked all over with cottages, where honest folk find a home and the stranger is ever welcome. And then the fair valleys between, with the peaceful steads where men are born and die in sight of their fathers' graves, and the old thatched roofs, and the stonecrop on the walls, and the roses clambering over the casements, and oh, the little kyloe cows coming home at night, and the poultry"—

She paused abruptly and threw her apron over her face. Myles carefully knocked the ashes out of his pipe, laid it upon a ledge above the bench, and taking his wife by the arm led her into the house where he might seat her upon his knee with no risk of scandalizing chance spectators. Then he calmly said,—

"The worst of quiet creatures like you, Bab, is that a man never knows the fire's alight till the house is in a blaze. Now as you, or was it Priscilla Alden, said once of me, 'A little pot's soon hot,' and all the world is forced to know it, but you,—art homesick for the old country, lass?"

"Nay, Myles, there is no home to be sick for; all is changed there; but I would like it better if we had a little holding of our own, and our own cow, and some ducks, and a goose fattening for Michaelmas."

"But you share the great red cow with Winslow's folk, and have milk enough for your furmety, sweetheart!" And the grim warrior smiled as tenderly as a mother upon the flushed wet face so near his own. Barbara smiled too, and wiping away the tears sat upright, but was not allowed to leave her somewhat undignified position upon her husband's knee.

"There, Myles, 'tis past now, and I will be more sensible"—

"Prythee don't, child! I like thee better thus."

"Nay, but we're growing old folk, goodman, and it behooves us to be sober and recollected"—

"Nonsense, nonsense, Bab; there's no lass among them all that shows so fair a rose upon her cheek, or such a wealth of sunny hair, as my Bab, and as for thine eyes, lass, they are a marvel"—

"Now! now! now! well then, dear, I'll behave myself, after all that sweet flattery, and—come, let us go out and look at Manomet."

"Nay. Your longing for a place you may call your own, and have your kine and poultry and all that about you, marries so well with a thought I've been turning over and over in my mind for a month or more, that I'll e'en give it you now, and Manomet and the furmety may wait another ten minutes, or so."

"Well, then, let me but take my knitting"—

"No. You shall do naught but listen, and you shall sit where you are! For once I'll have your whole mind"—

"For once, Myles!"

"Ay, for once,—look as grieved as you may out of those eyen of yours! Well enough do you know that Alick, and little Myles, and now Mistress Lora have well-nigh pushed their poor old dad out of their mother's heart"—

"Myles! Dost really think it, love?"

The captain held his wife as far from him as her seat upon his knee would allow, and eagerly read her fair troubled face, her tender blushes, quivering lips, and lovely, loving eyes, where the tears stood and yet were restrained from falling—read and read as men devour with incredulous eyes some voucher of almost incredible good fortune. Then he slowly said,—

"Truly God has been very good to me, my wife. His name be praised."

It was a rare aspiration from those bearded lips, not innocent of the strange oaths and fierce objurgation well known to the soldiery of that day,—'our army in Flanders,'—and over Barbara's face came a look of such joy and peace as transformed its quiet comeliness to true beauty. But it was she who with woman's tact dropped a veil over that moment's exaltation before it should degenerate into commonplace.

"What is your plan, dear?" asked she, and her husband, with a half-conscious feeling of relief, drew a long breath, and said,—

"Oh—yes. Well, Bab, I, as well as you, would be content to live a little farther from some of our townsfolk; it is not here as it was at first, or even when you came. Then we were all of one mind and one interest, and if I could not belong to their church as they call it, at least I respected their beliefs, and they let mine alone. But now, amid all this bickering with Lyford and Oldhame"—

"But Oldhame has gone, and so has Lyford, and are forbidden to come hither again," interposed Barbara, and her husband slowly and dubiously replied, "I know, Bab, I know; but for all that somewhat of ill feeling in the town has grown out of that affair, and though there's no man on God's earth so near to me as William Bradford, and none I reverence more than the Elder, or had rather smoke a pipe with than Surgeon Fuller, there are others that are to my temper like a red rag to a bull, and it's safer all round that we should not day by day be forced to rub shoulders. So the long and short on't is, Bab, for I'm not good at speechifying, it needs Winslow for that, I have spoken to Bradford about taking possession of that sightly hill across the bay"—

"The one you fired a cannon at, the other day?" interrupted Barbara slyly.

"Yes—that is, you goose, I fired toward it, just to see how far the saker would carry."

"Nay, I think it was a sort of salute you were giving to some fancy of your own, Myles, anent that hill."

"Well, then, since you will have me make myself out no older than Alick, I had been marking how the headland stood up against the gold of the western sky, and it minded me so of Birkenclyffe at Duxbury, and of my boyhood at Chorley and Wigan, and of fair days gone by"—

He paused, and Barbara knew that his thought was of Rose, the sweet blossom of his youth, Rose, whom he had carried in his pride to the neighborhood of the stately domain that ought to have been his and hers, and spent there with her almost the only idle month of his life. She knew, and her heart contracted with a slow, miserable pang, but she only said,—

"Yes, it does look like Birkenclyffe. And you think you could be happy in living there, Myles?"

"Happy!" echoed the soldier moodily. "I should be happy if the wars would break out afresh, and Gideon and I might hear once more the music that we love. We rust here, we two."

"But the children, Myles! The boys so like their father, and Lora—would you have them orphans, and me"—

"Ah, Lora! I did not tell you when I came home from England, wife, for I did not want to hear any jibes and gainsaying"—

"Oh, Myles, do I jibe at you?"

"Well, no,—no Bab, not jibes; but you know, lass, we never were quite of a mind about the Standish dignities"—

"Dear heart, we have left all that behind us in the Old World! Here we Standishes have dignity and observance in full measure, because we belong to thee, love. Captain Standish, head of the colony's strong men, is the founder of a new race in this New World."

"Nay, nay, Barbara, you talk but as a woman, and you never did rise up to the lawful pride of your birth"—

And the captain all unconsciously put his wife off his knee, and rising, strode up and down the room, tugging at his red beard, and frowning portentously. Barbara, her hands folded in her lap, and a sad smile upon her lips, sat watching him.

"It is as well to tell you now as to keep it for years," broke out the captain suddenly. "Nothing will change it, that is, nothing but Alexander's death"—

"Alexander's death! Not our boy, Myles!"

"No, no, no, child! Alexander, son of my cousin Ralph Standish of Standish Hall. When I was in England I went to see him as I told you."

"Yes, dear."

"I went to enforce upon him, newly come to the estates, my just and honest claim to my grandfather's inheritance which Ralph's grandfather juggled out of the orphan boy's hands, and which they have kept ever since."

"I supposed that was your errand, but as I saw naught had come of it I asked you no questions, Myles."

"And therein showed yourself the kindly sensible woman you ever were, wife. But there is more to the matter. Ralph is an honest fellow, and after some days of looking into the matter he confessed the justice of my claim. I tell you, Bab, we went through those old parchments like two weasels from the Inns of Court; Morton of Clifford's could have been no subtler; we had out the old deeds from the muniment-room, and sent to Chorley Church for the registry book, where are set down the marriage of my father and mother and my own birth and baptism; and I showed him Queen Bess's commission to her well-beloved Myles Standish, born on that same date, and at the last, over a good pottle of sack, he confessed to me that I was in the right, but added, with a smile too sly for a Standish to wear, that I should find it well-nigh impossible to prove the matter at law, for, as he was not ashamed to say to my beard, neither he nor his lawyers would help me, and he knew, though he had the decency not to say it, I have no money to tickle the palms of the judges, the commissioners, the court officials, and the Lord Harry alone knows who they are, but all too many for me."

"Then your cousin is a knave and a robber!"

"Nay, nay, Bab! Nay, I know not that one could expect a man to strip himself of half his estate if the law bade him keep it"—

"You would, Myles."

"Ah, well, I was ever a thriftless loon, with no trader's blood in my veins to show me how to keep or to get money. Ralph's grandmother was fathered by a man who made his money in commerce."

And the captain smiled as one well content with his own chivalrous incapacity, then hastily went on. "But though Ralph would not give me mine own, nor even let me take it if I tried, he had an offer to make on his part. His oldest son, Alexander by name, was then an infant of two years, a sturdy little knave already scorning his petticoats, and Ralph proposed that we should solemnly betroth him then and there to our Lora"—

"But Lora was not born when you were in England five years ago, Myles."

"No; but I knew that our two little lads must in course of time have a sister, and counted on her. Truth to tell, Barbara, Ralph and I picked a name for her off the family tree. Lora."

"If I had known it, the child never should have borne the name, and if I could I would change it now!"

And Barbara, seriously angry, rose from her chair and would have left the room, but her husband detained her.

"There, look you, now! I knew you would take it amiss, and told Ralph so, and he bade me keep it to myself, at all odds till the girl was born and named, and so I have. And yet I do not see what angers you so, Barbara, except that you ever favored your mother's family, and held your Standish blood too cheap."

"That quarrel well-nigh parted us ere ever we came together, Myles. Haply it had been better if we had been content to rest simply cousins and never married."

"Commend me to a good woman for thrusts both deep and sure when once she is angered," cried Myles, flinging out of the house and up the hill to his den in the Fort.

But when Alick and Betty Alden raced each other thither to tell him that supper was ready, the choleric captain had fully recovered his temper, and found his wife so placid and quietly cheerful that he supposed she also had both forgiven and forgotten.

Which shows that the great Captain of Plymouth understood the strategy of battle better than that of a woman's heart. Nor did he ever note, that from that day Barbara never spoke her daughter's name if it could possibly be avoided, calling her generally "my little maid," and as the child grew, addressing her as May, the sweet old English contraction of maiden.

A few weeks later, as Barbara set the stirabout that sometimes served instead of furmety upon the table, her husband entered, and throwing his hat into Lora's lap said in a tone of well deserving,—

"There, Bab, I've bought out Winslow's share in the red cow for five pounds and ten shillings, to be paid in corn, and I've satisfied Pierce and Clark for their shares with a ewe lamb apiece, so now it is mine, and I give it to you. She's not the kyloe cow you were longing for, but she's your own."

"Thank you, Myles," replied Barbara, flushing with pleasure. "And is it quite settled that we are to go over to the Captain's Hill as they begin to call it?"

"Duxbury, I mean to call it in due time. Yes, dame, the men and I are going over to-morrow morning to fell timber, and you shall have some sort of shelter of your own over there before you're a month older."

CHAPTER X.

THE UNEXPECTED.

It was just as true in 1625 as it will be in 1895 that nothing is certain to occur except the unexpected; but the idea had not yet been phrased, and even if it had been, William Bradford's turn of mind was absolutely opposed to the epigrammatic, so it was in sober commonplace that he remarked,—

"I never thought to have spoken with you again in Plymouth, Master Oldhame, but sith you urge pressing business as your excuse for coming hither, I am ready to hear it."

The governor sat in his chair of office, and the Assistants were ranged each man in his place. At the end of the platform stood John Oldhame, and behind him Bartholomew Allerton and Gyles Hopkins, each carrying a pike, and looking very important.

But except for these nine men the great chamber where we assisted at the Court of the People was empty, and the sad afternoon light fell across the vacant benches, and glimmered upon the low-browed wall upheld by sturdy knees of oak, with a sort of mournful curiosity quite pathetic; this curiosity was, however, reflected in the minds of the townsfolk of Plymouth in a degree far more ludicrous than pathetic, man often falling short of the dignity of nature.

All that they knew, these good people, was that about noon a Nantasket boat had rounded Beach Point, anchored in the channel, and sent a skiff ashore under command of William Gray, the elder of two brothers, representing the solid men of Nantasket at that day. Stepping on the Rock, Master Gray demanded to be led to the governor, a demand complied with the more readily that as he declined to communicate his business to any one else. Dinner-time came and went, and as the town returned to its posts of observation it noted William Gray rowing back to the vessel, receiving a passenger into his skiff, and bringing ashore the very John Oldhame whom Plymouth had so ignominiously dismissed some two years before. The same, and yet a very different John Oldhame from the drunken ruffler of that day, or the blustering bully who a year before that had been solemnly exiled from Plymouth; yes, a strangely meek and quiet John Oldhame this, who, looking neither to the right nor the left, strode up the hill to the Fort, apparently not noticing, certainly not resenting, the attendance of the two men-at-arms who escorted or guarded him, as one might elect to call it.

So much had Plymouth seen, and Helena Billington, arms akimbo, and head inclined to one side, was beginning to vituperate the tyrants who had beguiled an unfortunate gentleman into their clutches, and now would clap him up in jail, when those very tyrants severally appeared coming out of their houses and leisurely climbing the hill.

"The governor, and the Elder, and the captain, and the doctor, and Master Winslow, and Master Allerton," counted she breathlessly, and not without a certain awe at sight of all the authority of the colony paraded before her eyes; and as the last doublet disappeared within the gate, she sagely shook her head, with the conclusion, "Well, gossip, it passeth my comprehension or thine, and I'll e'en hie me under cover when it rains, for only a fool will stay out to get drenched."

From which somewhat blind apothegm we may perhaps evolve the theory that Goodwife Billington was not one of those whom our modern slang declares "don't know enough to go in when it rains!"

"Seat yourself an you will, Master Oldhame, and speak your errand," repeated the governor a little more indulgently, for in fact Oldhame's weather-and-timeworn face and somewhat bowed shoulders suggested ill health or great suffering, a look supplemented by his voice, as dropping upon the bench which young Allerton pushed forward he slowly said,—

"My thanks, Governor Bradford. I have come here to-day upon an errand so strange that I can scarce credit it myself, and I know not that in my half century of years I have ever charged myself with the like.

"Man, it is to crave pardon for my ill offices to you, and these your associates, and to all the town of Plymouth, where I repaid kind entertainment and many good turns with as much of evil and malevolence. Can you, as Christian men, forgive me?"

"As Christians," began Bradford, after a pause of unfeigned astonishment, "we are bound to forgive injuries greater than those you have offered us, which indeed did not harm us as you intended. But as prudent men, we would fain know before receiving you again to our confidence what are the grounds of your repentance."

"Right enough, Master Bradford, right enough! It behooves every man to be prudent, and the burned dog dreads the fire. But the matter is here. A year or more agone I and other men loaded a small ship with goods, bought mainly on credit from the French and English vessels at Monhegan and Damaris Cove, to truck them at the Virginia colony for tobacco and other matters which sell well to the sailors and fishermen; but outside the Cape here, we fell upon Malabar and Tucker's Terror, and all those fearsome shoals and reefs that drove back your own Mayflower from the same voyage, and to cap our misfortunes a shrewd storm out of the northeast seized us at advantage, and shook and worried us as you may see a dog torment a wolf caught in a trap, and sans power to defend himself.

"Now in that extremity some of the mariners bethought them of God, who verily was not in all their thoughts, and so fell on prayer, making loud lamentations of their sins and professing desire of amendment and satisfaction. So as I listened, and marveled if those men were verily worse than other men, or than me, of a sudden a flash as of lightning pierced my soul and showed me mine own enormous wickedness, and how it well might be that I was the Jonah for whom an angry God would slay all this company. Natheless I did not cry out as Jonah did, for I knew not if there was a great fish prepared to swallow me when my shipmates should fling me over, nor did I feel within myself the prophet's constancy and courage to abide three days alive in a fish's belly; so I held mine own counsel, and getting behind the mast I fell upon my knees and heartily abased myself before God, confessing my sins, and most especially my ill-doing toward you men of Plymouth, and as the heat of my devotion bore me on, I vowed that so God would spare me alive, and not make shipwreck of all this company for my sin, I would humble myself before those I had wronged, and would, if I might, do them as much good as I had done harm. Then, sirs, believe it or not as you will, but as I finished that prayer and made that vow, the wind fell, as though some mighty hand had gathered it back, and held it powerless; the ship that had lain all but upon her beam-ends, and in another moment must have capsized, righted herself, and stood amazed and quivering, like a horse curbed in upon the very brink of a precipice; the sea still ran high, but the tide so bore us up, and carried us so kindly, that two men at the helm could manage it again, and the master, recovering his spirit that had been well-nigh dashed with the imminent peril of his occasions, so ingeniously manœuvred his course in and out among those sholds as to fetch us through into the open sea, although so crippled and battered that we could no more than make back to Gloucester for repairs.

"There I found another vessel bound south, and took passage with my venture, secure that now my voyage should be prospered as indeed it was, and I stayed in Virginia something over a year, trading and laying by money.

"And now, masters, here I am in fulfilling of my vow. I have, and I do crave pardon and forgetfulness of my former wrong-doing, and to prove that my repentance is fruitful, I here bring you in solid cash for the use of the colony five-and-twenty rose-nobles, good money, honestly gained."

And with a smile of self-approval not unmixed with surprise at his own position, Oldhame brought a grimy canvas bag from the depths of one of the pockets of his pea-coat, and planted it with a pleasant thud and jingle upon the table in front of the governor, who raised his hand as if to push it back, but restrained the gesture, and after a moment's hesitation rose, and taking the penitent by the hand said in his grandly simple way,—

"No man can do more than to confess himself sorry for wrong-doing, and to offer satisfaction for sin. Zaccheus did no more, and the Son of God became his guest. Master Oldhame, we receive you again as our friend and comrade, and make you welcome to our town whensoever you may see fit to visit us. As for this money, if you will retire for a little, I will take counsel with my advisers here, and tell you our mind. Will you walk about the town, or will you await our summons outside? Bartholomew, Master Oldhame is no longer a prisoner but a guest; go with him where he will, and Gyles, wait you without to summon him, when we are ready."

But Oldhame went no farther than a sunny angle of the Fort, where, seated upon the section of a tree-trunk set there by Captain Standish, he lighted his pipe, folded his arms, and fixing his eyes upon Captain's Hill sat smoking in stolid silence, rather to the disappointment of Bart Allerton, who was a sociable young man, and would have liked the news from Virginia.

The penitent's mood had changed, however, and he was suffering from the reaction consequent upon most unwonted acts of self-sacrifice. He really was sincere in his contrition, and had honestly offered that bag of gold as satisfaction for the injury done and intended toward Plymouth. But five-and-twenty rose-nobles, representing more than forty dollars of our money, meant in that day and place four or five times as much, and was a sum neither lightly won, nor lightly to be spent; so that Oldhame half unconsciously fell to meditating how far it would have gone toward purchasing English goods for another voyage to Virginia, or for his own maintenance while resting from his labors. He had told his story, and made his peace-offering in a moment of exaltation, and now the exaltation was all gone, and a certain flat and disgusted mood had seized upon its vacant place. Human nature is not essentially different in the nineteenth nor will be in the twentieth century from what it was in the seventeenth.

"The governor prays your company, Master Oldhame," announced Gyles Hopkins; and knocking the ashes out of his pipe, Oldhame pocketed it and followed into that dusky chamber, where still the Court of the People seemed to fill the benches with ghostly presence waiting to hear and confirm their governor's decision.

"We pray you be seated, Master Oldhame," began Bradford, motioning to a chair beside the table. "Bartholomew and Gyles you are dismissed, and see that we are not interrupted."

He paused while the men-at-arms withdrew, closing the door with a heavy bang, which echoed gloomily through the empty room.

Then Bradford, referring now and again to his associates, told the grisly penitent that the opportunity he craved of doing a good turn to Plymouth was at hand, and the money he proffered would aid in carrying out the enterprise. This was no other than the transportation of Thomas Morton to England, and there delivering him to the authorities who waited to punish him for offenses committed before seeking the shelter of the New World. After his capture by Standish, Morton had been brought to Plymouth, but as he was too troublesome a prisoner to be held there, some brilliant mind had hit upon the idea of marooning him upon one of the Isles of Shoals, where, having no boat, he was perfectly sure to be found when wanted, and at the same time quite out of danger. The season for the return home of the English fishing-vessels had now arrived, and Plymouth was already in treaty with the master of the Dolphin to carry their rebellious prisoner as passenger; but it was most desirable that some competent person should accompany him, and perhaps none could be found more suitable than Oldhame, to whom the position was now offered. If he chose to accept it, the five-and-twenty rose-nobles, "said to be contained in this bag which we have not opened," and at the words Bradford laid a hand upon the bag and threw a penetrating glance at Oldhame, whose face flushed guiltily, for one of those nobles had indeed been so grievously clipped as to lose a good third of its value, and he knew it, although the governor only guessed it, "this money, be it less or more, shall be used by you, Master Oldhame, to pay Plymouth's proportion of the expense of this transportation, and the remainder shall be our recognition of your services and loss of time. Do you accept the offer, friend?"

"Gladly and gayly, Governor, and gentlemen all," cried Oldhame, laying an impulsive clutch upon the bag. "And truth to tell, I was purposing a voyage into England when occasion should serve, so that your proposal jumps with my desires most marvelously, and you shall find that once there I will do you good and manful service in whatsoever you desire. I am not unknown to Sir Ferdinando Gorges, the Governor of Old Plymouth, whither the Dolphin is bound, and I will so present this Morton's offenses that we shall have him hanged over the battlements, a prey for gleeds, before he has well tasted English air."

"Better to shoot him before he goes," growled Standish. "'Tis bad venerie when you have trapped a wolf to let him go free on the chance some other man will finish your work."

"Morton hath committed no offense worthy of death on this side the water," suggested Allerton in his crafty voice. "If he hath in England, let English law decide."

Standish cast a look of impatient dislike at the speaker, but Doctor Fuller interposed,—

"Fair and softly is a good rule whereby to walk, and I know not if the right of life and death except in combat is fairly ours. I fear me one hundred men though led by Standish would hardly cope with Old England's forces if she sent them hither."

"My brethren," said Bradford, lightly tapping the table with his finger-tips, "why waste time thus? There is no question of life or death in the present matter; we are to send this dangerous rebel home to England for trial, and John Oldhame is to be surety for his safe arrival, and to receive this money to defray Plymouth's proportion of the expense. Am I right, sirs?"

"You are right, Governor Bradford," said the Elder solemnly, and the conclave broke up.

CHAPTER XI.

GOVERNOR BRADFORD PAYS A VISIT.

"Now mind you, goodman, you are to put on your ruff, and the goodly wrist-ruffles, and see that your doublet is fresh brushed, and your hosen tight and smooth, and your hair well set up, and your beard newly combed,—I wish I might but put a thought of ambergris and civet upon it"—

"Nay, dame, not while I live, and I think when once you have killed me with kindness you'll have no heart to send me to the grave smelling like a civet cat"—

"Oh, Will, Will! How can you!"—

"How can I die, or how can I forbear civet upon my beard? Nay, then, my dame! Wilt cry over it—there, then, sweetheart, there, there!"—

"'Twas that you talked of dying, Will, and if thou wert dead"—

"Men who talk of dying never die, Elsie; but take courage, take courage, and for thy sweet sake I'll don the ruffles, and brush my doublet, and re-garter my hosen, and set up my hair; nay, then, I'll even clean my shoes and anoint them afresh, which is more than you bade me do."

"Why certainly, of course you must do that, dear; and, laugh at your poor wife as you will, I'm sure enough you'll pleasure her by going brave, and showing a good front to these fine new-comers; and if you come to see Lady Arbella Johnson be sure to mark all the items of her clothes, for she will have the latest modes out of England."

"Oh, wife, wife! Oh, woman, woman! 'Twas but yesterday we were driven to make coats of deer-skins, and shoe ourselves with the hides of wolves and bears, because we had no other clothing, and to-day you are all agog for the latest modes out of England, and send me to take inventory of a titled lady's raiment that you may copy her silks in kersey, and her velvets in homespun."

"Nay, then, sir, I'm none so poor as you would make me out, but have more than one robe of say of mine own, only they have never been aired in this rude wilderness, and are a thought antiquated. But now that we hear of Governor Endicott of Salem, and Governor Winthrop of the Bay, I mind me that I am wife of Governor Bradford of Plymouth, and it is my duty, my bounden duty, Will, to magnify thine office, and show myself abroad as a governor's lady should."

"Ay, dame; but methinks the wife of a governor should show herself more governed than other women; more meek, and recollected, and chastened, rather than more arrogant."

"Nay, Will, do I lack in these matters?" And Alice looked up in her husband's face, her blue eyes so swimming in tears that she could not see the smile of tender malice upon her husband's lips as he folded her in his arms and whispered tender reassurances needless to set down.

Yes, our governor was going a-neighboring to his brother potentates at Boston, for a great change had almost suddenly befallen that pleasant region where William Blackstone had dwelt as a solitary for so long. Let us, as briefly as may be, freshen our memories of these early arrivals, and so understand more clearly the new relations suddenly involving the Pilgrims of Plymouth.

It was in 1628 that Governor Endicott with a large and aristocratic following arrived at Naumkeag, and speedily dispossessed Roger Conant and the other old settlers both of their proprietary rights and their privilege of trading with the natives. The next step was to name the place Salem, and ordain as Independent ministers the men who had left England proclaiming their fealty to her Established Church.

But Salem did not long claim the seat of government, for on the 17th of June, 1630, Governor Winthrop, with near a thousand colonists under his command, sailed into Boston Bay and landed at Charlestown, where a deputation from Salem had already prepared for them. Neither numbers, nor home protection, nor wealth, nor aristocratic pretensions could, however, save this great colony from the very same enemies that had assailed the glorious hundred of Mayflower Pilgrims ten years before, and cut down one half of their number. Ship fever, scurvy, and other diseases incident to the horrors of a sea-voyage in that day seized upon the new-comers, who aggravated their own danger by improper food, treatment, and, so long as they lasted, terrible drugs. In six months Charlestown had become a village of graves and of loathsome insanitation, complicated with the want of pure and sufficient water. Moved at length by the sufferings of his neighbors, Blackstone, who at first had scowled upon their invasion of his solitude, visited Governor Winthrop, and told him of a pure and unfailing spring of water near the southern foot of the hill upon whose western slope lay his own cabin and apple orchard, and suggested that it might be well for the settlement to be removed across the mouth of the Mystic, and reëstablished at Trimountain, as he called the peninsula hitherto his own.

Winthrop gladly accepted the suggestion, came over with Blackstone to view the proposed site, and liked it so well that in October, 1630, he caused the frame of his own house nearly ready for erection in Charlestown to be taken over, and set up close by the spring in question, or, as we might now describe it, on Washington Street, between the Old South Church and the corner of Spring Lane, under whose worn and dusty pavement one still fancies to hear the cool wash and gurgle of those imprisoned waters.

Was Blackstone sorry for his good-nature when, after a little, Winthrop and his council kindly set apart fifty acres of the domain to which he had invited them, as his property, and proceeded to divide the rest among themselves? Cannot one picture the reserved and somewhat cynical hermit smoking his pipe beside his solitary fire in the evening of that day, and smiling to himself as he considered the condescension of the new government? And did haply some herald of coming Liberty suggest certain pithy queries to be more plainly worded on Boston Common a century or so later? Did the lonely man ask himself what right Governor Winthrop or any other man had to come into this wild country and dispossess the pioneer settlers of their holdings? True, the King of England had given him that right. But where did the King of England himself get the authority to do so? He had neither bought the land of the natives, nor had he conquered them in fair fight; he simply had heard of a fair new world beyond the seas, and claimed it for his own by some arbitrary right divine whose source no man could tell. The land was his, he said, and so he had sent these men in his name to take possession, to parcel out, to give, or to withhold, from men as good as themselves who had borne the heat and toil of the earlier days, and who had paid the savages full measure for the lands they held. What was this right divine? Why should kings so control the property of other men—men who only asked to live their own lives, and neither meddle nor make with kingcraft? Why? And as William Blackstone, the forgotten pipe burned out, pondered this "why," the yellowing leaves of the young Liberty tree a few rods from his cottage door rustled impatiently, as though they felt the breath of 1775 already in their midst.

It did not last very long. Not only were there disputes and heartburnings about proprietorship, but the Puritans who had come to New England professing a stanch adherence to the church, and almost immediately proved false to her, could not forgive the quiet man who made no parade of religion, but never swerved from his adherence to his ordination vows. They tried to persuade him, they tried to coerce him, and at last received the assurance that he who had exiled himself from England to avoid the tyranny of the Lords Bishops was not disposed to submit to that of the lords brethren, but would leave them to dispute with each other.

So selling all that he had, except a plot of land around his old home, Blackstone invested the thirty pounds of purchase money in cattle, packed his books and some other matters upon his cows' backs, and driving the herd before him passed over Boston Neck and out into the wilderness; nor did he pause until upon a tributary of Narragansett Bay he found a lonely and lovely spot, so far from white men or their ordinary line of travel as to rival the Isle of Juan Fernandez in solitude. Naming his domain Study Hill, Blackstone built another house, planted some young apple trees carefully brought from the old orchard, set up his bookshelves, filled his pipe, and settled himself for forty years of happiness, dying just in time to escape King Philip's war.

But in September, 1630, when Governor Bradford went up to pay his first visit to Governor Winthrop, Blackstone still lived on Boston Common, and looked upon the new-comers as his guests. They had not yet presented him with the fifty acres of his own land.

With the Governor of Plymouth came Elder Brewster, and Captain Standish, Thomas Prence, and Doctor Fuller, who was already well and gratefully known by many of the new settlers; for when the pestilence broke out in Salem about a year before, Governor Endicott dispatched Roger Conant to beg, in the name of Christian fellowship, that the doctor of Plymouth, who had already met the grim enemy at home, would come and aid his brethren. Fuller was not slow to respond, and not only cured some of the sufferers in spite of the deadly methods of his day, but so set forth the religious beliefs and practices of the church of the Pilgrims that Endicott, who was still a Puritan Churchman, and soon to be a Puritan Independent, wrote a cordial letter to Bradford, telling how glad he was to find that the Separatists were not so bad as he had supposed them to be.

Again, when in the summer of 1630 the settlers at Charlestown, Boston, Dorchester, and the neighboring country fell into the same disaster, and with the earliest victims lost Doctor Gager their only physician, Plymouth was appealed to for assistance, and Doctor Fuller at once responded. But the scanty stock of drugs brought by the emigrants was already exhausted, and Fuller's own supply soon went, so that his treatment was principally confined to blood-letting, and after writing a homesick letter to his brother-in-law Bradford, he returned to Plymouth.

At the wooden wharf where the Pilgrims disembarked in Charlestown, they were met by Governor Winthrop, Dudley his Deputy and successor, and the Reverend Master Wilson, who, as he cordially grasped Elder Brewster by the hand, cast a hurried glance over the group of visitors, and felt a sensible relief at not perceiving the face of Ralph Smith among them. For this reverend gentleman, persecuted out of Salem for opinion's sake, and refused shelter in Boston or Charlestown, had found an asylum among the liberal Pilgrims who presently invited him to the position of their first ordained minister.

Mr. Wilson need not, however, have been alarmed, since Bradford, whose character singularly united the wisdom of the serpent with the innocence of the dove, had not thought best to include a person so likely to be unwelcome to his hosts in this visit, at once friendly and official; for the Governor of Plymouth had been invited to assist at the first formal session of the Bay authorities, convened at the Great House built by Thomas Grove, the architect "entertained" by the Massachusetts Company under whose auspices the new colony came out.

To this inauguration feast came also Governor Endicott from Salem, with Master Isaac Johnson, whose wife, the Lady Arbella, lay sick unto death in her new home, and never more would don the brave attire in which Alice Bradford had expressed such womanly interest. With these were assembled Sir Richard Saltonstall, Master Bradstreet, soon to be Governor of the Bay Colony, and Pynchon, ancestor, perhaps, of Hawthorne's Hester; all the magistrates in fact of New England, all the representatives of legal or spiritual authority upon this side of the broad seas; for these men were about to test their right to self-government, and to exercise jurisdiction over the liberty, the property, the persons, nay, the very lives of others, and doubtless felt that in case this right were to be called in question from the throne or the Star Chamber, it might be well to secure the strength of numbers and authoritative consensus.

But we, like Bradford and his company, are only guests at Mishawum, as they still called Charlestown, and must hasten back to Plymouth. Enough to briefly note that Morton of Merry Mount, who had audaciously returned to his "old nest" and his old ways, after Allerton had been forced to dismiss him from his house in Plymouth, was brought before the magistrates, somewhat unfairly tried, and sentenced to be "set in the bilboes," and afterward sent prisoner to England. His entire property was to be confiscated, and his house burned in presence of the Indians whom he had robbed and insulted, and so speedily was the first portion of the sentence carried out that, as the court left the Great House at noon, they passed close beside the criminal already seated in the stocks with a party of Indian squaws staring at him, half in dismay, half in satisfaction.

"This way, Bradford! Don't look upon him; 'tis no punishment for a gentleman," muttered Standish, seizing the governor's arm and dragging him in a sidelong direction, while Parson Wilson, and Increase Newell the Elder of the Charlestown church, stopped to administer a "word in season" to the defenseless prisoner.

The business of the Bay Colony finished, Governor Bradford begged the attention of his fellow magistrates to an affair in his own jurisdiction: one as important as life and death could make it, for it was a question of enforcing the death penalty upon a murderer, fully convicted and offering no plea of extenuating circumstances.

The culprit was John Billington, already notorious as the first person the Pilgrims had felt called upon to punish. Since that early day he had more than once come under discipline of the law, but now his offense exceeded all human bounds of forgiveness, and by the stern code of Old Testament justice merited nothing short of death.

The victim was a young man named John Newcomen, a somewhat rough and lawless companion, who had persisted in trapping and shooting over ground which Billington claimed as his own monopoly, although neither man made any pretense of ownership. The end was a bitter quarrel, after which Billington armed himself, and, lying in wait until Newcomen appeared, deliberately shot and killed him.

A solemn trial by jury ensued, whereat the crime was fully proven and no defense was attempted. A verdict of willful murder was brought in, and no recommendation to mercy was offered by the stern foreman. The trial could not have been more deliberate or more just, but sentence was not immediately pronounced, for as Bradford frankly declared to his fellow magistrates, he shrank both before God and man from pronouncing the words that should deprive a fellow mortal of life, and before doing so he desired the counsel and concurrence of the other New England authorities.

"Who killeth man, by man shall his blood be shed," quoted Endicott in the silence which followed Bradford's solemn appeal. "It is the law of God."

"And haply," added Winthrop, "a sharp example in these early days may hinder the loss of more valuable lives hereafter."

"With God is no respect of persons," spoke Elder Brewster in tones of stern reproof; but Parson Wilson, with almost a sneer, retorted,—

"Then let him die as one of the princes, even as Zeb and Salmana."

A little more discussion followed, but the result was obvious, and the next day Bradford turned his face toward home with a heavy heart, and yet a mind resolved upon the terrible duty soon after fulfilled.

CHAPTER XII.

SIR CHRISTOPHER GARDINER.

It was several days after the governor's return to Plymouth, and Alice had wondered more than once if aught beside the gloom and sorrow of Billington's execution lay upon her husband's mind, when, after noon of one of those heavenly days in late September, in which one's whole life goes out to the joy of living, Bradford after hesitating a moment at the door, turned back and said,—

"Come, Elsie, do on your hood and walk with me a little."

"Gay and gladly, Will," replied she, and in a few moments they had passed down by Elder Brewster's house toward the brook, and then turning to the right crossed on the stepping-stones, and striking into the Namasket Path strolled along until, reaching a lovely intervale, afterward called Prence's Bottom, and now Hillside, they sat down upon a fallen tree trunk, and Bradford abruptly asked,—

"Was it not one Sir Christopher Gardiner that our Pris spoke of when she first came as some sort of sweetheart of hers?"

"Yes. He gave her that lordly neckerchief she wears betimes. She calls him a Knight of the Golden Melice, and then again Knight of the Holy Sepulchre,—poor maid!"

And Alice laughed as matrons do at the follies of maidenhood. But Bradford shook his head, and plucking a great frond of goldenrod softly smote his own palm with it, while he said,—

"'Tis a bad business, Alice, a bad business, and I fear worse may come of it."

"Worse! Worse than what, Will? There's no harm done as yet. The girl's not wearing the willow, nor needing pity; it's not likely she'll see or hear of him again, and after a while she'll wed William Wright, who woos her honestly and openly."

"Alice, the man is here."

"Here! What man?"

"Sir Christopher Gardiner, Knight of the Golden Melice and the Holy Sepulchre, and of what you will beside. I've seen and spoken with him, wife."

"You! When and where, for pity's sake?"

"Softly now, and I'll tell you. When we left the Bay people the captain would have us stop at Squantum Head to visit Mistress Thompson in her widowhood and see if she lacked aught, or wished us to recommend her to the good offices of her neighbors of the Bay, and so we did"—

"How is her child, Will?"

"Well and hearty, as is she herself, and farming her island, which Standish would have us call Trevor's Island, but we would liever name Thompson's Island in his honor who was her husband and father of the boy. Now while we talked with the widow, I remembered me that Winthrop had mentioned some new settlers hard by Squantum, a gentleman, as he said, named Gardiner, who claimed some title, and who, besides several servants, entertained as housekeeper a comely young woman whom he called his cousin.

"Master Winthrop had not seen them, but when I said we would tarry a little with the Widow Thompson, he asked me if it were in my way to take a look at this Gardiner, and let him hear my judgment of him. Truth to tell, I did not at the first mind me of our Prissie's story of her Knight of the Golden Melice, for such toys get cast into the dark corners of a man's mind"—

"Unless it be his own case, Will," interposed Alice with tender jibing in her voice.

Bradford smiled reply, but went on with his story. "So while the rest drank a cup of metheglin, and ate some of Mistress Thompson's curds and cream, Standish and I clomb the brave headland ever I hope to be known as Squanto's Point, and presently came upon a new cabin fairly seated above a rising ground some half mile south of the Neponset's River; a pretty home as one would wish to see, with a posy bed under the window, and vines from the woods trained over the door and casement, this last set with glass and swinging open, for all the world like a cottage of Old England.

"Well, we came to the door, and Standish rapped with his sword hilt after his own masterful fashion, so that there presently run out a—well, I was about to say a maid, for she was young and very comely to look upon, but in sad certainty I know not—she may be the man's wife, and charity will not have us suspect ill that is not brought home by proof."

"How was she so very fair, Will?"

"Why, her hair was of yellow gold, and her eyes blue as a June sky, and the white and red of her face so cunningly mixt that it minded me of the may in our hedges at home, or of the mayflower that we find here in Plymouth woods, and her shape was lissome and delightsome as those young birches, and her little hands were white and soft, and her voice as sweet as— Why, Elsie, woman, what is it?"

"'Tis naught, 'tis naught! Leave go my hand I pray you, sir. I'm for home, but you need not haste!"

"Now, now, now! What, is mine own true-love jealous that I find another woman fair? Why, Elsie, I go well-nigh to blush for you! Come then, to punish you I'll not say the words that were springing to my lips. I'll not tell how the frighted, guilty look of those blue eyes minded me of other eyes steadfast and pure and serene as the evening star, nor how the fluttering, broken tones of that sweet voice brought to the ears of my heart a voice as sweet as that, but calm and steady, and full of the assured peace of a clear conscience"—

"Nay, then, Will, tell me naught, but let me creep close to thy knee like a chidden child and hide my face thus, for indeed I'm shamed to show it."

"Nay, let me look once upon thee in sweet penitence, since 'tis so seldom one may find the chance! Well there, then, hide it an thou wilt, sweetheart, for if I look too closely on't I forget all else. Well, then, this lady, we will call her, ran to see who knocked, and meeting Myles's grim face, which he had forgot to deck for lady's gaze, she uttered a sharp little cry, and fell back to give place to the gay figure of such a cavalier as we used to see strutting up and down Paul's Walk in London, hand on hips, and mustachios curled up to either eye, and beaver cocked a' one side, and laces and fine needlework, with velvets and silks, and all scented like a posy bed, or the civet cat you love so well."

"I mind me of the gallants of Paul's Walk, Will; but did this man really have laces and needlework and scent and all those matters?"

"Well, he had the air of having them, sweetheart, and that is still the main point, you know. So out he came, hand on sword hilt, and eyes so terrific that I, poor wight, shrunk back affrighted"—

"You affrighted, indeed!"

"Ay, but you don't know how terrific a mien this paladin put on, dame! Our captain bristled at sight of it as the wolf hound does at sight of the wolf, and I feared me for the moment that they would fall to before I could cry, 'A list, a list, good gentles'!"

"Oh, Will, how can you! But go on."

"Well, seeing the peril, I stirred myself as best I might to avoid it, and elbowing Standish aside, I doffed my hat and said,—

"'Pardon, good sir, but we have come to change courtesies with our neighbors. We are men of the Plymouth Colony, and have been to visit the new-comers at the Bay, who told us you were here.'

"Upon that our host's visage relaxed, and he made some sort of civil reply, although none could doubt he would liever our room than our company; but he had us in, and as the young woman lingered near, he spoke of her presently as 'My cousin, Mistress Mary Grove, who of her kindness keepeth my house.'

"'And your name, sir, is Gardiner?' queried I; and he, cock-a-hoop in a moment as one insulted, set his hat on 's head, and twisting his mustachios to a needle's point, pouted his lips to say,—

"'I am Sir Christopher Gardiner, sirs, Knight of the Holy Sepulchre, and Chevalier of the Golden Melice. And your names and quality, if I may make so bold?'

"But so insolent was the tone and so belligerent the manner of this announcement that before I could find words for reply the captain stepped before me, his own hat set aside, and, Heaven save the mark! twisting his own stubbly russet mustachios as fiercely as the other, the while his hand on Gideon's hilt, he cried,—

"'This gentleman is Master William Bradford, Governor of Plymouth Colony; and I am Myles Standish, commandant, for want of a better, of the colony's military force.'

"Now this bold assumption, which would have made some men laugh, and set others upon opposition, just jumped with the humor of our new friend, and taking off his hat, he held out a hand for ours; saying, handsomely enough, that he had heard marvelous tales of our captain's prowess, and also of the wisdom, and I know not what, of Plymouth's governor. Faith, I know not but he said he had crossed the seas to look upon two such marvels! Certes, he gave no other motive, since in religion he seems of that convenient stripe which fits with any pattern, and for hard work he is no better fitted than is his cousin and housekeeper, whose lily-white hands could ill trundle a mop or work a churn-dasher."

"And what do they honestly seek here in the wilderness?"

"Why, truth to tell, I fear me they seek nothing honestly, but the rather a dishonest refuge from judgment. If ever woman wore a guilty and shamefaced look, it was that poor wench when first she met us; and as for the man, although he vapored much about his desire for a quiet life, far from the setbacks and downfalls of worldly affairs, and his love of sylvan solitudes and the like, I trust him not,—nay, not so far as just out of reach of a tipstaff's clutch; he's false, so false that even as he talked he seemed to sneer at his own professions."

"But our Prissie, Will! If this is indeed the man she talked of"—

"Ay, that's where the matter sits close to our hearts, wife. Did ever she talk of him to you, in the way of picturing out his face and mien?"

"Nay, for after that once I never would let her talk of him; but still she gave me the notion of a gay cavalier, such a man as haunts the king's court, and as you say struts in Paul's Walk,—a man who well might be the one you and the captain saw."

"But—Mary Grove?"

The matron's fair cheek flushed a little, for the purity of that age was of the order that hates sin without having learned to love the sinner, and shrinks back from the sight or touch of evil instead of fearlessly examining the hurt, and applying the oil and wine. The world does grow in good, let the pessimists deny it as they may.

"Pris will never know that the man is on this side the sea, unless we tell her," said Alice presently.

"No. And I will caution the captain not to mention the matter."

"Oh, he will have mentioned it to Barbara, and she to Priscilla Alden, before this!" exclaimed Alice. "They are like one household, the Standishes and Aldens, and Priscilla loves to talk."

"But Barbara is very prudent, and if she has heard so ill a story will think twice before she spreads it. I never knew a woman less given to gossip, except mine own wife. I'll tell thee, Alice, I'll ask Myles if he has told the tale; and if he has, I'll ask him to speak to Barbara and find how far it has gone."

"But do not tell even the captain of our poor maid's folly," interposed Alice.

"Nay, child, I'm as jealous for Prissie's good name as if she were mine own sister. Come, you are shivering, and the night dews begin to fall. Let us go home."

CHAPTER XIII.

ONE! TWO! THREE!　　FIRE!

Alice Bradford's instinct had correctly foreseen that Myles would narrate his adventures to his wife just as Bradford had to his; but the governor's reason was also correct in arguing that Barbara would be likely to keep such a story to herself, and the rather that Pris Carpenter had once spoken the name of Sir Christopher Gardiner in her presence with so much of maidenly flutter that Barbara felt there was a story underneath.

So when Bradford took occasion, over a pipe in the captain's den, to suggest that it was as well for the present to keep the story of the knight of the Golden Melice from the public, Myles replied with a laugh,—

"So says Mistress Standish. I told her, as indeed I tell her most matters; but when she had listened, her first word was, 'I hope neither you nor the governor will noise this story abroad, for it might do much harm, and could do no good.' A prudent woman is"—

"From the Lord," said Bradford. "And you and I have cause to thank Him for the gift."

The talk drifted to other matters; and as the weeks and months went on, the subject was not resumed until March came in with all the chilly rigor of a New England seashore spring, and yet with certain fitful gleams and promises of better things in store. It was in the midst of one of those tempestuous storms incident to March, and always reminding one of a fascinating naughty child's passionate burst of temper, that Hobomok appeared at the Fort, escorting a stranger Indian.

"Weetonawah wants head chief," announced he succinctly.

The captain looked up from his Cæsar, and laid down his pipe.

"Weetonawah is welcome," said he in the Pokanoket dialect, which he had acquired in perfection. "But Hobomok should not bring him here. The head chief's wigwam is below the hill."

"Pokanokets like The-Sword-of-the-White-Men best," replied the stranger in a final sort of manner, and Hobomok's suppressed "Hugh!" seemed to indorse the sentiment. Standish smiled,—for who does not love to be trusted above his fellows?—and, rising, he threw his cloak about his shoulders, saying,—

"Well, we will seek the head chief together, and take counsel upon thy matters, Weetonawah."

So, unmindful of the rain, as men who live close to Nature will still become, the three went down the hill, and found Bradford in his study reading the Georgics, until such time as the weather would permit him to plough his own fields; for now that "oxen strong to labor" had immigrated, their fellow-colonists were able to improve upon the earlier methods of agriculture, and the plough had superseded the hoe whose rude labors had slain John Carver. Laying aside the book, but with its pleasant influence upon his face, Bradford received his guests, gave a cup of metheglin to each of the Indians, who would rather it had been Nantz, and asked Standish what he would take, but the captain shook his head.

"I've had my noon meat, and care for nothing until night. Now, Weetonawah, tell out your tidings to the head chief."

So Weetonawah, who spoke no English, told in his own tongue—Standish now and again translating for the benefit of Bradford, who never became as apt an Indian scholar as the captain—how he and a Massachusetts brave, while hunting, had come across a white man seated beside a camp-fire, and leaning his head upon his hand as though sick or sorry, they knew not which. Approaching with due precautions, they found him friendly, and willing to change tobacco for some birds to make a broth, for he was so fevered as not to crave solid food. But when they had parted from him a little way, the Massachusetts man halted, and choosing a war-arrow from his quiver, gave Weetonawah to understand that this was a criminal fleeing from justice, and that the white men at the Bay had bade the Indians search the woods between Shawmut and Piscataqua for him, promising a reward to whoever should bring him in.

Still, during the brief interview beside the camp-fire, both red men had silently marked how thoroughly armed, and how alert in spite of his illness, the fugitive remained, and the Massachusetts man felt that at close quarters he might fare even as Wituwamat or Pecksuot in combat with The-Sword-of-the-White-Men; so, even in their friendly parting, he had laid his plan to turn back and shoot the sick man as he crouched over his fire; and lest his comrade should claim any part of the reward, he would go upon the war-path alone, and rejoin him at the wigwams of the Namasket village.

But Weetonawah was brother to one of the men killed at Wessagussett, and he had imbibed such a terror of The-Sword-of-the-White-Men and his vengeance upon those who molested the palefaces that he would rather have killed his Massachusetts friend, and taken the chances of punishment from Massasoit, than to be named as companion of an Indian who had killed a white man. So, half by argument and half by threat, he led away the assassin, and forced from him a promise to suspend his purpose until orders should be obtained from Plymouth; consenting that if the head chief and The Sword gave permission, he should alone slay the fugitive and claim the reward.

So far, Weetonawah spoke and Bradford listened, but at this point he started up and exclaimed,—

"An Indian promise! Who knows but that even now the wretch has stolen back to slay yonder poor fugitive? Horrible! What warrant have you, Indian, for believing this murderer will refrain?"

Sternly repeating the query, and receiving the reply, Standish grimly smiled.

"He says that the Massachusetts swore upon his totem, but to make the matter sure he brought him along hither, promising him a good noggin of strong waters, and he is even now in the kitchen, waiting."

"Have him in! Hobomok, fetch him in!" cried Bradford, still in dismay. "Kill a white man in cold blood! Shoot a sick man shivering over a campfire! Standish, they are savages and heathen to the end, and we may as well preach Christ to the wolves and bears as to them."

"Your best Indian preacher is still a snaphance," replied the captain grimly, as his mind glanced back to Pastor Robinson's strictures upon the Wessagussett chastisement.

"Here they come! Now speak to this man in his own tongue, and make him understand that if he kills this white man we will require it at his hand, and that, after no stinted measure. Terrify him, Myles, as you well know how! They fear you more than all the power of the Bay Colony put together."

Now the fact remains that so long as Myles Standish lived his was a name to conjure with among the red men; and although, except at Wessagussett, he seldom, if ever, was engaged in actual conflict, or was guilty of their blood, the rumor of his coming was enough to disperse many an angry party, and to restrain many incendiary counsels. Nor was it fear alone, for the savages admired and emulated, yes, and loved the man; he went freely among them, slept in their wigwams, ate beside their fires, smoked the pipe of peace with their warriors, and showed human and friendly interest in their concerns. Never at any crisis did he forget to exempt women and children from the fortunes of war, and it was under neither his leadership nor his counsels that the Pequot atrocities were committed by the soldiers of the Puritan Bay Colony.

So now, as he sternly addressed the Shawmut Indian in his own tongue, the latter visibly quailed, and, not daring to reply directly, slunk behind Hobomok, and in a torrent of muttered gutturals besought him to assure the Sword that his voice was as the voice of the Great Spirit, and he would obey it as implicitly, for if he did not his own totem would turn upon him and destroy him, as indeed he should well deserve, and— But here Standish held up a hand and impatiently interrupted with,—

"There, there, that's enough! You understand me, Shawmut, and you know that what I promise I perform. Now then, Bradford, what is to be done?"

"Why, the man must be taken and brought in as gently as may be. Doubtless he is in some sort a lawbreaker hiding from the justice of Governor Winthrop, and it may be our duty to return him to the Bay; but the first thing is to discover who he is and of what accused. Explain, if it please you, to both these Indians that they are to find this man, and take him by force of numbers or strategy, but without violence, and bring him safely to this house. What reward have the authorities of the Bay offered for his capture?"

"A kilderkin of biscuit, a horseman's cloak, and five ells of scarlet cloth," reported Standish after a good deal of discussion with the two Indians.

"The Bay is rich," replied Bradford dryly. "Tell them if they bring in this man unharmed we will give twenty pound weight of sugar, and that is a large reward, be the man who he may."

The Massachusetts Indian listened as this proffer was repeated, and then in his guttural and sullen voice muttered something at which Standish frowned and answered angrily, while Hobomok gave way to a derisive chuckle. As the two turned and glided stealthily out of the room, the captain also laughed and said,—

"The red rascal wanted a piece and some powder and shot, or at least a pottle or two of firewater, as he calls it."

"Ay! there's the outcome of Thomas Morton's work," replied Bradford. "The Bay people dealt hardly with him, yet none too hardly when we see the despite he has done to all of us by arming the savages."

"Hardly, do you call it?" echoed Standish. "Well, I know not. Had I been the judge the sentence should have been shorter and less spiteful. To my mind it is too much like the savages themselves to crop a man's ears, and set him in the stocks, and pelt him with garbage, and burn his house in his own sight, and mulct him of his money, and ship him out of the country, and after all leave him at liberty to pull the wool over the eyes of the big-wigs and come back again to plague us as he did before. 'Tis womanish to invent so many ways of tormenting an offender, and yet not put further offense out of his power."

"And if you had been judge?" asked Bradford with a shrewd smile.

For answer the captain raised an imaginary piece to his shoulder and gave the word of command,—

"One! Two! Three!   FIRE!"

And with the last word he brought down his right foot with full force upon his own pipe, which had fallen unheeded from his pocket. The governor laughed, and Standish ruefully picked up the amber mouthpiece, exclaiming,—

"Now, by my faith! there goes the meerschaum that Jans Wiederhausen carved on purpose for a parting gift to me when we left Leyden ten year ago. And serves me right for wasting time on such boys' tricks as yon brag of what I might have done had all been other than it was. Well, well! Sorry and sad I am to lose that pipe! Now I must turn to the one Hobomok has carved out of what I take to be a jasper stone, but 't is heavy, and cannot drink up the poison of the tobacco as my meerschaum did. There's naught for a pipe like meerschaum, Will."

"Clay is well enough for me," replied the governor with a smile, as he brought a new clay pipe from the cupboard and presented it to Myles.

Nor shall we be surprised to hear that when, a year later, Captain William Pierce came over in the Lyon to Boston Bay, he brought a fine meerschaum pipe as a present from Governor Bradford to his friend Captain Standish.

CHAPTER XIV.

SIR CHRISTOPHER ENJOYS THE CHASE.

Five days later, Priscilla Alden sat in the gloaming of the wild March day before a fire so cheerful as to be truly perilous to the chimney of sticks laid up with mud attached like an elongated hornet's nest to the outside of the house. Upon her knees lay little Sally, future wife of Alexander Standish, but just now a child of two years old, with a bad cold upon her lungs and a tendency to croup, or, as her mother called it, quinsy; and it was by way of an ounce of prevention that Priscilla was roasting the little thing before this huge fire, and at the same time diligently rubbing her chest and throat with goose grease. The child, hardly knowing whether to be amused or annoyed at the process, kicked and struggled, uttering little cries varying from crowing laughter to indignant squeals, while the mother made all the play she could of the affair, now tickling the small creature in her fat neck, now answering her cries with counter-cries and merry Boo! Boo! Boo! and anon,—

"See, Sally! See the pretty fire! Shall mother throw Sally in and burn her all up?" rubbing away meantime, until the child's white skin glowed like a rose and glistened like a mirror.

"She looks like the suckling pig you roasted last Thanksgiving, mother," remarked John junior, who stood drying his feet before the unusual fire, preparatory to rushing out and wetting them again.

"Why so she is, mother's darling little piggie-wiggie, mother's little suckling piggie-wiggie, and she shall be all nicely basted and set down to roast for daddy's supper, so she shall! Now, now, now! One more little rub to drive the basting well in! Now, now, now, mammy's little Sally! Phew! who's at the door, Johnny? Run and shut it before the air reaches little sister!"

"It's only Betty," remarked John with brotherly indifference, but still running to help his sister close the door against the playful south wind which insisted upon coming in along with his playmate, who laughed aloud as she closed the door in his face, set her back against it, and pulled off her hood to rearrange the soft red hair blown all over her face. Glancing toward her, the mother smiled with involuntary delight in her child's beauty; and truly Betty was very pretty, very pretty indeed, having selected her features and coloring from her father's pure Saxon type and her mother's Latin traits, with rare eclecticism; for her deep and rich red hair was far more beautiful than John's blond locks or Priscilla's dusky tresses, and her eyes, halting between his blue orbs and her dark ones, had resulted in that sparkling brown we all love to watch in the woodland brook stealing out from the roots of trees. Her complexion, neither pale nor dark, was at once glowing and delicate, the white values bordering upon cream rather than snow, and the reds suggesting carnations rather than roses. As for the mouth, it was too young yet to have got its expression, but the lines were noble and clear, sweet and pure, promising much for their maturity. A winsome little lassie, and so her mother knew, but was far too wise to show it. In fact, her tone was almost reproving as she said,—

"Why, Betty! How you are blown about! You are growing too big a girl to play the hoiden."

"Goody Billington calls me a tear-coat," replied the child, laughing in a blithe, fearless voice very pleasant to hear.

"Goody Billington"—began the mother, flushing a little, but checking herself as she sat Sally up and pulled her little red flannel nightgown over her head, while she asked in quite another tone, "Did you see father, Betty?"

"Yes'm, and he sent me to tell you he'd not be home for a little while. Oh, mother, what do you think! I was running out north to find father, as you bade me, and just as he stepped out of the woods with his axe and Rover, we saw two Indians coming down the trail, and they were driving a man, a white man, in front of them; and he looked so tired and so sick, and all bent over as if he would fall down, and no hat or cloak, and his doublet tattered and torn like the scarecrow we dressed for the cornfield, and his poor hands all cut and bleeding and tied behind him with a strip of deerhide, and one of the Indians holding the end of it, and every once in a while jerking it to make the poor man go on; for indeed he looked fit to fall every minute, and, cold as it was, the sweat dropped off the dark points of his hair and rolled down his poor dirty face. Oh, mother, I was like to cry at such a sight, and father"—

"Ay, what did your father do?" asked Priscilla eagerly, as, lapping the child close to her breast, she turned half round toward Betty, who with fixed eyes seemed witnessing again the piteous sight she described.

"Oh, father! He talked with them a little, but you know he is none so quick at the Indian, not like the captain"—

"Never mind," interrupted Priscilla impatiently. "'Tis not for you to say another man's quicker at aught than your father, but what came of it?"

"Why, when father had talked a little he shook his head and said in English, 'Nay, I can make naught on't; you must come to the governor;' and then we all came on toward the housen, and daddy said to me that I should run home like a good girl, and tell you he would be here anon, when he had seen the governor."

"Ay, he'll not think of himself till every one else is served, but I'll not let him balk himself of a good supper if I cook a dozen, one after the other."

And Priscilla, stepping into the little bedroom off the kitchen, laid the sleeping baby in her cradle, and had no more than returned to the larger room when the door again opened to admit her husband, with a look of considerable perplexity upon his genial face.

"Well, goodman, and what's it all about?" demanded Priscilla with her usual impetuosity, as, coming within the radius of her influence, John's brow cleared, and an expectant smile softened his mouth.

"Why, dame, 'tis a coil, for you to unravel if thou canst. Betty told you, mayhap, of the prisoner the Indians brought in."

"Yes?"

"Well, the governor and the captain and Hobomok are off to the woods after deer, and not yet home, and Dame Bradford and her sister are in the woods looking for wintergreen and sassafras for the spring beer the dame makes so famously after thy recipe"—

"Nay, she makes it better than I," interrupted Priscilla, replying to her husband's proud smile. "Well?"

"So Christian Penn would not let me leave the savages and the captive there, for the Indians couldn't, and the white man wouldn't, speak a word of English, and so"—

"You brought them home, goodman?"

"Why yes; how did you know that, Priscilla?"

"By art magic. Where are they now?"

"I left them in the cowshed until I knew thy mind about it, wife."

"Nay, then, John! When was my mind other than thine in a deed of charity?" asked Priscilla tenderly. "Fetch them in, I pray thee, with no more ado."

And in a moment more John had ushered in a figure at sight of which Priscilla exclaimed indignantly,—

"Why did you not unbind his arms, John Alden? The shame of seeing a white man so used by savages, and you not to make in to his rescue!"

"He would not have it, nor would the Indians," expostulated John helplessly.

"Would not have it!" repeated his wife contemptuously, while with the scissors hanging at her girdle she cut the thong of deer-hide painfully binding the wounded wrists of the captive. As she approached, one of the Indians growled a remonstrance and muttered something, of which Alden understood only the words "Big Chief," but with one stride he placed himself between his wife and the remonstrant, and first laboriously evolving Indian words equivalent to "Stand back! It's all right!" he added in English,—

"The Big Chief isn't at home, but I'm here, and my wife will do as she sees fit. It'll be bad for the man who tries to hinder her."

"And did not you want my husband to unbind your hands, friend?" asked Priscilla, as she gently removed the thong which had sunk deep into the bruised flesh.

"My thanks to you, fair dame," replied the stranger, breaking silence for the first time. "No, I did not wish to be released until the Governor or the Captain of Plymouth had seen my plight and told me if it was by their command these savages had thus dealt with me; I knew not what might be the authority of this gentleman"—

"My husband is John Alden, lieutenant of the colony's forces, and second in command to Captain Standish."

"My service to you, Lieutenant Alden, and I crave your pardon for what may have seemed surly silence under your first advances; but truth to tell, I am a little overborne with fatigue and annoyance"—

"Indeed, sir, you are fit to drop," broke in Priscilla indignantly. "Here, sit you down in the roundabout chair, and say not a word more till I fetch you a cup of cordial-waters. John, do get rid of these Indians. I hate the sight of them! Let them go wait at Master Hopkins's until the governor comes home to take order with them"—

But at this moment, and while Priscilla, half filling a small silver cup with Hollands gin slightly tempered with water, held it to the lips of the fainting man, the door suddenly opened, and Bradford, followed by Standish and Hobomoc, entered the room.

"My wife and Christian Penn sent me up to ask about—ah yes—why—Captain, this gentleman is—Your name, good sir?"

"My name is Sir Christopher Gardiner," replied the captive, rallying his strength to reply with dignity. "And as you seem to recall, we met once before at my poor home in the Massachusetts. Well enough I know that my hospitality then was not such as befits either your quality or mine, and yet methinks your response is even less courteous."

"We knew not who the fugitive might be of whom the Indians told us," returned Bradford gravely. "But evil entreated though you seem to have been, your case would have been even worse had it not been for us."

"They went about to kill you, man," broke in Standish bluntly. "And if the hound the Bay Colony laid upon your track had not fallen in with one of our own Indians, you had long since tumbled across your own camp-fire, with an arrow through your heart."

"Say you so, Captain," replied Gardiner faintly. "'Tis but another proof that a man seldom knows his best friends; but why do the Bay people seek my life?"

"That is best known to yourself, sir," began Bradford somewhat severely; but Priscilla Alden interposed,—

"I pray your pardon, Master Bradford, but this man needs care and tendance rather than catechizing just now. Look but at those arms and hands!"

"Ay, look!" exclaimed Gardiner, holding up his arms, yet forced at once to drop them through pain.

Bradford and Standish stared in amazement, for through the tattered and stripped sleeves of the knight's doublet and fine Hollands shirt could be seen many and cruel weals as of stripes, some of them still bleeding, others crusted with dry blood, and others lividly bruised. The hands were in even yet more pitiable case, discolored, swollen, and cut so that they hardly looked like hands at all.

"What is this? What has chanced to your hands and arms, sir?" demanded the governor.

"Ask those red devils there," replied Sir Christopher bitterly. "And let me ask if it was not done by your own orders."

"By my orders! Never, so help me God!" cried Bradford; and then turning upon the Indians he demanded,—

"Is this your work, Weetonawah, or is it the Shawmut's? Did I not warn you both to bring in the man with all care and humane tenderness?"

The Indians looked at each other, drew their skin mantles closer about them as if in assertion of their own dignity, and finally uttered a few words which Standish as briefly translated:—

"They say they did but a little whip him with sticks, and it is no harm."

"But why did they whip him, little or much?"

"My faith! they could never have taken me alive, had not they beat my last weapon out of my hands," broke in the knight. "When they are gone and I am a little refreshed I will tell you the whole story, gentlemen; but if you indeed wish me well, drive away these assassins and leave me to this comely matron's tendance for a while, at least."

"'Tis well spoken," replied the governor in his usual placable voice. "John Alden, will it suit you to keep this man over-night, if no longer, and will you, Priscilla, give him the care he needs and you so well understand?"

"If the goodwife says yes, I'll not say no," declared Alden; and Priscilla added a little sharply,—

"'Tis the best word said yet."

CHAPTER XV.

AND DESCRIBES IT.

Not until the next afternoon did Priscilla Alden allow her husband to report the patient ready to receive the visitors who awaited her summons, but when the governor, the captain, the Elder, and the doctor were finally admitted they found him a very different looking person from the captive driven into town by the Indians, who had already been paid their reward and dismissed.

Like most of the colonists, John Alden had enlarged his house from the rude shelter of the earliest years to a dwelling suited to a growing and thrifty family, so that at the other side of the door opening into the great cheerful kitchen with its southern and eastern windows lay a new room, more carefully finished than the first, its floor nearly covered with rugs of Priscilla's own manufacture, its fireplace decorated with Dutch tiles, its woodwork painted, and its casement window set with real glass in leaden bands, instead of the oiled paper or linen which sufficed for the kitchen windows.

Here were collected the few pieces of furniture which William Molines and his wife had managed to bring over from France, Holland, and England, the three homes of their years before the Pilgrimage. The deep and wide carved chest of black oak, with cunningly wrought hinges and a key nearly as large as that of the Bastile, stood on one side of the fireplace, its depths well stored with damask and napery, bed linen and window curtains, some of Priscilla's own spinning and some of her mother's, while certain articles of fine damask wrought upon looms of Flanders, and bought even there at a great price, were hereditary treasures.

On the other side of the fireplace stood a "buffet," of English make and quaintly carved with heads of beasts and gaping gargoyles which were the terror of Betty and her brothers on the rare occasions when they were allowed to penetrate the solemn solitudes of this state apartment. This buffet was not as well supplied as that of the governor's wife, and boasted no Venetian glass, although there were four plain glass tumblers, or rummers, as they were then called, and a few pieces of Delft ware with a china bowl so precious that Priscilla seldom dared to look at it. Around the neck of one of the gargoyles projecting from the cornice of the buffet hung a string of curious Indian, or rather Ceylonese beads, each carved into semblance of an idol's head, a fact happily unguessed by their owners, or indeed by Plymouth, which would have demanded an auto-da-fé of them in the town square; but by some unconscious cerebration Priscilla had decorated the other gargoyle with a string of wampum, thus balancing the superstition of oldest eastern idolatry with that of newest, or rather latest discovered, western. Later on, this string of wampum became quite an appreciable bit of property, but at present it was scarcely more than a curiosity; for although it had been recommended to the Pilgrims some four years previous to this date by Isaac de Razières, the delightful Dutchman who visited Plymouth with overtures of friendship and menace from New Amsterdam, it had not as yet become the circulating medium it did later, since both the New England Indians and the New England colonists had to be educated to its use,—a use invented by those unhappy Pequots and Narragansetts upon whose shore the quahaug shells were found in perfection. The thrifty Dutchman in his visit to Plymouth had brought a quantity of wampum for sale, and the Pilgrims, after listening to his account of its uses and value, invested fifty pounds with him at the rate of a penny for three bits of the blue, or six of the white shell, this price bringing the blue pieces nearly to the value of a cent of our currency.

But we must linger no longer over the description of Priscilla's "withdrawing" room, as it might very literally be called, but stand aside to allow the Fathers of Plymouth to enter and find Sir Christopher Gardiner seated in an invalid-chair beside the fire, writing in a little pocket-book which at their entrance he closed and hid in his breast.

Grave salutations passed, the guests were seated, and Alden, who had ushered them in, would have left the room, but was bidden to remain by the governor, while Standish with one of his rare smiles added,—

"I can answer for my friend John's discretion as for mine own." At which pleasant word the giant looked foolishly glad, for it was the most friendly speech Standish had vouchsafed since the night when Alden's ill-timed slumbers had so nearly dishonored his captain.

"And now, sir," began Bradford in a tone finely mingled of magisterial authority and benevolent hospitality, "if you are sufficiently recovered from the hardships of your journey hither, we should be glad to hear some account of your coming into such straits, and especially of what complaint the rulers of the Bay Colony may have against you."

"A truly reasonable inquiry, Master Governor, and one which I shall find joyful content in gratifying," replied the knight, assuming an easier position, and stretching his shapely legs, clad in a pair of John Alden's best hose, toward the fire. The action attracted Bradford's notice, and, with Pris

Carpenter's fancies in his mind, he scrutinized his guest with more attention than men generally bestow upon one another's personal appearance.

Tall, dark, with a hawk's eyes, and an eagle's nose above an enormous mustache, which could not, however, conceal a riotous and sensual mouth, with dark floating hair now carefully dressed, and a smooth-shaven cleft chin telling of both will and courage, the knight was beyond controversy a handsome man in spite of his forty or fifty years, and one well suited to turn the brain of a romantic girl. His expression of reckless and jeering self-assertion, thinly veiled under a mask of deference and deprecation, was less propitious than his features, but as Bradford shrewdly told himself was by no means the expression he would wear in conversation with a young maiden whom he wished to please.

"Yes, I shall be most happy, most content, to tell you whatever in your opinion, sir, it imports you to know of my poor history," pursued Sir Christopher in a vague fashion, as if inwardly employed in concocting a romance to serve instead of the truth. "But I know not well where to begin. Shall I tell you that my father is a wealthy gentleman of Gloucester in England, and is, or was, poor man, nephew of that Bishop Gardiner, Lord of the see of Winchester, who did God service under Queen Mary"—

"Peace, ribald!" broke in the stern voice of Elder Brewster. "If indeed you are of kin to that bloody persecutor and servant of a yet more murderous mistress, boast not of it here among those who have fled into the wilderness to escape the cruelties of the Scarlet Woman and those who serve her."

"Lo you now! I do most humbly crave your pardon, most worthy—nay, then, what do they call men who are no priests, and yet take upon them the priest's office under John Calvin and his fellows?"

"Sorry should I be to seem discourteous or inhospitable to a wounded man," exclaimed Bradford indignantly, "but men have been set in the bilboes and worse for less offense than such words."

"Do I not know it?" retorted Gardiner. "Did not I, with these eyes, see mine own friend Thomas Morton set in the bilboes and direfully insulted in yon village of Boston, for less,—nay, for naught—for naught—but scaring a pack of saucy Indians by firing some hail-shot over their heads to fright them into bringing him a canoe? And did I not see him, less than two months gone by, haled down to the quay and put by main force aboard a skiff which rowed him out to the Handmaid, a crank leaky old tub, not half victualed or half found, and no provision for his comfort, nay, for his very life, but a handful or two of corn out of his own provision, stolen out of his house at Merry Mount before it was set afire? Yes, sirs, set afire as the

Handmaid sailed out of port, as a taunt and a gibe to a helpless prisoner! Ha, ha, though! That word 'helpless' minds me of a merry joke even in the midst of such dolor. When our friends yonder had got poor Morton into their boat, and rowed him to the side of the Handmaid,—and marry, she's much such a handmaid as Hagar of the Bible, turned out into the wilderness with neither meat nor water enough to keep poor Ishmael alive"—

"Profane man! Do you dare"—began Brewster, but with an uplifted hand and deprecatory bow the knight interrupted him:—

"Pardon, your reverence, though 't was a most apposite quotation and surely more scriptural than profane,—but let it pass. As I was saying, when the boat reached the Handmaid's rotund sides and a rope was thrown over, Morton was bidden to seize it and climb aboard; but, as he himself might say, he put in a demurrer, and represented that having no business on board the Handmaid he hesitated to intrude where perhaps he was not wanted. The tipstaves persisted, Morton desisted, until in the end the rope was drawn up and a noose let down instead, wherein they netted him and so hoysed him on board, he laughing like a fiend at their toil and rage."

"They should have put the noose around his neck, and not hasted to pull him inboard," growled Standish; and Sir Christopher, turning airily upon him, cried,—

"Say you so, Captain Sh—nay, Captain Standish? Well, and truly there's little love lost 'twixt you and Morton. He had a story that you pleaded hard for leave to shoot him with your own hand, when he was down here at Plymouth a prisoner as I am now."

"I would have been glad enough to meet him man to man, and let him who was the better marksman shoot the other."

"And a very pretty main it would be between two such fighting cocks as"—

"Enough of this!" exclaimed the governor, silencing with a gesture not only the captain, who had sprung to his feet, but the Elder, who with a slow red mounting to his cheek where it showed like the color in a hardy apple frozen and withered, yet clinging to the parent tree, seemed about to speak.

"Sir Christopher Gardiner, if that is indeed your name and degree, we men of Plymouth claim no titles, nor are we courtiers, skilled in cunning fence of word, but we have our own dignity as rulers of this little commonalty, and our self-respect as men. Be pleased, therefore, to lay aside all these quips and cranks, and tell us briefly who you are, and why you are found fleeing from the Bay, even at risk of your life."

Somewhat impressed by the simple dignity of Bradford's manner, and perhaps a little ashamed of his own levity, the knight at once threw it off, sat more upright in his chair, and fixing his eyes steadily upon Bradford's face as if to avoid the challenge of Standish's eager gaze, replied courteously,—

"I have already told you, Sir Governor, that I am Christopher Gardiner, son of a worthy gentleman of Gloucester in England. Early in youth I wandered away from home, and sojourned so many years among Jews, Turks, and other infidels, as the Prayer Book hath it, that my father disinherited me and gave my estates to a brother who clung to him—and to them. On the other hand, a certain potentate whose name you love not made me a Knight of the Holy Sepulchre and a Cavalier of the Milizia Aureata, commonly called the Golden Melice."

"The Pope of Rome has no power to appoint a Knight of the Holy Sepulchre!" exclaimed Brewster, recalling worldly lore which he had thought forgotten. Gardiner bowed low and mockingly.

"Pardon! No doubt, reverend sir, you are better acquainted with His Holiness than I can be, but I go on with mine account of myself. Coming back to England after well-nigh thirty years' absence, I find my father dead, my brother and his brood in possession, and naught left for the poor exile, should he ever return, but a beggarly thousand crowns and a nook beside the hall-fire so long as he should behave himself!

"Well, well, 't is not good for me to dwell on those days; so to cut the matter short, I took my thousand crowns, and a few more that had hidden among the tatters of my knightly robes, and came hither to the New World, hoping to escape from men and the weariness of their ways. I bought a bit of land from a copper-colored gentleman calling himself Chickatawbut who professed to own it, and who made much complaint that the men of Plymouth had stolen from his mother's grave the choice bearskins laid over it to keep the good gentlewoman warm through the storms of winter"—

"We bought some bearskins of a native, but knew not where he got them," said Bradford with an air of annoyance, and Sir Christopher's great mustache stirred in malicious glee at seeing that the pin-prick had reached the quick.

"I bought my land, and I built mine house, and I planted my garden, and I hired some Indian guides to show me the haunts of the game and fish, and I began to live much such an innocent and beneficent life as that of Adam in Paradise"—

"With yon fair lady as your Eve?" demanded Standish. The knight turned his eyes upon him and the spark kindled in their depths, but again Bradford interposed,—

"Leaving aside tropes and metaphors, Sir Christopher, may we ask what relation the gentlewoman we found at your house sustains toward yourself?"

"She is my cousin, my housekeeper, my poor little friend. Ah, indeed, gentlemen, you may leave her alone with no fear but she will suffer enough both for her own peccadillos and mine, since those gloomy bigots of the Bay have seized and hold her close prisoner, with low diet, and questionings like those of the Holy Office, day by day."

And the man's voice took on so genuine a tone of pain and fear as he thought upon his helpless companion that even Brewster forbore to press the subject further, and Bradford not unkindly inquired,—

"And why didst thou flee from this poor paradise of thine?"

"I heard by my friendly Indians, the same who afterward told me that Mary was a prisoner, that there was mischief plotting against me in the council chamber at Boston, and one fine morning when I saw a boat filled with tipstaves and bum-bailiffs crossing the river half a mile or so from my house"—

"Neponset the Indians call it," murmured John Alden; and Gardiner nodded good-humoredly.

"Ay, so they do, yet at that moment I tarried not to discover if Winthrop's men had learned its name as well as its navigation, but, throwing my shot-pouch and powder-flask around my neck, thrusting my compass into one pocket and a full flask into the other, I bade my poor little cousin good-by, and well armed, as you may be assured, I plunged into the forest, and set out for the New Netherlands, some sixty or seventy leagues to the southwest of Boston Bay."

"They thought you would try to reach Piscataqua, where Hilton and others are seated. Church of England men, they, and more of your own fashion."

"Why, of course they so thought, Master Governor, and that is why I went not thither; nor did I seek to come here because I felt myself in need of some air less pure and less attenuate than that which circles round a conventicle; I pined for the company of ordinary mortals like myself."

"You hardly reached the New Netherlands, however," suggested Bradford dryly.

"No. I fell sick the first night, from sleeping on the bare ground in a pitiless storm of rain and sleet, and I rested for a day or so with some natives whom I knew. Besides, had they much harmed her I left behind, I would have gone back and revenged her by at least John Winthrop's life."

"Come, now, that's spoken man fashion!" exclaimed Standish, and the two soldiers exchanged an almost friendly glance and smile. But the smile quickly faded from the knight's face as his thoughts went back to his terrible experience in the wilderness, and resting his elbow on his knee, with his chin in the cup of his hand, he stared gloomily into the fire, and went on:—

"I heard once and again from Boston, and I sent a token to my poor girl, bidding my messenger lie, and say that I was safe and well; then I went on, and wandered for days, nay, for weeks, up and down, hither and yon, fevered, wounded, helpless, yet unbroken. I met natives who told me of a great river in the Pequod country,—Canaughticott they called it; but I could not cross it save by the favor of those savages, the most bloody and the most implacable of any in the country, and I saw it would be but madness to attempt it. Then I was minded to linger about in the forest until summer, when I might make my way north to Piscataqua, or perhaps ship aboard some vessel bound to the New Netherlands, or even come hither and ask shelter,—in very truth I knew not what I would be at, for every way seemed barred, and I was too dazed and fevered much of the time to concoct a plan beyond the next meal, or the next lodging. At last the Massachusetts runner who had dogged the path to Piscataqua for two or three weeks tried another trail and came upon me. I since hear that he would have murthered me but for your influence, and I am beholden to you, one and all; for, sad as is my plight, I am not yet ready to make venture of a country even stranger to me than New England. But since the Bay had set a reward upon my head it might not safely rest even upon the dank leaves of the forest; and two days ago, while Samson so slept, the Philistines came upon him; that is to say, I wakened suddenly with a most uncomely savage bending over me, and trying to steal my snaphance which I hugged close to my breast. Alive in a moment, I sprang to my feet, dashed my fist into the fellow's mouth and heard his teeth split off like icicles, even as I sprang for the other side of the thicket to make ready to shoot him. Now beyond that thicket lay a stream whose name I know not, but broader than the Thames at London"—

"Taunton River, we have named it," again suggested Alden.

"Ay? Well, there lay a canoe pulled up on the bank, with the paddles in it. To seize that canoe and paddle across the river was my game, and haply so reach the New Netherlands; but as I put my shoulder to the bows the enemy fell upon me, a half dozen at least of hellish whooping savages with all their murderous motives uppermost. With one mighty heave I pushed off and sprang in, at the same moment presenting my piece now at this, now at that one of the savages. Well I knew that any one of them might hide behind a tree and pick me off with an arrow, and I found time to marvel that they did not, for how was I to know that they had been ordered to take me alive and unharmed? but even as the canoe felt the stream and swerved away from the shore, even as a delusive hope of escape danced before my eyes, the stern of the tittlish craft ran upon a rock, and presto! I was in the water, and what is worse, my piece and my rapier were at the bottom of the stream! I stooped to grope for the good blade, but it lay too deep, and as I rose they were upon me, yelling like fiends. One weapon remained, my little dagger of Venice, which I would not have lost for a gold piece, sith it is a dagger of happy memories and hath carved me many a puzzling knot, even as the great Alexander untied the Gordian knot with his own good blade"—

"Your dagger is safe, and shall be restored. I pr'ythee get on," remonstrated Bradford.

"Sir, your impatience is flattering to my poor powers of narration, and sooth to say, I found myself much interested in the story as it went on. Well, I drew the dagger and I shook it in their faces after a most terrible fashion, and I swore most roundly that the first man who came within reach should taste its point; and so fearful and so truthful was my mien that they slunk back, and I even began to cast lightning glances toward the canoe as it lay stranded not many feet away, when some direct emissary of Satan whispered a plan to those imps of the same master, and two of them, retiring to the bushes, cut half a dozen or so of long poles and stripped them of their leaves and little shoots; then each man seizing one, they began to try to knock the dagger out of my hands, and as I swiftly changed it from side to side, and turned every way to shelter it, their dastardly blows rained down upon my hands and arms until the sleeves were cut to tatters and the skin beneath to ribbons of most unseemly hue. I held on so long as a man's will may conquer flesh and blood, for I fancied that, knowing me to be a man of some daring and endurance they fain would take me alive to test my courage under torture, and I had liever provoke them to kill me then and there; but in the end, when the dagger was beaten out of my numb and swollen fingers, they closed in upon me like foul wolves upon a wounded stag, and all was over.

"They bound my arms, as Master Alden can tell you, most cruelly, and so soon as themselves were refreshed—although not so much as a drop of water gave they me until at night I managed to drink from a pool where we lay for a few hours—they set off for Plymouth; and the rest you know."

"And the man is over-weary for safety. 'Tis best to leave him to rest, and to Mistress Alden's ministrations."

So spake Samuel Fuller, the kindly surgeon and physician of the Pilgrims; and Bradford cordially replied,—

"Yes and indeed, Doctor. Sir Christopher, we do not make you any answer just now, except that we are beholden to you for your courteous reply to our inquiries, and we will now leave you to repose. To-morrow we shall know better what to reply. We wish you good-e'en."

"Good-evening, Sir Governor, and each of you gentlemen. Captain Standish, it would please me much if by and by you would waste an hour in talk with me of the stirring adventures we both have known in those realms of heathenesse beyond the seas."

"It will give me singular pleasure so to do, Sir Christopher," replied Standish; and so in amity and sympathy parted two men who with equal pleasure would have fought hand to hand until one lay dead upon the field, or, as they that evening did, over a tankard of strong ale, rehearsed for each other's benefit their battles of old time.

CHAPTER XVI.

A MILLSTONE FOR SIR CHRISTOPHER.

"Here, Betty woman! You shall help mother and carry the strange gentleman's breakfast to him. I'm too put about with my baking to redd myself fit to see him. Put a clean towel over the sarver, set the salt and pepper pot upon it, and take father's beer-mug to fill him out a measure of my oldest home-brewed. He said but yesterday he loved a cool tankard better than strong waters of a morning."

"Shall I take one of the real damask napkins for him, mother? There are two in the drawer of the dresser newly laundered."

"Yes. Give him of the best, poor fellow, while he's with us, for he goes from us to prison, and mayhap to worse."

"What worse, mother?" demanded Betty, pausing as she shook out the folds of the Antwerp damask napkin, and turning her face toward her mother, whose quick eye marked its sudden pallor.

"Pho, child! I did but shoot at random; there's no harm coming to the man that I know of. Here, now, here's the little bird done to a turn, and some manchets of wheat bread, and a cup of honey, and the tankard. That's enough for any man's breakfast, be he sick or well. What's that, now?"

"Just a bit of mayflower, mother, that I found yesterday in the nook south the hill, you know."

"Yes, yes, but—well, have thine own way, poppet,—thou 'rt a good child."

And the tray, decorated with a little silver cup holding the two or three reckless sprigs of epigæa, which had ventured before their time into a world not yet ready for them, was carried into the fore-room, where Sir Christopher stood at the window impatiently considering his swollen and discolored hands from which he had removed the bandages.

Before we attend to him, however, let us here note that the *Epigæa repens* still blooms in Plymouth so early, that by May-day it is gone; and it is not, and never was, and never will be an arbutus, although a world which chooses to say "commence" instead of "begin," and "locate" instead of "build," insists upon calling it so, and probably will so insist as long as time endures.

"Ah! Good-morrow, little maid!" exclaimed the knight, a smile replacing the scowl of vexation. "I have not seen you before. Are you Master Alden's daughter?"

"Yes, sir," replied Betty, placing her tray upon the table, and then turning to make her little curtsy, for Betty knew her manners as well as any young gentlewoman alive. "Mother was over-busy this morning to attend you, and so sent me with your breakfast."

"And a right tempting breakfast, too!" declared Gardiner, seizing the pewter beer-mug and half emptying it at a draught. "Ha! 'tis good! A right honest strike of malt!" added he, carefully wiping his long mustachios and smiling upon Betty, who stood solemnly regarding him. "And a posy, too! A posy that looks marvelously like thyself, child, so sweet and tender, yet blossoming from out austere and rigid foliage. What is thy name, little one?"

"Elizabeth Alden, sir; but I'm mostly called Betty."

"Ay, then, this flower is the Bettina, or the Betty-belle, or the Bettissimo, is it not?"

"Nay, sir; we call it mayflower, because father says it minds him of the English may that blooms in the hedges where he was born. But the doctor, who is wondrous wise about herbs, will still give it some hard name I cannot remember. He knows botany, the doctor does."

"Ay, does he? Well, I would he knew a way to make me a well man and a free one." And the knight, hastily pushing aside his half-eaten breakfast, began to pace up and down the room in restless anger and impatience. Betty, halfway to the door, stopped and regarded him pitifully, then timidly said,—

"I would I could help you, sir. Shall I bring my kitten to see you? or mayhap you'd like Shakem better?"

"And what is Shakem, thou pretty child?"

"He's father's little dog that catches rats and shakes them so merrily, and he knows tricks, too: he'll stand up and beg, and he'll catch the bits on his nose, and he'll play at being dead"—

"Nay, then, Betty, he's not for me! I need no mimic deaths to mind me of mine own. Ohé!"

"Is that the 'worse' that mother meant? Oh, I'm so sorry, sir!"

"Worse that thy mother meant? Now what's that riddle, child?"

"Mayhap I should not have told it again; but mother made the manchets and broiled the bird, while we had but bean soup and coarse bread for breakfast, because she said you'd go from here to prison and it might be to worse."

"Said she so? Ha! is it resolved upon, then? But no, no, no! Winthrop and the rest would not dare, especially with Gorges at my back. I can make them see 'twould be but self-murther for them to give him and the council so excellent a weapon against them. There's no danger, no danger of death, but I must write to Sir Ferdinando"—

"Is he at the Bay, sir, and will he serve you if you can make him know?" asked Betty eagerly; and the knight, who had forgotten her, turned with a sudden smile and uplifted eyebrows.

"What! we're in council together, are we, Betty? Nay, Sir Ferdinando Gorges is in England, and— Come, now, child, I read thine honest eyes, and I know thou 'rt sorry for me, and would not add to my discomfort, hadst thou the chance of doing it."

"Nay, sir, indeed and indeed I would not do so."

"I am sure of it. Well, then, Betty, promise me thou'lt not say over again what just slipped my lips, and most particularly the name. I'll be sworn thou hast even now forgotten"—

"Nay, sir, I've not forgotten; 'tis Sir Ferdinando Gorges that would befriend you, but he's in England and may not be reached, but an the Bay does you an injury he'll revenge it."

"Thou hast too good a memory, Betty, and a wonderful quickness for thy years," replied the knight, biting his lip, and staring almost angrily at the child. "Yet I must e'en trust thee. Thou'lt not lisp one word of that lesson thou hast so pat? Mind you, child, 'twas not meant for your ears!"

"I'll not say it over to any one, sir, and I did not want to hear it." And Betty, with a pretty air of dignity, took up the tray and was leaving the room when Sir Christopher recalled her:—

"Betty, you're taking away my posy! Was not it meant to tarry with the poor prisoner, and comfort him a little?"

"Yes, indeed, sir. Will you be so gentle as to take it off the tray?"

"Ay, and thank you, Betty. Good-by, my pretty turnkey."

"I know not what that is, sir. Can I bring you aught else?"

"Yes, Betty. I fain would have pens and ink and paper, if I may; and will you or some other ministering sprite redd up the room a little?"

"I'll ask mother, sir," replied Betty comprehensively, and disappeared, leaving Sir Christopher plunged in meditation both perplexing and futile.

"I must wait and see how much they know before I frame my reply," at length said he aloud; and throwing off the weight with a shrug of his broad shoulders, he took a small dressing-case from one of the inner pockets of his doublet, and began to comb, to perfume, and to curl the long dark hair which was in itself an abomination to the Puritans, and an object of scorn to the Pilgrims.

"The right mustachio still excels the left," muttered he discontentedly, as by help of a tiny pocket mirror he carefully scrutinized the result of his labors, and separating the hairs of the left-hand mustache tried to give it a more formidable appearance, although it already nearly touched his eye and covered his cheek. A gentle tap upon the door disturbed him, but without interrupting his occupation he cried, "Come in," and a moment later, "Oh, 'tis my little Betty again! She has brought some paper and pens, and she finds me at my toilet. What think you of my lovelocks, little Betty?"

"I never saw such on a man before, sir."

"Nay, that's no answer, madam! I asked how liked you them."

"I would like them"—

"Well, say it out, thou strange child."

"I would like them on a woman right well, sir."

"But not on a man?"

"Nay. Even Alick was shorn long since."

"And who is Alick, pr'ythee?"

"Alick Standish, the captain's oldest son."

"And your little sweetheart?"

"Nay, sir, mother says 'tis not pretty to talk of such things, though like enough we'll marry when we're old enough, for our two fathers are close friends."

"And how much older must you be, mistress, ere you may speak of such things?"

"Well, Susan Ring is no more than fifteen, and she is to marry Thomas Clarke so soon as he has William Wright's house finished, for he's a carpenter, and William Wright would fain marry Prissie Carpenter, the governor's wife's sister"—

"Ohé! I had forgotten! So, so, indeed, and so it is! Now, then, here is a coil!"

Betty, perceiving that her prattle was no longer heard, ceased abruptly, and in silence completed the spreading of the bed, and dusting and arranging the furniture with all the mature and responsible methods not uncommonly characterizing the oldest daughter of a large family, especially in those early days. Suddenly the knight broke silence:—

"Betty, you know Mistress Carpenter?"

"Prissie?"

"Yes."

"Oh, yes, sir, I know her very well. We have merry games of play together, and I am main fond of her."

"Well, child, I also know her a little, and I too am fond of her, but that is another of the things you may not tell abroad."

"And yet you have never been here before, have you, sir?"

"No, thank the Lord, I never have, nor shall I willingly come again, I promise you, my Betty; but being here, I fain would change a word or two with Mistress Carpenter, whom I knew in England before ever she or I came hither."

"And that will not be hard, sir, for she often runs in to have a chat with mother, and I will tell her"—

"No, no, no, child, that will never do!" broke in Sir Christopher impatiently. "Did I not tell thee 'twas a secret?"

"Yes, sir, but you would speak with Prissie, you said," replied Betty, her eyes wide with wonder and a growing instinct of wrong-doing. "You had best tell mother about it, sir."

"Nay, Betty, I thought thou wert my little friend, and felt sorry that those cruel men at the Bay will presently serve me worse than they did my friend Master Morton."

"He was here, and I liked him not at all. He miscalled Alick's father, and mother would not make jelly for him though he asked it of her."

"So! What a little partisan thou art, Betty! and I'll venture thy mother is, too. But, Betty, there was another man there at Boston, whom they whipped until the blood ran down to his heels, and then they cut off his ears, and laid a hot iron on his cheek"—

"Oh, sir!" And Gardiner paused, startled at the power of expression developed in that little flower-face by horror, and anger, and pity beyond its years. His own face softened to perhaps its best expression as, laying a hand upon the glittering hair, he kindly said,—

"Nay, then, 'tis not a tale for the ears of a little maid; but thou'dst not like to have me so served, if thou couldst hinder?"

"Oh, sir, but how can I hinder?"

"Why, I know not that thou canst, and yet—the first way is to keep my counsel even from thy mother."

"I always tell mother, and sometimes father, all I do, but—I will not tell what can harm you, sir; only please tell me no more."

"But, Betty, dear little Betty, I was just going to ask you to do me one little kindness, and tell nobody about it. Won't you be the friend of a poor wretch who is to be so cruelly used if you do refuse to help him?"

"Indeed and indeed, sir, I would help you at one word if I could, but I may not tell a lie, even though to save you and me too from a den of lions."

"Daniel, eh? Well, little Daniel, I ask thee to tell no lies, nor to do anything to hurt thy tender conscience, but only to carry a little folded bit of paper to Mistress Priscilla Carpenter, and fetch me another which she will send."

"Oh, I can do so much as that, sir," replied Betty, relieved at what seemed to her a very harmless proposition.

"But you must give her the billet when she is all alone, Betty, and you must not let any one—not any one, mind—know a word about it from first to last. Can you do that?"

"Oh, yes, easy enough,—but"—and Betty pondered, finger on lip; then suddenly turning her brook-brown eyes upon the dark face of the man of the world, she demanded, "Is it right for me to do it, sir? Since I may not ask mother or father, you must tell me, sir, is it right?"

Nobody knows why Sir Christopher Gardiner fled his native land, nor why he dreaded to put himself in reach of its authorities; but whatever may have been his crimes, I believe none injured his own soul more, none at the last day will hang more like a millstone around his neck, than the offense he now offered to the little one who made him for the moment her arbiter of right and wrong; for he said, but turned away from her eyes while he said,—

"Yes, child, 'tis right, and so would your mother say if you could ask her; but she would far liever you did not, for she would then feel that she must tell your father, and he the governor, and so I should be balked of what will be a comfort to me while I am burned and bleeding in the hangman's hands up yonder."

"Oh, sir! oh, sir! The pity on't—and—and—indeed, I'll carry your token."

"There, then, there, then, dear little maid,—don't cry! I pr'ythee don't cry! Come, now, I'll give it up! I'll say no more about it."

"Nay, sir, I'll do it, and I'll not tell, and 'twill be a comfort to you when— oh dear, oh dear,—but sith you say 'tis right, and mother would call it right"—

"Nay, I'll not do it,—and yet—and yet"—

"But why will you not, sir? 'Tis not that I was naughty and did refuse at the first? Sometimes when I've been froward, father will not let me fetch his pipe or his dry slippers, and says, 'Thank you, Elizabeth, but I'll serve myself,' and I'd rather he'd beat me, or scold, as mother will."

"My child, I'm not vexed, and—well, there—wait a bit—now, here it is, just these half dozen lines thou seest, Betty; surely there's no harm in such a scrap of paper, is there, child?"

"You say not, sir," replied Betty submissively, yet sadly, for she liked not her errand, although resting in the confidence of a nature itself upright, upon the assurance of her elder that she was doing right in obeying him.

At dinner time, with the tray came Betty, again with an apology from her mother; and when she had set it down she took a scrap of paper from her bosom and handed it to the knight, who, impatiently unfolding it, read in a very rude and Gothic scrawl the two words,—

"*Ask Betty.*   PRISCILLA CARPENTER."

"'Ask Betty,'" repeated the knight aloud. "That is all there is in it, Betty. But what is the message that I am to ask?"

"Prissie cannot write much, but she made shift to read your billet, and she sends her love and kind remembrance," repeated the child glibly. "And she said if you got leave to walk out, and I went with you, we should go to look for the mayflowers just below the Fort Hill, down near the palisades, and mayhap she would be there about three hours after noon. And if you cannot go to walk, or father goes with you, she will pass by this window while they are at lecture in the Fort, but it would be no more than to say good-by."

"Now that goes almost too well to be true, little Betty!" exclaimed the knight, rubbing his hands, and wincing as he did so, for they were not yet healed, while Betty, sadly changed from the careless and merry little maid of the morning hours, withdrew without a word.

After dinner, as he had expected, Sir Christopher received a visit from his host, who told him that the governor still awaited a reply to the letter he had sent by Indian runners to Governor Winthrop at the Bay, and that meanwhile Sir Christopher was to rest content where he was, or, if it better suited him, to walk about the town.

"That proposal jumps well with mine own fancies," replied Gardiner smilingly. "Your little daughter brought me these posies this morning, and told me of how and where they grow, and I should well like to study them in their habitat. I cherish a singular love for herbal lore, and have the theorics of Fuchsius and Bauhin at my fingers' ends."

"You should talk with our doctor, then," replied Alden. "He is marvelously learned in all such matters, and can pluck you to pieces the prettiest posy that grows, and break your head with the learned names he'll find in it."

"Ay, I doubt not," returned Gardiner coldly. "But in my captivity I better love the company of a prattling child than of a man who may be mine enemy."

"Nay, friend, we're none of us enemies of yours, nor of any but those who are enemies of God and the king; still so far as my will goes, Betty is free to walk with you if her mother needs her not."

"And may I ask of your courtesy that you will put the matter before your dame, as I am not like to see her?"

"Surely, although the mistress bade me say that she is presently coming to look once more at your wounded hands and arms."

"Oh, they are all but well. Sound flesh and good blood like mine heal apace." And Sir Christopher, with a self-approving smile, held up his well-shaped hands and straightened his comely figure.

John Alden looked and listened, but made no response, unless a slow smile that began almost imperceptibly, and widened and widened until it showed nearly all his broad white teeth, could be called so. But before it gained its full development he had left the room.

CHAPTER XVII.

"TWO IS COMPANY, THREE IS TRUMPERY!"

And so it fell that about three o'clock that afternoon, as Sir Christopher Gardiner and Betty Alden wandered along the southern foot of Burying Hill, then called Fort Hill, searching under the lee of every rock and clump of bushes for the epigæa, as often to be found by its pure spicy fragrance as by sight of its coy clusters of pink and white blossoms, Prissie Carpenter, a little basket in her hand, came strolling along the brookside, rather ostentatiously bound upon the same errand.

"Now would I like the skill of a painter fellow I knew in Holland, one Martin Ryckaert, a man I could take by the heel and eat him body and bones as I would a prawn; but give him his charcoal and his paints and his canvas, and he'd picture out this scene for you as if you saw it."

So spake Sir Christopher, who, old swashbuckler though he was, possessed a real love of nature and a real appreciation of beauty in whatever form it revealed itself, as he stood upright with folded arms and looked about him, while Betty, her little fingers grimed with soil and scratched with briers, delved amid the thickset ground pine to find the flowers hiding there.

It was one of those early April days which redeem the character of the froward month, and make one almost love its capricious yet prophetic gleams better than the assured joys of June. A high wind from the west drove before it great white cumuli, glittering like silver in the strong sunlight, and careering across the sky and dropping down behind Manomet as if in an illimitable game of hide-and-seek and catch-who-catch-can. The waves, uneasy at beholding liberty they might not have, and games they might not join, leaped as high as they could toward that azure playground, laughed back to the sun who laughed with them, or, breaking hoarsely upon the shore, sent up their voices of sturdy discontent. The trees, moved by such gigantic melody to bear their part in the grand antiphony, clashed their bare branches in a rhythm too vast for the human ear to comprehend, while the evergreens murmured and sobbed and whispered together, lamenting that they had not even dried leaves to send whirling down that wondrous dance. The brook, its icy winter shroud still clinging to the banks, rose up to assert that life defies the shroud, and that there is a power of spring which shall vanquish death again and again forever; and as the brown waters went tumbling and leaping down toward the ocean which the icy shroud can never compass, their sweet voices joined in the universal song like children in the choir. On sheltered slopes and sunny hillsides the grass was springing green, and though no flowers disputed the epigæa's precedence, the violets and anemones, the snowdrops and the Solomon's seal, stood with finger on lip and foot on the threshold, waiting for courage to cross it.

Coming up the brookside in her blue skirt and mantle, a white handkerchief tied over her hair, which in spite of it escaped in a hundred little dancing tendrils, Prissie seemed a part of the great sweeping harmony of sky and wind and sea and shore, and the knight, as with his extended right arm he swept in the lines of a magnificent imaginary landscape, felt, as his eyes first lighted upon that figure, more as if it were the fitting centre and *motif* of his piece than a real personage.

"A red cloak would be better," muttered he. "And yet no,—no,—the cold purity of blue is more harmonious, and marries well with sky and sea, but— Aha, Betty, there's your friend Mistress Carpenter!"

"Is it? Oh, yes! I'll call her."

"Nay, we'll stroll that way and see the brook near at hand, and you may search for gooseberries while I exchange a word with pretty Prissie."

"There are no gooseberries as yet, sir," replied Betty, bewildered; but the knight only laughed and strode farther down the hill toward the brook.

At that very moment Myles Standish pushed his round head and square shoulders through the trap door leading from the interior of the Fort to the flat roof, along the parapet of which his beloved guns were ranged, and lightly stepped off the ladder, saying,—

"Come out hither, Wright, and I'll show you through the perspective glass the beginnings of my new house. Ha! Does not the hill show fairly against the sky?"

"The Captain's Hill, all men call it," said William Wright, carefully coming out upon the roof, and shading his eyes with his hand as he looked across the water to the bold eminence, tree-crowned and majestic, upon whose skirts Standish had already erected a summer cottage soon to be solidified into a dwelling.

"I know they do," replied his companion absently, while he adjusted the clumsy glass solemnly deposited in his charge by the chiefs of the colony. "But I better like to call it Duxbury, for it minds me of hills I knew of old."

"I know no hills called Duxbury in England," objected Wright cautiously.

"Nay, the hills are called Pennine, but the place where I first saw them is in the manor of Duxbury. Ha! look you here, Wright, here's matter close at hand more nearly concerning us than the Pennine hills. See you yonder?"

"'Tis Mistress Carpenter and—and the man Gardiner," stammered Wright, staring down into the valley at his feet.

"Ay, and little Betty Alden picking posies so far away that she might as well be at home. Mind you, now, my friend, how close the rascal walks to the maiden's side, and how those hawk's eyen of his stare into her fair face; and by my faith, he's grasping her hand and she, poor maid, knows not how to pull it away!"

"She might an' she would," muttered William Wright jealously.

"Oh, I know not, I know not," retorted Myles, teasing him. "She's but a withy lass, and mayhap afraid of him. Is it true she's troth-plight to you, Wright?"

"Yes—that is no; she never would give her promise sure and fast, but I had hoped"—

"Then, man, if you will be said by my advice, you'll make down to the brook at best speed and secure that faltering hope before it is floated away like the flowers the silly maid is stripping off and flinging into the brook, not knowing what she's about. Go down, Wright, and claim your own."

"Nay, Captain," returned Wright, whose thin face had grown tallow-pale, and whose thin lips refused to take moisture from a tongue almost as dry. "If Mistress Carpenter finds her pleasure in such company and such folly I'll not trouble her with mine. No, I'm not for a young gentlewoman who brings such manners and such morals from the wicked courts of kings."

"Come, come, Wright, I'll not listen to your light-lying of Mistress Bradford's sister. 'Tis a good girl as ever stepped and a pure maid as lives in Plymouth, but she's young, man, a score of years younger than you, and doubtless she's known the man in England, and they've met by chance, and he is parley-vooing after the fashion of his kind, and she knows not how to be rid of him. Come, go you down, man! Or go with me, if it suits you better."

"No, Captain, I'll not go." And the stubborn face hardened in the utterly discouraging way some faces can. "But I'll ask this much of your kindness, friend: go you and meet them, and find out, as you so well can do, what is the meaning and the intent of it all; and especially tell me if you as an honest man will say to me that this maid is such a maid as a cautious, God-fearing man may crave for his wife. I will trust to your discretion rather than to mine own fears, Standish."

"Well, man, I'll try to warrant your trust," replied the captain, laughing a little, "although I do not feel it in myself to be the judge in a Court of Love such as they hold in France and those parts. But you may be sure I'll deal fairly both by you and the maid. Come after sunset and I'll tell you how I have fared."

"Nay, Pris, sweet Pris, 'tis such a pretty name I fain would dwell on't since I may not take sweeter dews upon my lips, believe me, fairest, I have forgot nothing of that fair memory; all I then said I say now and again and again! I came to New England for naught but to find thee once more, and to woo thee for mine own dear wife and lady paramount so long"—

But upon the smooth and dulcet tones of the knight suddenly intruded a strident and mocking voice:—

"Good-e'en to you, Mistress Prissie; so you are looking for mayflowers already?"

"Ah! Oh, Captain Standish, how you startled me! I knew not you were here."

"Nay, I'm grieved to have startled you, mistress, but why should not I take my walks abroad and look for mayflowers as well as you, or at least as well as this gentleman, whose walks in life have not always led him in such pleasant paths, more than mine own. How say you, Sir Christopher? We did not gather posies much in those stirring days among the Turks wherein I first met your knightship."

"I do not remember meeting you, Captain Standish, before I came to New England," replied the knight coldly.

"No? Well, you are an older man than I, and your memory more laden, so like enough a little matter may well slip out of it. But when I saw you there at Passonagessit t'other day I was sure 'twas not the first time. And how is the fair lady we saw with you? Your wife, is she not?"

"No, sir, she is not my wife!" thundered Sir Christopher, and the captain's face assumed an expression of dismay and embarrassment.

"Not your wife!" echoed he. "Nay, nay; if I'd known that, I would not have named her in presence of this modest gentlewoman. But how is it, then, that she spake of you as her lord? Nay, I'll not push the matter, sith I see 'tis an over-delicate matter. Wow! this wind cuts through one's blood. Mistress Prissie, I much fear me you'll catch a megrim if you linger longer by the brookside, and Betty, 'tis high time thou wert helping thy mother with the supper; run home, little maids, and Sir Christopher, I'll show you something more to your taste than spring flowers and young lassies. Come up to the Fort and help me fire the sunset gun."

Sir Christopher's face was very dark, and possibly enough the captain had not so easily taken his captive, but that Prissie Carpenter, ashamed and terrified at the meaning she suspected under the captain's debonair look and voice, had already fled toward the village, followed by Betty with a basket full of flowers, but a conscience full of thorns.

Seeing that resistance had thus become useless, the knight gloomily accepted his defeat, and clomb the hill beside the captain, whose jovial manner suddenly dropped into silence, nor did he speak until the two men stood upon the roof of the Fort. Then, while the sun, disdaining the mantle of gold and purple officiously presented by the western clouds, sank in undimmed glory to the horizon, and resting there an instant seemed to view once more the fair domain he now must abandon, Standish, his lighted match in one hand, laid a finger of the other upon his companion's breast.

"Sir Christopher Gardiner," said he, "we breed no Mary Groves in these parts, and yon young gentlewoman is the sister of our governor, and the promised wife of one of our worthiest citizens. 'Twould go hard with the man that trifled with her, and well do I hope no more hath been said than is soon forgotten and will leave no blot behind."

"Since when hath Myles Standish added the duty of father confessor to his other cares?" demanded Gardiner with a sneer.

"Ask rather, what sin hath he committed so notable as to call for the penance of listening to thy confession, my son?" retorted the captain good-humoredly. "Nay, man, take my hint in good part, as indeed 'tis meant. This maid is not for thy fooling, and thine own affairs are like to give thee trouble enough without mixing and moiling them further. Ha! the sun is going"— Puff! and the dull boom of heavy metal resounded across the quiet town, and startled the eagle circling above his nest on Captain's Hill.

Then the two men went silently down the hill, and whatever may have been the knight's secret resolves of virtue, he never again found the opportunity to test them.

"Now, Betty," said her mother, as the family rose from that meal we call tea, but they named supper, "I will put the babies to bed, and then step up the hill to Mistress Standish's to see little Lora, who is worse of her measles to-night, and thou wash up the dishes and redd the kitchen, and then go to bed like a good little lass. I'll take in the gentleman's supper, and ask what he fancies for his breakfast. John, you'll find me at the captain's when 'tis time for lecture."

"Ay, dame; and meantime I'll smoke a quiet pipe here with Betty and dry my wet feet."

But hardly had the mother disappeared when John Alden felt two tender arms about his neck, and heard a broken whisper,—

"Oh, father! I'm so sorry!"

"What! Betty, child, is't thou? And crying! Nay, then, little woman, what is it all about? Come sit on father's knee and tell him thy trouble. What makes thee sorry, my little maid?"

"I—don't—know—father."

"Don't know! Nay, how canst thou be sorry and not know why? That's naught but foolishness, Betty."

"Please, father, will you speak to mother, and not have me carry the gentleman's sarver into the fore-room, nor make his bed any more?"

"What! what!" exclaimed Alden, pushing the child back until he could look into her wet and troubled face. "Nay, then, Betty, I'll have the truth of thee; has the man been rude to thee, or said a word amiss?"

"I—oh, don't look so angry, father; you frighten me."

"But I will be answered, Betty! Why dost thou fear to go into this man's room? What has he said to thee?"

"He's said naught but kindness, father; he never spoke a cross word, not one. What should he scold *me* about?"

And the innocent wonder of the sweet face filled the man with fear lest his child might have understood him. Yet still with his own persistence he asked,—

"But why dost thou not want to take him his victual, poppet?"

"I may not tell you, daddy dear, because I promised sure and fast I would not tell, but I'd rather he asked mother or you"—

"Asked us what, child?"

"To help him— Nay, father, please do not ask me, for I promised I would tell nobody, and he said they'd cut off his ears and burn his cheeks"—

"Tut, tut, he's been scaring thee, thou silly little maid, and I doubt not asking thee to help him escape. Now isn't that the great secret?"

"No, daddy—that is, perhaps he thought Pris would help him escape"—

"Pris? Why, what has she to do with this man, or thou with either of them?"

- 122 -

"Mother's coming, and I don't want to tell her, for she'd chide me so sharply if I did not give up the secret, and I promised, father dear, I promised, and you said I ought to die rather than tell a willful lie."

"And so I did. Well, I'll think on't; go back to thy dishes now."

And as Priscilla bustled into the room and hastily put on her outdoor gear she noticed neither how grave her husband looked, nor how little progress Betty had made with the dishes.

A little later, as John Alden brought his wife home from the lecture, he said,—

"William Wright was telling me that he saw Prissie Carpenter and our Betty with Sir Christopher Gardiner by the brook picking posies this afternoon."

"Why 'twas you that bade me send Betty out with him!" exclaimed Priscilla, forestalling the objection in her husband's voice.

"I know it, and I'd better have left the matter to you, wife. It was ill thought on, and we'll not have our little maid called in question if the man is plotting an escape"—

"Talking with Pris Carpenter, was he?" interrupted Priscilla sharply.

"Yes"—

"Then it wasn't escape he was talking of, but his own captivity to her charms. She knew him in England, John; she told me so, and showed me a token he gave her. Mayhap he's come to marry her!"

"And the woman Mary Grove, what make you of that, wife?"

"Oh, a body must have charity, and many a mare's nest is naught but a tangle in the hedge. We'll see."

"Ay, but we'll not have our Betty mixed in with any such matter, Priscilla, and I pray thee keep her away from this man while he is in our house. Do not send her to the fore-room again; one of the boys can carry in the sarver, or I will do't myself, but Betty is not to go in thither again."

"As thou sayest, John," replied Priscilla with a meekness reserved for the rare occasions when her husband chose to assert his authority; so thus it came about that not again during the week he remained at Plymouth did Sir Christopher Gardiner find speech with the child, who never to her dying day revealed the secret she had promised to keep, and never quite comforted herself for the duplicity into which she had been led.

CHAPTER XVIII.

THE LITTLE BOOK.

An uneasy and difficult week passed over Plymouth, its shadow resting especially upon John Alden's house, when one fine sunshining morning Jo, the second boy, rushed into the house, with the news,—

"Mother, there's a big boat down from the Bay, and a captain in it, bigger than our captain, and the governor's son, and a mort more of men come to get the man in our fore-room."

"And where's thy father, Jo?"

"Oh, he's down there at the waterside, and all the other men, talking with the Bay folk, and I ran off to tell you, mother."

"That's my brave boy! He doesn't forget mother, does he?" And Priscilla turned to look fondly at her second-born, a fine, manly little fellow, with a marvelous likeness to his uncle Joseph Molines, victim of the first winter's pestilence, the brother whom Priscilla had so fondly loved, so deeply mourned.

"Well, poor man, if he's to be carried away prisoner by so many warders, I'll e'en toss him up a dainty dish for his last dinner with us," continued she busily. "Jo, my man, run down and ask father if any of the Indians have brought in oysters to-day, and if not, to get some clams or a lobster; and be quick, my boy, for it's hard on noon. And, Betty, see if there are some fresh eggs in the hen roost,—I'll make an omelet with herbs; and there's a fine salmon to serve with cream sauce and a sallet"—

"We might kill a chicken, mother," suggested John, the grave first-born, so like his father in everything.

"Nay, not to-day, Johnny," replied Priscilla, somewhat embarrassed, for her mind reverted to a little discovery of her own, and her eyes glanced toward the high mantel where lay a small brown-covered notebook much worn at the edges, and although apparently of trifling value, just then a greater weight upon the mind of the mistress than even her silver cup, or her six teaspoons.

It was but the day before that Betty had picked up this book just outside the house, and bringing it to her mother said she thought the gentleman had dropped it out of his pocket, for she had seen it in his room upon the table. Opening it at random, Priscilla read a few words only, but those so strange that, instead of at once restoring the book, she laid it aside until she should have time to consider her duty in the matter. On one side lay hospitality and honor, but on the other was the obligation to justice and to the common weal, which to those early settlers was a matter far more vital than to us, for it included not only their own interests, but perhaps the very lives of all belonging to them. If here indeed was "a snake in the tender grass," had she a right to let him wind his beautiful deadly way out of reach of justice? But on the other hand, was the danger deadly enough to warrant her in betraying the man who had eaten her salt? This controversy of mind, sufficiently perplexing to a woman of Priscilla's day and training, was suddenly resolved by the news brought home by John Alden that the Boston boat would return directly after noon-meat, and that Sir Christopher Gardiner would return with her.

"Then come you in here a moment, John," said Priscilla, rising from her almost untasted dinner, and leading the way to her bedroom.

John ruefully rose, his eyes upon his plate, where lay a huge segment of suet pudding which he had just begun to absorb in his own slow and methodical fashion. Betty's quick eyes saw the whole.

"I'll turn a basin over it, father, and set it by the fire till you're ready for it," said she with a flashing smile; and her father, smiling also, replied,—

"Thou'rt ever a good little wench, Betty!"

"See here, John! See this little book!" exclaimed Priscilla, shutting the door so promptly as nearly to catch her husband's last foot in the crack. "'Tis the man's, and mayhap the governor ought to know he's a Catholic for one thing. See, see! Isn't that what this page meaneth?"

"Ay, he was reconciled, as they call it, on such a day and"— But as Alden pored over the scribbled entry, murmuring vaguely such words as more clearly presented themselves, his impetuous wife interrupted him:—

"I gave him fish for his dinner to-day, sith I would not have a dog lack meat to his mind in mine own house, but still I remember how those fiends of Catholics murdered my grandsire in cold blood, and his wife after him, for naught but that they were Huguenots, as we are, and I must hate Catholics forevermore."

"Nay, wife, not hate them,—not hate whom God has made and still spares for repentance," suggested John; but Priscilla impatiently tossed her head.

"God is God, and I'm but poor Priscilla, his creature. I cannot love and hate all in one breath the same thing."

"Nay, wife, but thou didst give the man what meat his conscience called for on a Friday?"

"Yes, of course I did."

"And now will deliver him to death, if so it be?"

"Oh, I cannot tell; but I hate Catholics; my father bade me do so."

"And yet thou dost feed them, and I'll be bound thou'lt see that this man's tender wounds are well covered from the cold before he goes aboard."

"There, now, I'm glad you spoke on't, John! I'll lap his arms with a good woolen bandage, and you must lend him your old horseman's cloak to wrap himself withal. The governor'll fetch it some day when he goes up to visit the Bay governor again."

"Nay, wife, I don't see but thou dost humbly follow thy God, and love the sinner while thou dost hate the sin." And John slowly and fondly smiled down upon the petulant brown face of the wife he still loved as well as when first he wooed her.

"Oh, I know not how that may be, my Jeannot," replied Priscilla, laughing and blushing a little as she saw herself trapped. "But here's the little book."

"Ay, here's the little book, and to my mind the best thing is for me to carry it straight to the governor and let him do with it as he lists. 'Tis a matter too weighty for us to handle alone."

"Doubtless you're right, John, and here it is," and Priscilla, with a little sigh of vague regret, handed the book to her husband, and watched him as he at once left the house to carry it to the governor.

But Betty kept the pudding warm for his supper.

That afternoon Sir Christopher Gardiner, formally made over to the custody of Captain John Underhill and Lieutenant Dudley, son of the deputy-governor, sailed out of Plymouth wearing John Alden's cloak, in which he sullenly muffled the lower part of his face, while a slouched hat nearly covered the upper.

"Are you sick?" bluntly demanded Underhill, who had orders to treat his prisoner honorably and kindly.

"Nay, I'm sorry," retorted the knight.

"Fortune of war, comrade," returned the Puritan captain not unkindly, "and there's no very sharp measure laid up for you, as I take it. Our governor bade me have a care for your comfort, and the Plymouth governor hath writ a long letter to Master Winthrop, all in your favor, as I know from what he was saying to Alden."

"'Have no fear,' says he, 'it shall do him no harm;' and t'other returns, 'We did but our duty, and yet would be right loath to hurt the man.' Now what make you of that, man?"

"Read the governor's letter and you'll know more than I do," replied Sir Christopher gloomily.

"Read it! Nay, that's not my business. But 'tis a hugeous letter."

And from the pocket of his doublet Underwood drew forth a little packet carefully sealed and superscribed,—

To

MASTER JOHN WINTHROP,

Honourable Governor of the Massachusetts Bay Colony these:

As he turned the package over and over in his hands, the knight, who at first had glanced at it in moody indifference, roused to intense attention, and finally, while a streak of dusky red animated his sallow cheek, extended his hand, saying as carelessly as he could,—

"Let me look at the governor's seal, captain. Has it an heraldic device?"

"Nay, I know naught of such follies," returned Underhill, holding out the packet; but even as his fingers touched those of the knight, trembling with impatience, a glance at his face, or perhaps only the soldier's instinct of peril at hand, suddenly diverted his attention, and snatching back the dispatch, he began to replace it in his doublet, saying gruffly,—

"Marry, 'tis no business of mine or thine what these governors say to one another."

"Nay, but I'm sick—make way, man, make way"—and throwing himself across Underhill, as if to reach the side of the boat, Sir Christopher, what with his long arms flying all abroad, and what with the great cloak that swept across Underhill's face and breast, came very near knocking the packet out of his hand and sweeping it overboard.

"Have a care, man! Have a care!" cried the captain angrily. "Though you're squalmish all of a sudden, you needn't fling yourself nor me overboard." And thrusting the inclosure containing Sir Christopher's notebook and the kind and gentle letter accompanying it deep into his pocket, the future slayer of "Pequods" recovered his equilibrium and made room for Sir Christopher, who, leaning his head upon the gunwale of the boat, effectually hid his face from view, and made no reply to further efforts at conversation.

A week or so later another Boston boat came down to Plymouth, and brought John Alden's cloak and a letter to Bradford from Governor Winthrop. It tells its own story in its own quaint phraseology:—

> S^R.: It hath pleased God to bring S^r. Christopher Gardener safe to us with thos that came with him. And howsoever I never intended any hard measure to him, but to respecte and use him according to his qualitie, yet I let him know your care of him, and y^t he shall speed ye better for your mediation. It was a spetiall providence of God to bring those notes of his to our hands; I desire y^t you will please to speake to all y^t are privie to them not to discover them to any one for y^t may frustrate ye means of any farder use to be made of them. The good Lord our God who hath allways ordered things for ye good of his poore churches here directe us in this arighte, and dispose it to a good issue. I am sorie we put you to so much trouble about this gentleman, espetialy at this time of greate imploymente, but I know not how to avoyed it. I must again intreate you to let me know what charge & troble any of your people have been at aboute him, y^t may be recompenced. So with the trew affection of a frind desiring all happines to your selfe & yours, and to all my worthy friends with you (whome I love in ye Lord) I comende you to his grace & good providence & rest
>
> your most assured friend
JOHN WINTHROP[4]

BOSTON *May 5, 1631*

FOOTNOTE:

[4] True copy.

CHAPTER XIX.

A MUCH-MARRIED MAN.

The spring had ripened into midsummer, and under the sad and foreboding eyes of Governor Bradford a most ominous hegira of some of his dearest friends and Plymouth's most valued townsmen had taken place, nominally for the summer only, but as Bradford too plainly foresaw not to end with the summer.

Standish's house upon the foot of his own hill was complete, and not far away Jonathan Brewster, the Elder's oldest son, had put up a summer cottage and established his wife and children. This might have passed, but when the Elder himself, with his two sons Love and Wrestling, also built a cottage close beside Jonathan's upon a pretty inlet called Eagle's Creek, the governor's heart sank within him, and, calling a Court of the People, he proposed a legal enactment to the effect that those colonists who should build houses outside the town limits for the convenience of grazing or farming should return to the town at the beginning of winter, and abide there until spring; also, that they should week by week come into town to attend divine service on the Lord's Day.

To this all consented, even Winslow, who, in spite of his frequent and protracted absences in England, had found time to view the land beyond Duxbury, and to appropriate a lovely and fertile tract at Green Harbor in what is now Marshfield. Building a temporary cottage here, he named the estate Careswell after his ancestral home in England, and in true family spirit gathered around him his brothers: John, now husband of Mary Chilton, Josias, and Kenelm, who, married to Ellinor Newton of the Fortune, settled upon a gentle eminence by the sea in a spot so fertile and so beautiful that it was fitly named Eden.

Where Standish chose to lead, John Alden was in the habit of following, nor was this migration to Duxbury an exception, for in this very summer of 1631 Alden took up a large tract of land on the south side of Bluefish River, and built his house upon a pleasant rise of land near Eagletree Pond; and although two other houses have at different dates replaced the one he built, his children of the eighth generation live to-day upon the spot where Betty Alden grew into her fair maidenhood, and brothers and sisters made home happy, and life a quiet joy.

All these things and more had William Bradford been rehearsing to his friend Captain William Pierce of the Lyon, who had looked into Plymouth to leave some passengers and merchandise before proceeding upon his voyage to England, until the sailor, sorry for the depression and foreboding Bradford did not disguise from him, cast about for some pleasanter topic, and finally cried,—

"Oh, let me tell you, Governor, of the hornets' nest I found myself caught in, awhile ago in Lun'on; and by the way, Master Isaac Allerton was in it as well. Didn't he tell you here of the two wives of Sir Christopher Gardiner?"

"Nay, we have had but little pleasant converse with Master Allerton for a long time past," replied Bradford heavily, and Pierce hastened to proceed:—

"I know, I know, it would seem as if Allerton with all his pious texts had never learned that the man who faileth to care for his own is worse than a beast; for he cozened his own old father as much as he did you. But this is another matter. It was in February that I was stopping at the Three Anchors down by Wapping Old Stairs, and Allerton came in and said he had a message from a woman calling herself Lady Gardiner, who fain would have speech with him because he came out of New England; but he, prudent man, would go to see no fair ladies unknown to himself without a reputable witness to his honest intent, and so he was come for me. Be sure, Bradford, I did not let the chance slip to pass some merry jests upon our sour-visaged friend, and brought the blood to his tallow cheeks as it has not been seen for many a day; but in the end I gave my word to go and protect him as best I might from any designing Lindabrides who might assail him. So at once we went to the address written on the billet that was sent him, smelling of musk and ambergris and civet, worse than the hold of the Lyon after a ten weeks' voyage. Coming to the house in the Strand, we found in a very fair lodging not one but two fair dames; and the merry jest of it is that both the one and the other are honest women, and married by ring, book, and bell to this same gay knight whom Winthrop found living so meekly in the woods of Neponset River with his cousin Mary Grove."

"Nay, Pierce, but this passes a jest!" exclaimed Bradford, much disturbed as he recalled his little sister's pale face, and his wife's anxieties on her account. But the jolly mariner mopped his red face and laughed amain while he replied,—

"Nay, nay, Governor, I'm no church-member, and I suppose you saints were men before you were saints, and how can you help to see the mirth of it?"

"Well, tell me how it was."

"Why, the first fair dame,—and a pretty creature she was, with soft eyes like those of your wife's pet doe, and yellow hair, but a mouth too sad for kisses, and a cheek too thin and white for my taste,—she showed us her marriage lines, and told how she was married some six years ago to this Sir Christopher in Paris, and there abode until a few weeks before that speaking, when, hearing strange rumors of her husband's proceedings, she came over to seek him in Lun'on, and found the scent warm indeed, but Master Reynard fled over seas; and as she sought him up and down, her quest crossed that of this other lady, who had been indeed more deeply wronged than herself. And at that word, Number Two, a fine bouncing well-set-up figure of a woman, black eyes and hair, and a cheek like a sturdy rose, and a mouth I'd rather have seen at peace than trembling with rage, she took up the word, and told how not six months before, she too had wed Sir Christopher Gardiner, and she too showed her marriage lines, which if not so binding as the first ones had at least the merit of being writ in English; and furthermore she showed us schedules of jewels and coin, and silver- and goldsmith's work, and much rare and costly apparel both for men and women, for she was a widow, and all of it gone over seas with Sir Christopher, who, it seems, after sending her for a day or two to visit friends in the country, had made a clean sweep of everything, and the same night set sail for Monhegan with Mary Grove, for whom, poor wench, she could find no name vile enough, laying all the blame, as is the wont of women, upon her, and making Sir Kit a victim of her wiles."

"You saw the marriage lines of both these women?" asked Bradford, leaning his forehead upon his hand as he sat beside the table, and sighing heavily.

"Oh, yes," returned Pierce, wondering at the effect of his story, but rather attributing it to the morbid sensitiveness of a church-member. "Yes, they were both of them as safe as a chain-cable; and though Sir Kit does seem to have slipped them, he couldn't have parted them so long as the anchor of common law found holding-ground. Well, both women were clamoring to have us two catch the man and bring him back; but while the soft sweet first wife would have him brought back to duty and gently wooed into a better life, the full-rigged to'-gallant-s'il gallant buccaneer of a second wife only yearned to get him within reach that she might write the ten commandments on his face with her pretty little nails, and if she couldn't recover her jewels, plate, and apparel, she would have the worth of them out of his hair and hide, and as for Mary Grove,—wow! man, you should have heard her! The ducking-stool, and the bilboes, and the white sheet, and the cart's tail, and I know not what, were but the beginning of the blessings she longed to pour upon that poor little sinner's head, oh me, oh me!"

And again the sailor, recalling the scene, threw back his head and laughed aloud, but meeting no response checked himself suddenly and continued:—

"Well, Allerton and I, when we might be heard, assured both the one and the other dame that we compassionated their sad estate most heartily and would willingly see them avenged, but that we had no power except to bring the matter before Governor Winthrop, within whose jurisdiction Sir Christopher had settled, and in the end both ladies resolved to write to His Excellency, and promised to send the letters betimes next day to the Three Anchors at Wapping; which, to cut the yarn short, they did, and I gave them to Winthrop, and he as you know coursed the hare, or rather, hunted the fox, and ran him down, here at Plymouth."

"But he has not been sent home, or so I heard the other day!" exclaimed Bradford.

"No; and why, I know not," replied Pierce. "They kept him clapt up for a while, but finding nothing worse against him than that he is a friend to Sir Ferdinando Gorges, who wants the Massachusetts lands for himself, they gave him the run of the town, and he has been vaporing up and down there for months more than one or two. But now, Bradford, now here's a merry jest that even you cannot but smile at if there's a drop of red blood in your veins.

"A week or two ago a stalwart fellow called Thomas Purchase, who has taken up land at the eastward at a place called Sagadahoc, on the Kennebec River,—or is it the Androscoggin?"

"Both, since they come to a confluence. We have been thither trading for beaver, and will have a port there soon, if God will."

"Well, this Purchase is a big man down there, and meaning to be bigger; so, having a house, he came to Boston to purvey himself a wife; and who should he pick from among all the fair and godly maids and widows of that pious village but Mary Grove, who has been waiting there until the magistrates should settle within their own minds which of the Lady Gardiners might claim the plucking of her feathers. Yes, sir; Thomas Purchase, with his eyes and his ears open, chose Mary Grove to be his wife, Sir Christopher gave his consent and his blessing, and the lord's brethren, as Blackstone calls them, hailed with joy so clear a course out of the muddle they'd fallen into with this woman. So Winthrop himself married them, and Purchase, having his boat at hand, well stocked with the barter of the beaver he had brought up, carried his bride aboard, and also,—now mark you well, for here's the very moral of the jest,—also he took aboard Sir Christopher Gardiner himself, and away they all sailed for Sagadahoc. There, what think you of that, gossip?"

"I think Master Thomas Purchase a singularly charitable man," replied Bradford with a dry smile. "But let us hope that Mary Grove convinced him that she was more sinned against than sinning, and had not done the wrong this villain's second wife imputed to her."

"Ay, ay, doubtless you as a church-member are bound to find some such way out of the thing; but to the mind of a plain old sea-dog like Bill Pierce 'tis a marvelous merry tale, with no moral tacked to the end on't."

And possibly this conversation had something to do with the fact that when Thanksgiving Day came round, Priscilla Carpenter became the wife of William Wright.

CHAPTER XX.

BETTY'S JOURNEY AND THE GARRETT WRECK.

"Betty, child, thou'rt not well. Thy little face is so peaked and pined I hardly know my winsome lassie. What is't, maiden?"

"Oh, father, I don't know"—

"Nay, don't cry, my poppet! Come here and tell daddy all the trouble."

"Well, father, I'm so tired of seeing our neighbors carried up the hill, and I'm looking for them to carry us too."

"What! Here, mother, come and tell me what our little maid may mean. She says she's tired of seeing our neighbors going up the hill, and she cries as if her little heart would break."

The mother did not at once reply, but, laying her hand upon the child's head as it nestled upon her father's breast, she looked sadly out of the window, and said, "We had better have stayed over at Duxbury another month, John."

"Why, so we would have done, wife, and indeed 'tis a loss to come back to the town so early; but you know the governor desired it, because in so much sickness our good doctor could not go far afield, and when Jo was taken down he bade me bring you all in. Another year, if God will, I mean to establish our home for winter as well as summer by the Bluefish. But what about the hill, Betty?" persisted the father. "Why does it daunt thee to see the folk go up the hill?"

"Because they're dead, father, and they carry them up to bury them!" cried Betty in a wild burst of sobs; and Priscilla, nodding, pointed out of the window to a little procession just passing the house, where four men bore upon a rude hand-bier a coffin covered with a black pall, the corners held by four younger men. Behind walked a score or so of mourners, all men, with long crape scarfs tied around their hats. No clergyman attended, for religious solemnities at funerals were studiously avoided by the Separatists, lest haply they might seem to infringe upon the hidden councils of the Almighty in regard to souls withdrawn from the sphere of human influence. A gloomy and a hopeless affair they made of death, those men who dreaded popery as they did Satan, and loved John Calvin, recently gone to test his own sunless theories.

"Betty, dear," exclaimed the mother suddenly, "there's little Molly crying in her cradle! Run, dear, and hush her, and sit by the cradle till I come."

The obedient child sprang to obey, and so soon as she was gone Priscilla softly said,—

"'Tis all these buryings, John, that work on the child's tender heart, and she heard us talking last night of poor Fear Allerton's passing. 'Tis she that's going up the hill now; and see! they've got Thomas Prence and Philip De la Noye and Thomas Cushman and John Faunce for pall-bearers, and Isaac Allerton and the Elder are chief mourners. You should have been there, John, for Allerton was ship-fellow with us in the Mayflower, and she was a dear gossip of mine always."

"And so I would have been but for that spike running into my foot and making a cripple of me," replied Alden with a rueful look at his bandaged foot.

"Shouldst not have left thy harrow lying on 's back with its teeth grinning up to the sky," suggested Priscilla absently, and then taking from the mantelshelf a bit of stick and a sheath knife she cut a notch at the end of a long line, and counting said,—"Eleven on my tally-stick already, and some of the best, alas! Peter Browne,—mind you, John, how he and Goodman roosted in a tree all night for fear of the 'lions,' and ne'er a one here? And Francis Eaton, he's gone, and left Christian Penn a widow. I'll warrant me she'll go back to the governor's kitchen. Then there's the captain's two little boys. Poor Barbara! Truly I believe, John, of the hundred Mayflowers that came ashore there's not a score left."

"There's two and twenty of us, counting them who were children, like Henry Samson and Peregrine White," said John sadly.

"Ah, you've kept the tally in your head better than I with my stick," said Priscilla, laying it aside. "And to think of Pris Carpenter, widowed almost as soon as she's wed. William Wright has left her all that he had, Alice Bradford says."

"Ay; and glad am I that Sir Christopher Gardiner hath gone back to his two wives in England before she came into her fair estate."

"Nay, Pris would not have looked crosswise at him after she heard the story Captain Pierce gave the governor. She was too sound a maid to listen to any such golightly cavaliers as this man proved himself. But, John, did you hear of the will that Widow Ring has made, and tied up everything on her boy Andrew? And there's Susanna Clark and Betsey Deane been the best of daughters, and tended her hand and foot, and she as full of whims as an egg is of meat; and when she'd for very shame' sake given Susan a pair of pillows, she had to tuck in that Andrew was to have the feathers out of 'em. Think of that for a mother! And Susan Clark, she's to have the making of a baby's bearing-cloth out of a piece of red cloth the widow had laid up, and Betsey Deane's child, she's to have the rest on't. And who's to have the widow's three say gowns, one of green and two of black, I mind not, but all Betty told me of getting was one ruffle that her mother bought of Goodman Gyles, who had it out of England in a present, and she gave him four shillings for it, but"—

"But what's to be done with our Betty?" calmly inquired John, stemming the tide of his wife's eloquence, apparently all unconsciously.

She, standing open-mouthed for a moment, looked at him, colored a little, then laughed, and nipping his arm retorted,—

"What's to be done with our goodman, that's lost his wits as well as lamed his foot? Didst not know that I was discoursing of Widow Ring's will?"

"But she's left naught to us that I've heard, nor are we even called to distribute her goods as I can hear, so were it not the part of wisdom to attend to our own concerns instead of hers, good wife?"

"Well, as for Betty, the child's growing too fast, and mayhap has been a little too straitly tied at home, what with little Molly's coming, and Jo's fever, and the rest. So now that you're laid up from work, John, why don't you take her up to Boston in the governor's boat that's set to go two days from now, and tarry the night at Parson Wilson's, as he so kindly asked you when he was down here with Governor Winthrop and his folk? Marry come up, 'twas a good supper I set before their high mightinesses that night, and our own governor did thank me kindly for so pleasantly entertaining the guests of the colony. 'Twas a better supper than they had at the Winslows' or the Howlands' or the Allertons', for I know all about it. As for the Standishes, I was helping Barbara all day, and the merit of that feast lay between us, but"—

"And dost think Mistress Wilson would welcome our little maid?"

"Surely she would, and why not? You'll not find our Betty's marrow among the pick of the Bay maidens, not forgetting Master Winthrop's own; no, nor Simon Bradstreet's Anne that you were so taken with when we went up to see Mistress Winthrop."

"Then if you'll make her packet ready I'll see the governor about the boat," concluded John, carefully putting his wounded foot to the ground, taking a cane in each hand, and hobbling out of the room, just as the roll of a muffled drum announced the death of Samuel Fuller, the much-prized and well-beloved physician of Plymouth, deacon of her church, brother by marriage to Bradford and Wright; the constant friend of his townsmen, and valued by many an one in the new settlements about Boston Bay. Faithful to the last, he had attended the sick-beds of those who were only a trifle worse than himself, until of a sudden he succumbed, and died almost before his friends knew that he was ill. Few deaths could have been more deeply felt in that little colony, and few were noted in William Bradford's diary with more solemn and affectionate feeling.

But before the doctor was laid to rest in his nameless grave on Burying Hill, Betty Alden, full of delight, and yet soberly attentive to her mother's last charges, both as to her own conduct and her care of her father's foot, was on her way to Boston, where she saw many new faces and made many new friends. Of one of these, a girl of her own age named Christian Garrett, there is more to tell, for so close was the friendship springing up between herself and Betty, and so good and commendable a little maid did Christian prove herself, that John Alden, on parting with Richard Garrett, the father, cordially invited him to visit Plymouth at some near date and bring his little girl to visit Betty, and this he promised to do.

Why the luckless man should have selected mid-winter for this expedition no man now can say, but so he did, and in spite of urgent warnings sailed from what is now Long Wharf upon a bitter-cold morning, with a north wind catching the crests off the waves, and hurling them in needlepoints of ice in the teeth of the doomed company whom Richard Garrett had persuaded to accompany him. One of these, named Henry Harwood, was a passenger, and the other three were Garrett's hired servants. As the day wore on, the wind freshened, working round to the northwest, so that arriving toward night off the Gurnet the exhausted men thought best to anchor until morning. The killock, a rude anchor consisting simply of a stone bound in a network of rope, was thrown over in twenty fathoms of water, and not resting upon the bottom the stone soon worked out of the rope, and left the boat to drive. No lighthouse upon the Gurnet, no beacon upon the beach, then protected the mariner of Plymouth Bay, and as the horror of thick darkness fell upon the scene, and the boat flew before the wind which now came laden with sleet, freezing as it fell, Garrett exclaimed,—

"Now may the Lord have mercy upon our sinful souls, and forgive me that has brought my motherless child here to die!"

"And more than that, Richard Garrett, you that have involved us in the same disaster," replied Harwood angrily. "Do you suppose, man, I would have adventured with you and paid my two shilling for a passage, had I known what manner of shallop this is, and nothing but a stone and a rope for killock?"

"Peace, man!" retorted Garrett sternly. "How dare you go before your Judge with revilings in your mouth! Get you to your prayers, or be silent."

"Father, the water freezes around my feet!" moaned Christian, nestling close to his side in the darkness.

"My poor little maid! Here, sit on my knees and I'll lap thee in my cloak!"

"Nay, thou'lt take it from thyself, daddy," remonstrated the child; but the father had his way, and all through that cruel night sheltered the little maid upon his knees and under his cloak, while his own feet first ached bitterly, and then grew numb, and then died.

"Let us pray!" cried a voice from the forward part of the boat, and, mingled with the howling of the storm, the hissing of the brine as it rushed savagely past the wreck, and the rattling of the frozen rigging, there rose upon the midnight air one of those stern, strong, abject yet self-assertive prayers that the Puritans were wont to address to their vindictive and implacable Deity; confessing their own enormity of sin, yet beseeching Him to forego his rightful vengeance and to lift his scourge from their backs because his Son had already borne the penalty of their sins, and suffered to appease the Father's annihilating wrath.

The prayer was strong and eloquent after its own rugged fashion, and as the hearers breathed "A-men" they felt that their chances were better than before, and were not surprised when, as morning broke, the low line of Cape Cod lay before them, and the sail, partially blown from the gaskets, filled just enough to carry them gently upon the shallow beach.

"We are saved!" exclaimed Harwood, staggering to his feet and clinging to the mast. "Come, men, tumble over and wade ashore! We can be no wetter than we are."

As he spoke he stepped over the gunwale into water almost up to his middle and turned shoreward, but Garrett cried to him,—

"Hold, man, if you have a heart of flesh and not of stone! Take my child out of my arms and carry her ashore, for I am utterly spent. I shall never reach that land."

"Give her to me, then, some of you," replied Harwood grudgingly. "I know not if I can hold her in my numbed arms, but I'll try it, though she never should have been here."

"Tut! Prut! Master Harwood!" retorted Joseph Pierce, Garrett's foreman. "None but a sour temper would flout the master with his misfortunes just now! I'd carry little mistress myself and spare you the trouble, but my feet are froze fast into the wash at the bottom of the boat."

"And so are mine!" exclaimed another, making ineffectual efforts to release himself from his icy bonds.

"And I know not if I have feet or not," added Garrett drowsily. "But I beseech you, men, to care for my little maid."

"Be sure we will, master," replied Pierce cheerily. "Here, Brastow, give me that hatchet to cut away the ice from my feet; but no, first help Mistress Christian over the side. Now, then, Harwood, take her, and God's blessing if you get her safe ashore. Have you a hold? Put your arms round his neck, there's a brave maid. Now hold fast."

No sooner was Harwood off than the others began to move, and although Garrett himself only reached the shore by the help of two men, and at once fell down never to rise again, all at length stood upon the barren and shelterless sand-bank, at that point running down from the scrub forest to the water, and looked around them in dismay. Garrett, the leader of the expedition, was evidently dying, and one of his men was in scarce better case. Harwood and Pierce, the strongest of those who remained, yet hardly able to bestir themselves, gathered some sticks and lighted a fire, but for want of a hatchet could not cut any substantial fuel. "We must e'en wade it again to the boat, and fetch off some victual, the hatchet, and some rugs, if nothing more," declared Pierce, when the fire had a little revived his chilled frame and flagging spirit; and Harwood gloomily acquiescing, the two once more made their perilous journey, and so loaded themselves that the hatchet, most precious item of all he carried, dropped from Pierce's numbed fingers and fell somewhere among the rocks upon which the boat had now drifted. To find it was impossible, and to stay longer in the freezing and rising water was as impossible, so the two were fain to stagger ashore, and fall with their burdens upon their backs beside the fire, where their companions lay mutely regarding them with the apathy of dying men.

The day passed, and the night, those who survived could never quite tell how, but in the morning Joseph Pierce and Thomas Barstow set out to walk toward Plymouth, lying as they supposed some six or seven miles to the westward, but in reality about fifty. Several miles on their journey these two encountered two Indian women, who ran away from them, but carried intelligence of the encounter to their husbands, encamped near at hand.

And now Plymouth's just and generous policy toward the Indians bore fruit. The savages both loved and feared the white men of the Old Colony; they knew that kindness would be rewarded, and offenses surely punished; so acting accordingly, they hastened to overtake the footsore wanderers, and discovering whither they would go, one of the Indians went forward as their guide, while the other turned back to the camp, where beside the last embers of a fire lay the lifeless body of Garrett, his child crouching beside him, dazed and dumb with cold and terror. At the other side of the exhausted fire lay Harwood and the other man, only half conscious, and quite unable to move or to help themselves. The Indian, making the most of his few words of English, stopped only to promise help and to assure the sufferers that their comrades were safe, and then sped away to his wigwam, whence he presently returned laden with rugs, a hatchet, and some sort of reviving draught which he heated over the renewed fire, and administered to each in turn. Then, covering them warmly, he cut saplings, pointed them, and built a hut over the prostrate bodies of the sufferers. Last of all he hewed a grave in the frozen soil with his hatchet, and respectfully raising Richard Garrett's dead body in his arms laid it to rest, carefully crumbling the soil to cover it, and raising a cairn of stones and brushwood to protect it from the beasts of prey then prowling up and down the waste of Cape Cod.

As the warmth increased, however, the apathy of the frozen men turned to anguish and torture, and Harwood, dragging himself out of the hut, had the resolution to thaw his feet in the water of a neighboring pool, and so kept life in them; but his companion, too far gone, remained by the fire, and when the pain was eased died, so that Harwood and the little girl remained alone with the Indian.

The two men who had gone toward Plymouth were no more fortunate. One died upon the road; the other so soon as he had told his piteous story to Bradford and the rest who ministered to him so tenderly, yet could do nothing to detain him. Within the hour a boat well manned, and carrying the Indian for guide, was on its way to the scene of the disaster, and the next day returned, bringing Christian Garrett, Henry Harwood, the body of their comrade, and the Indian who had so faithfully cared for them, and whom Bradford liberally rewarded and praised for his benevolence.

Harwood was billeted upon Stephen Hopkins, but Betty Alden pleaded with her parents that Christian Garrett might come to their house and be her own especial charge; and this boon being easily granted, the spare-room where Sir Christopher Gardiner had wearied and plotted became the happy abiding-place of these two innocent young creatures, the one so active and helpful, the other so languid and so sorrowful, and yet both of them the happier and the better for their companionship.

When the spring had come, Harwood, with a good crew of Plymouth men to help him, attempted to sail Garrett's boat up to Boston, but caught in a wild spring storm was nearly wrecked again; and with some strange gloomy idea of having suffered from his association with Garrett he sued his estate for damages, and actually recovered twenty nobles, or about thirty-three dollars, which was duly paid to him out of the pittance left to Christian, who, although she went back to Boston and the care of an aunt, never ceased to be one of Betty's dearest and most intimate friends.

CHAPTER XXI.

"AH, BROTHER OLDHAME, IS IT THOU!"

It was a day in June, one of those lovely, nay, perfect days when heaven appears at once nearer and farther off than ever before: nearer, for we seem already to taste its delights; farther off, because earth has suddenly become so satisfying that we ask for nothing better.

A little southwest breeze loitered over Burying Hill, stirring the long grasses, wooing sweet kisses and incense from the balm o' Gilead trees, and finally floated down The Hill, past the closed and deserted homes of Standish and Alden to the governor's house, grown wide and stately in these days, boasting two parlors besides the great common room, and furthermore a recent extension toward The Hill consisting of one wide low room with an outside door and a loft overhead. This was the governor's study or office, where he kept his books and papers and transacted the colony's business. More than this, in the large closet and in the loft overhead were stored the colony's goods, both the peltrie for export, and the shoes, textile fabrics, and other matters which were brought back from England in exchange; and as every man or woman who had obtained a beaver, or mink, or otter skin brought it to the governor and asked him to send to England for a pair of shoes, a new doublet or kirtle, pewter platter, or horn comb, the adjusting these accounts, and remembering every one's wishes and instructions, consumed so large a part of the gubernatorial time that one cannot wonder that now and again Bradford "by importunity gat off" from reëlection, especially as his services were altogether gratuitous, and must have interfered with the necessity of living, pressing not only upon every man individually, but on husbands and fathers very imperatively. The casement window of the study was swung open to the soft June air, and the little breeze, peeping in, shrank back dismayed, yet, mustering the courage of a petted child, gathered a handful of perfume from Alice Bradford's bed of early pinks close at hand, flung it in at the open window, and then, laughing softly, flew round the corner and in at another casement, where Alice herself sat embroidering in green crewels the cover of a stool, and talking softly to her daughter Mercy, Desire Howland, and Betty Alden, who sat demure as kittens on three crickets, stitching fine seams or embroidering muslin or silk under Dame Bradford's skillful tuition; for among the fair memories this gracious woman left behind her, none seem fairer than her attention and kindly offices toward the young maids of the town.

A very different group was that at which the naughty breeze had peeped and flung perfume behind the swinging casement of the study: a group of men, mature and austere, as the fathers of unruly families are apt to become by the time the children wish to leave home and set up for themselves.

At the head of the old oak table with its twisted legs and lion's claw-feet sat William Bradford, his cheek resting on his left hand, while with the right he drew idle lines or figures upon a sheet of coarse paper. An inkstand hollowed from a square block of ebony stood before him, bristling with a thicket of quill pens standing in the sockets bored around the edge, and the Record Book of the colony, that same yellow and tattered book we reverently handle to-day, lay open beside it. Some papers and slips of parchment were scattered over the board, and one lay under Winslow's hand as he turned to speak to Myles Standish, whose flushed face and wrathful eyes showed that his hasty temper was stirred more than was its wont, now that Time had set his half-century mark upon the thinning hair and lined features.

Next to Standish sat Timothy Hatherley, his intimate friend and future executor, and opposite them were Thomas Prence, and John Jenney the miller, a man of substance and position, and father of two very pretty daughters. These five were the governor's assistants for the year, and to them, on this morning, was added the venerable presence of Elder Brewster, who, sitting at the foot of the table, and fixing his wintry blue eyes upon each speaker in succession, seemed to act as counterpoise and moderator to the more vehement moods of the younger men. A venerable figure truly, for the threescore and ten years of the promise were more than run out, and yet a form and face full of life and strength, and with a cleanly freshness of complexion and eye betokening a simple and abstemious life, enjoyed in fresh air and with moderate labor. Upon this reassuring face the eyes of the governor rested almost yearningly, as he listened to the captain's fiery words:—

"Yes, sirs, the Bay Colony and their friends have brought themselves into the mire by their own blundering, and now cry to Plymouth, 'Good Lord, deliver us!' Whose fault is it that the Pequots are risen upon them?"

"They have murdered John Oldhame, I tell you, Captain!" exclaimed Winslow impatiently. "Will you listen while I read Governor Winthrop's letter?"

"Yes, Captain Standish, I pray you to listen, and allow us to do so," added Prence in so peremptory a tone that the old soldier turned hotly upon him:—

"Thomas Prence, they say you are a dabster at handling the Bible in prayer-meetings and prophesyings; do you remember how King Rehoboam took counsel as to his dealings with the oppressed people of his realm, and the old men said, 'Deal softly and kindly with thy servants and they will remain thy servants for aye;' but with the folly of youth, Rehoboam turned to men with their beards still in the silk, and said, 'How shall I answer this people?' and they gave their counsel: 'Whereas thy father hath beaten them with whips, thou shalt scourge them with scorpions, and if thy father's yoke was heavy upon their necks, thou shalt add to it until they sink under it.' The boy king listened to his boy counselors, and the result was that ten tribes of—Pequots, we will call them, became his bloody foes instead of his cheerful servitors. We of Plymouth have held the whip behind our backs"—

"Yet brought it forward at Wessagusset," interrupted Prence good-humoredly, and in the moment of not displeased silence on Standish's part, Bradford hurriedly interposed,—

"Nay, Captain, let us hear the letter before we discuss this matter further."

"So be it, Governor; but naught that Master Winthrop can pen or Master Winslow read, clever craftsmen though they be, will fetch my consent to this wholesale slaughter of the Indians, Pequots, Narragansetts, or Pokanokets."

"Will you read, Master Winslow?" asked the governor in a patient voice, and, rather hastily, as if forestalling farther discussion, Winslow proceeded to read aloud the missive of the governor of Massachusetts Bay, who after certain grave greetings proceeded to tell the story, which we will enlarge a little from other sources, of how one John Gallop, founder of the guild of Boston pilots, and occupant of the island bearing his name in Boston Harbor, while trading to the plantation of Saybrooke in the Connecticut Colony, had been attracted by the strange manœuvres of a pinnace lying to off Block Island, and running in that direction recognized her as belonging to John Oldhame, late of Watertown, in the Massachusetts Colony, who had, about a week before, left Boston upon a trading tour, his crew consisting only of two English lads, his kinsmen, and two Narragansett Indians.

"John Oldhame must be very drunk to let his craft yaw about in that fashion," commented Gallop, watching the bark; and his sons, John and James, boys of twelve and fourteen, and Zebedee Palmer, his hired man, who composed the entire ship's company, dutifully assented, Zebedee suggesting that in the cold March wind then blowing he should not himself object to a drop of something comfortable.

"When is the day you would, Zeb?" inquired his master. "But lo you now! There goes a canoe from the pinnace to the shore heavy laden, and manned only by redskins. Be sure there's some Indian deviltry going on, and though the wind be contrary we will beat down and hail her."

But arrived within hailing distance, Gallop perceived the deck of the pinnace to be crowded with savages, who, so far from returning his hail, at once dropped their occupation of loading another canoe, and proceeded to make sail in so clumsy a fashion that the pilot's fears of the pinnace having been seized by Indians were reduced to certainty, and putting his own bark before the wind blowing off the land he pursued the captured craft, now driving wildly toward the Narragansett shore. Bringing up the two guns and two pistols comprising his entire armament, Gallop charged them with the duckshot he had brought along for purposes of sport, and so soon as they came within range began firing with no farther formalities into the dense throng of Indians, who on their part stood armed with guns, pikes, and swords, and as Gallop's bark drew near fired a scattering volley, happily of no effect; and then, as the incessant rain of duckshot—for the two boys loaded as fast as their father fired—became intolerable, they all fled below hatches, leaving the vessel to drift as she would. Seeing this, the pilot hit upon a new method of attack, and standing off a little he set his craft dead before the wind, now blowing half a gale, and coming down with full force upon the pinnace "stemmed her upon the quarter," as Winthrop has it, "and almost overset her. This so frighted the Indians that five or six ran on deck, and leaping overboard were drowned." Encouraged by this beginning, the pilot repeated his manœuvre, only this time so fitting his anchor to the heel of his bowsprit as to make a very good imitation of an iron-clad ram; then again striking the pinnace he crushed in her forward bulwarks, and sticking fast, began pouring in charges of his heaviest shot at such short range that they penetrated decks and sheathing, and reached the pirates skulking below. Finding that they refused to be driven out, and his two guns growing too warm to work, Gallop disengaged his anchor and again stood off; but this was enough, and five more Indians rushed up and threw themselves into the sea, preferring a death they well understood, to the tender mercies of a man who fought in such unknown fashions.

There being now but four of the savages left, Gallop boarded the pinnace, whereupon one of the survivors yielded, and was bound and stowed in the cabin for safe-keeping; another yielded, but leaving Zebedee to bind him the pilot dragged away a seine huddled in the stern sheets under which he had from his own deck perceived some horror to be hidden. It was the body of a white man, still warm, the head cleft, the hands and feet nearly cut off, and the face so covered with blood as to be unrecognizable, until

Gallop, dipping one of the garments stripped off but lying near, into the salt water flooding the decks, washed it and put aside the long hair; then gazing down into the staring eyes, he said as if in answer to their piteous appeal, "Ah, Brother Oldhame, is it thou! Truly I am resolved to avenge thy blood!" And, while Zebedee managed as best he could to fasten a tow-rope to the pinnace and make sail upon the bark, and John and James, pistol in hand, watched the hatches in case the Indians below should make a sortie, the pilot bound the mangled body of his friend in its clothes and in the private ensign lying at the foot of the mast, and launched it overboard.

"This man is wriggling his hands free, father," reported John Gallop, presenting his pistol at the last captive, a sachem of the Narragansetts and a very determined fellow.

"Say you so, Jack!" replied his father, turning back from the bulwark over which he had just reverently dropped the shrouded form of his murdered friend. "We'll take no chances! Lift you his feet and I his head and we'll put him in John Oldhame's keeping. Jim, stand you to your watch till our hands are free." And the sachem, stolid and silent now that the worst had come, went to rejoin his comrades. Two of the pirates remained below, but as they were armed and entrenched in the hold Gallop left them there as prisoners, although the night coming on and the sea and wind growing very violent, he was after a time compelled to cast off the pinnace, which drove ashore on the Narragansett coast.

Arriving in Boston, Gallop at once placed the matter in the hands of the government, who through Roger Williams and Miantonimo demanded the surrender of the murderers who had come safely ashore in the pinnace. In the end, Oldhame's two cousins, who had been kept prisoners at Block Island, were safely returned, and some of the stolen goods; but tedious negotiations revealed the fact that nearly all the Narragansett sachems had been privy to the conspiracy, and that some of them were in alliance with the Pequots to cut off the English and resume the country only sixteen years before absolutely their own. Not unnaturally alarmed at this report, Governor Vane and his council resolved upon what they at first called reprisals, but which soon became a stern scheme of extermination involving the entire Pequot nation, and such of the Narragansetts as refused to become tributaries and subjects of the English.

The murder of Captain Stone, the death by torture of Butterfield, and John Tilley and his man, came into the account and gave the air of righteous retribution to the Puritan severities; but the wrongs of the Indians, their natural temperament, their standard of morality, their ignorance of the gracious influences of Christianity,—none of these seem to have been considered or weighed in the councils of Vane and his associates, although more liberal Plymouth had set them the example of making friends rather than enemies of a people who had surely great cause of complaint in the loss of their homes and rights, and who simply sought to defend themselves according to their traditional methods.

It was in pursuance of this resolve that Winthrop, acting this year as deputy to Governor Vane, had written to Plymouth, setting forth all the causes of the war already begun, and requesting of Plymouth that aid and coöperation which one colony of white men and Christians would naturally afford to another.

The letter was read and laid upon the council board, and Bradford in his own grave, thoughtful, and well-considered manner took up the word:—

"Doubtless, brethren, we must find that there hath been much provocation offered to these Pequens and Narraganseds. We know somewhat of John Oldhame"—

"And naught that's good," muttered Standish in his red beard.

—"and we may be sure there was cause of complaint on the part of the Block Islanders before they so assaulted him. Jonathan Brewster hath held our post on the Connecticut River—Windsor, as the settlers from the Bay have named the place—for some four years now, and there has been no trouble worth the mention"—

"Save when the Narragansetts chased our friend Massasoit into the trading-house at Sowams, and I sent a runner for powder, but the enemy ran faster the other way than he," put in Standish. "And mind you, though John Winthrop let us have the powder out of his private store, that sour-visaged Dudley hauled him over the coals for it. Ever niggardly and domineering is the Bay, and my counsel is, let them fight out their own battles for themselves. When Plymouth has cause to complain of the savages, Pequens or who you please, I'll lead a handful of Plymouth men out to give them a lesson, and till then I say let-a-be. You have my counsel, Governor."

"And mine jumps with it, sir," added John Jenney heartily, but Winslow shook his head thoughtfully.

"It were but poor policy for us to fall out with our brethren of the Bay, seeing that they are so much stronger than we, and it may well chance that we shall need their countenance in some quarrel"—

"Like that of Kennebec when we called upon them to help us drive out the Frenchmen who had seized our post, and they did most civilly decline," suggested Standish, and Prence added,—

"Ay, that was but a scurvy trick they played us then."

And so the council went on, debating the question warmly, and yet with a brotherly love and harmony covering all differences, until in the end it was resolved that Winslow the diplomatist should be sent as envoy to Boston to declare in the first place the willingness of Plymouth to help her younger but more powerful sister against the common foe, yet at the same time bringing forward various causes of complaint as yet unredressed, and demanding more consideration in the future. These complaints were, first, the refusal of the Bay government to help Plymouth against the French who had seized her trading-post at Kennebec; second, their allowing their people to fraternize and trade with the usurpers; third, the insult and injury done to the Pilgrims at Windsor in Connecticut, where a great body of people from Watertown and Cambridge had swooped down upon the land bought by Plymouth from the Indians, and occupied by them as a trading-post, retaining forcible possession of it, and encouraged by the Bay to do so.

To these three unredressed complaints Winslow was to add a reminder of the fact, seldom forgotten by the Bay Colony, that they were much more numerous and much more wealthy than Plymouth, and apparently quite able to conduct their own quarrel through their own resources. For, as the envoy was especially directed to say, the Colony of Plymouth had hitherto lived at peace with the aborigines, and had no complaint to make of either the Pequots or any other tribe.

And now, this matter arranged for the moment, although much further trouble was to come of it, the Court turned its attention to a subject so much more personal, and near to their hearts as old friends and associates, that its presence in their minds had added austerity to Brewster's mien, and thoughtfulness to that of Bradford, while it acted as a spur to the captain's fiery temper.

Upon the table lay a formal petition, drawn by Edward Winslow, and signed by Myles Standish, John Alden, Elder Brewster and his two sons Jonathan and Love, Eaton, Soule, Samson, Bassett, Collier, Cudworth, De la Noye, and half a dozen more substantial men, who in decorous and respectful language represented that they and their families already composed a community equaling that of Plymouth, and begged to be incorporated as a town under the name of Duxbury, and to have the approval of the mother-church in their choice of the Rev. Ralph Partridge as their minister.

The petition had first been presented some four years before this time, but so deep and heartfelt was Bradford's opposition to this distinct separation of the original colony, and so varied his expedients to prevent it, that the motion had never fairly been carried until now, when an opportunity offered to secure the eloquent and devout Cambridge scholar as pastor, and it was essential that the town should have an assured being and resources.

Very few words were used upon this occasion, for all had been said that could be said, not once but many times before; and now as Bradford, after a brief and formal discussion, signed the act of incorporation, he laid down the pen, and looking around the council board solemnly said,—

"May this rending of his garment not provoke the Lord to wrath, as well I fear it may!"

Not even Elder Brewster found a word to reply, and the deed was done.

An hour later, as the Duxbury men prepared to return to their new home, Standish linked his arm in that of his old friend and led him up the hill, saying,—

"Nay, Will, for old time's sake put a better face on 't, man. Come over with us to Captain's Hill, as they call it, and tarry the night. We'll crush a kindly cup to the new town, and you shall be its godfather. Never look so glum, I pr'ythee, Will! You take all the heart out of me, old friend."

"See there, Myles, see that!"

"What, mine own old house? 'Tis going to ruin already, is it not, and yet 'tis no more than seventeen years since these hands with John Alden's aid laid it beam to beam."

"And why does it go to ruin, Myles?"

"Why? Why, because no man careth for it, I suppose."

"Ay, you've answered me, friend. No man careth for that home, nor for John Alden's hard by, nor for Edward Winslow's, and the Elder's great house is now but a half-hearted home, for he is more at Duxbury than here. I speak not of the rest, for they are of less account to me; and that is a fault which I confess, but nature is strong, and the carnal heart of man clings to its own."

"And why should not a man's heart cling to his old friends and comrades, Will, and why should not you value the Elder, and Winslow, and Alden, and a few more of us more than you do all these nimble Jacks that have sprung up to push us old ones from our places? Be a saint an' you please, old comrade, but don't strive to cease to be a man."

"And here is the Fort you loved so well, Myles. Shall you have a new Fort at Duxbury?"

The captain stopped, and squaring round laid a finger upon the governor's breast, and fixed his keen brown eyes upon the other's fairer face.

"Friend," said he in a tenderer voice than was his wont, "where a man is all but as good and as godly as a woman, he is apt to have some trace of woman's faults and follies, and that last speech of yours savors of woman's jealousy and spite. Play the man, Will, play the man, and smite me with thy fist an' thou lik'st not what I do and say, but never lower thyself to stinging with thy tongue."

The Governor of Plymouth turned his back and steadfastly looked over toward Manomet, green and glowing in the sunset of a June afternoon, her graceful young trees in their tender foliage as airy and as gay, and her forest monarchs as stately, as they had been before the white men saw these shores, or as they are to-day when Bradford and Standish are dust and ashes, and as they will be when the hand that writes and the eyes that read are even as those of the fathers. We love Nature so passionately and so persistently because it is an unrequited affection; at the most she only holds up the cheek for us to kiss.

This little interlude is but a piece of delicacy that Bradford may have time to recover himself, and now he turns, and folding Standish's patrician hand in a larger grasp slowly says,—

"'Let the righteous smite me friendly, but let not his precious balms break my head.' Come, Myles, let us mount the Fort."

"Yes, I must see if Lieutenant Holmes is carrying out my directions, for I promise you, Master Bradford, I'm meaning to hold a tight hand over you here in military matters. Mind you, I am always generalissimo of the colony's forces, whether of Plymouth, or Scituate, or Duxbury."

"I thank thee, Myles," said the governor quietly, and so they passed into the dusky Fort, over whose portal the skull of Wituwamat still stood, bleached by summer sun and winter snow, and sheltering year by year the wrens who had an hereditary nest in its hollow.

"And you'll come home with me, Will?" said the captain wistfully, as, a little later, they descended the hill.

"No, Myles, no; I'm not an Abraham. I can give my Isaac with submission and faith, but I cannot offer him up, nor feast upon the sacrifice."

CHAPTER XXII.

THE MOONLIGHT AND THE DAWN.

A clumsy boat, very different from the trim racing craft that to-day skim the waters of Plymouth Bay weltered slowly toward the rude pier just below the new home of Myles Standish.

The passengers were also very different from those of to-day, and perhaps a parallel might be drawn in both cases between passengers and boat, but as it would not be in our own favor I will not pursue it, merely mentioning that the solidly built, honest, safe, capacious, and unpretending boat first mentioned contained Elder Brewster, Captain Standish, Edward Winslow, John Alden, Thomas Prence, William Collier, and two or three more of the "Immortals" from whom we are so glad to claim descent, and so sorry to confess that it has been such a tremendous descent.

Upon the bluff where stood the captain's house, and scattered down the path to the shore, a path graded with military skill and precision, a merry crowd of men, women, and children stood waving hats and handkerchiefs and shouting words of welcome, whereat Standish smiled and Winslow remarked,—

"All Duxbury seems gathered to greet us; but how are they so sure that we bring the charter after so many disappointments?"

"I told them if we had it I would fly my private ensign," replied Standish a little complacently; and Winslow, glancing at the mainmast, perceived a small flag whereon was deftly embroidered the owl with a rat in his talons, then as now the crest of the elder house of Standish.

"Ha! That is something new, is 't not?" asked the master of Careswell, not well pleased that another should make heraldic pretensions before himself.

"Yes. My Lora embroidered it, and I told them all that if our errand to-day was successful I would fly it for the first time in honor of the birth of Duxbury."

"Daughter of our dear mother Plymouth," remarked Thomas Prence; and the captain somewhat uneasily replied,—

"God grant the daughter's birth may not cost the mother's life, as our good governor seems to forebode."

"Nay, Master Bradford would have the sun stand still in heaven, and lucky is it for Duxbury that he is no Joshua," retorted Winslow with a smile so near a sneer that Standish flushed angrily, and shouted with quite unnecessary vehemence to John Howard, who was steering,—

"Luff, man alive, luff! You'll never fetch the pier! Can't you see where you're going?"

"There's Hobomok waiting to catch the bowline," resumed Winslow pacifically. "What a good faithful creature he has proved, and how fond of you, Captain!"

"He is my friend, and I am one that looks for faithfulness in a friend," replied the captain significantly.

"You have a right to ask for what you give. And lo you now! there's a pretty sight!" pursued the diplomat, undisturbed. "Those little maids all in white and flower-crowned mind one of the maids of Israel coming forth to meet the captain of Judah."

"Or 'Benjamin our little ruler,' more aptly," laughed Standish, whose pride had no taint of personal vanity.

"Those two slips of May are your Lora, and Betty Alden, are they not?" pursued Winslow.

"Yes; they are fast friends, and always together. Fair lasses enow, eh, John?"

"Methinks we've naught to complain of, Captain," returned Alden placidly.

"They mind one of moonlight and dawn," said Winslow with honest admiration in his voice. "Lora does not look like a colonist's child, Captain."

"No. She favors her forbears. There's an old picture at Standish Hall that might have been painted for her likeness. Mayhap some day"—

"And Betty is a real rosebud of Old England. She does not copy her comely mother, Alden, and yet is as comely."

"No. Sally is more like her mother," replied John simply, and as the boat drew in to the wharf all three men looked approvingly at the two young girls just budding into maidenhood, and forming as sweet and pure a contrast as the moonlight and the dawn to which the courtly Winslow had compared them; for Betty in her wholesome growth had as it were absorbed color from the sunshine, willowy strength from the sea breeze, and fragrance from the epigæa, until her brown eyes sparkled and glinted like the sea in a sunny morning, and her crisp hair had netted the summer into its meshes, and her cheeks and lips throbbed with soft bright color like the petals of a wild rose. But Lora, as tall already as her friend, although several years younger, was slight as a flower stalk, her pale gold hair almost too heavy for her little head, her soft gray eyes almost too large for the pure oval of her face, the sweet color of her mouth too faintly reproduced in her cheeks. If Betty Alden resembled the dawn of a summer morning upon seagirt field and forest, Lora Standish brought to mind a garden of annunciation lilies bathed in moonlight.

And now as the fond fathers gazed, and Winslow's golden tongue dropped phrases sweet in their ears as honey of Hymettus, John Howard, ancestor of a grand line of Bridgewater yeomen, but at present in the household of Standish, deftly gave his tiller a turn that laid the boat's nose softly against the pier, while Hobomok, with an inarticulate grunt of welcome, seized the line tossed him by John Alden and made it fast around an oaken pile well bedded in the wharf.

In a few moments the boat was empty, and its passengers mingled with the eager crowd who pressed forward to greet them. Chief of these was the new pastor, Ralph Partridge, a "gracious and learned man," an alumnus of Cambridge and for twenty years a clergyman of the Established Church of England, but now, as Mather quaintly has it, he, "being distressed by the ecclesiastical setters, had no defence neither of beak nor claw, but a flight over the ocean. The place where he took covert was the Colony of Plymouth, and the Town of Duxbury in that Colony. This Partridge had not only the innocence of the dove, but also the loftiness of the eagle in the great soar of his intellectual abilities," etc.

To this gentleman as the principal person among his guests Standish addressed himself, and taking from the breast of his doublet a package carefully enveloped in oiled silk, opened it and showed a sheet of parchment, brief as to its contents and crude as to its chirography, but bearing some very distinguished autographs, and carrying with it an importance to that group of people similar to that possessed in the eyes of a young wife by the title deeds of her new home, her dower house, and the birthplace of her future children.

"Here is the charter, reverend sir, and now the people of Duxbury have a right to invite you to become their pastor," said the captain bluntly; but as Partridge took the parchment he looked at the man who gave it and said softly,—

"Shall I be your pastor, Captain Standish?"

"Nay, sir, this is no time for such questions," replied Standish, rather displeased, and turning away he entered the house to lay aside some of his heavy clothes and don festal attire. In the principal room, deep in whispered council, stood Barbara Standish and Priscilla Alden, two comely and gracious matrons, at sight of whom the captain's face softened into a merry smile.

"Now what mischief are you plotting, you two with your heads together like Guy Fawkes and Tyrrell?" exclaimed he. "Priscilla, never teach your rebel fashions to my well-trained dame, or I shall have her snatching at the reins!"

"And you'd rather she'd ride the pillion and cling to your belt with a 'Good master, have a care of me'!" cried Priscilla, her dark eyes flashing as brightly as they had done some sixteen years before while she said, "Why don't you speak for yourself, John?"

"'Tis a woman's rightful place, and I'll be bound, when all's said, you came over here to-day on a pillion with only your boy Jack to cling to."

"Nay, we all came in the boat, down Bluefish River and so round. You see there's so many of us,—John and Jo and Betty and David and Jonathan and Sally and Ruth and Molly; for I could not leave the babies at home without keeping Betty and Sally to mind them, and that was not to be thought of, says my Betty, who aye has her own way."

"And marvelous that she should, seeing she comes of so weak a mother."

"Oh, she takes after her father, poor child, and he would ever be aping the ways of his captain."

Doubtless the captain would soon have provided himself with a retort, but Barbara laid a hand upon his arm.

"While you two are changing your merry quips and cranks, the supper waits," said she. "Surely, Myles, you will wash your hands and straighten your hair; and Priscilla, is't not time for you to put the last touch to the whips and syllabub?"

"True enough, Barbara, and lo, I'm gone!" cried Priscilla, and disappeared into the great cool dairy with its northern exposure, where the milk of the red cow and the two young daughters now added to her was manufactured by Barbara into not only butter, but all sorts of dainty confections. On this occasion, however, Priscilla Alden had as of old been summoned to help the housewife, and lend not only her hands but her incomparable culinary skill to the work of providing entertainment for the two or three score persons who had gathered to celebrate the birthday of their town. With most of these, or at least with the heads of the families, we are already acquainted, but in the seventeen years since the landing of the Mayflower many who were then children have grown to maturity and married; as for instance, Love Brewster, who has been for three years husband of Sarah, daughter of that William Collier the only man among the London

Adventurers who proved his faith in the Pilgrims by coming to live among them. See him as he stands talking with Elder Brewster, his four fair daughters all within sight: Sarah Brewster, Elizabeth Southworth, Rebecca Cole, and Mary, whose sweet face and ample dowry have already comforted Thomas Prence for the loss of his first wife, gentle Patience Brewster.

So many of our friends are here collected that we may not mention half their names: Henry Samson, the little boy passenger of the Mayflower, with his bride, and his later come brother Abraham, soon to marry the daughter of Lieutenant Nash; the Howlands, not only stanch John and Elizabeth Tilley his wife, but John and Jabez their sons, and pretty Desire, fast friend of Betty Alden and Lora Standish. And here are some new-comers, the Pabodies, settled near John Alden on Bluefish River, but already owning land in The Nook, where the father promises to build a house for the first of his sons who shall marry. Three of the lads are here to-day, and William, a fine, manly young fellow of seventeen years, hangs around the group of laughing girls, and watches Betty Alden with all his eyes.

But we must not linger with the guests, although each one seems like a friend, nor may we pause to enumerate the dainties spread in graceful profusion upon the tables set between the house and the edge of the bluff; suffice it to say that Barbara has delegated to Priscilla Alden the part of caterer, and well has she sustained her reputation, using the abundant material placed at her service to the very best advantage, and winning from each of her assistants the very best service they knew how to render. Nor does the banquet fail to receive ample justice at the hands of the banqueters, beginning with those dignitaries seated in state at a table covered with Barbara's best napery, and provided with all the magnificence of silver, pewter, and china that she has been able to muster, not only from her own stores, but those of her neighbors. Here on either hand of the captain sit Elder Brewster and Ralph Partridge, with Winslow at the other end of the table, flanked by William Collier and Timothy Hatherley; at another table preside John Alden and John Howland, with Thomas Prence, William Bassett, and Jonathan Brewster, already a leading man in the colony: and at these two tables are seated nearly all the heads of families soon to be enrolled as the freemen of Duxbury, while their wives and younger children cluster around a third table, headed by Barbara and Priscilla, and the young people enjoy themselves amazingly at their own board, as remote as possible from that of the elders, their fun a little chastened by the presence of those young matrons Mistress Prence and Mistress Love Brewster, themselves no more than girls.

And so was Duxbury's birthday celebrated, and still the honest mirth and neighborly kindliness went on, until the sun dropped behind Captain's Hill, and the red cow lowed at the bars of her pasture hard by.

Then, after a little silence that made itself felt, Elder Brewster rose in his place and said,—

"Brethren and children, this is a day of solemn joy to us who now have become a town by ourselves, even as children going out from their father's house to begin a home of their very own; a day to remember, brethren, and to set down in our annals, that when in time to come our children's children shall ask, 'Why do ye these things?' they shall find an answer ready to their hands. Some of you upon whom mine eyes now rest were fellow-passengers with me in the ship Mayflower, and ye remember, as I do, the barren and comfortless shore whereon we landed and were fain to call it home. Some of us, turning our eyes to that southern shore, can almost see the hillside where in those first months we day by day laid away the forms of those dearest to our natural hearts, or most precious to the life of our little colony; we recall the suffering by sea, the suffering by land, the cold and hunger and misery and grievous toil we then endured; but do we recall them to lament, to sorrow like babes over our own distresses? Nay, men, we recall them in joy and praise, in wonder and admiration at His goodness who hath so wonderfully brought plenty out of famine, joy out of sorrow, the morning out of night. Well may we say with Israel, 'I am less than the least of thy mercies; for with my staff I passed over this Jordan, and now I am become two companies!'

"Is it not verily true? There lieth Plymouth, fair and prosperous, the mother of us all in this new land; and here stand we, sturdy, well-grown children, fit to take our own part in the world, ay, and to comfort her should she call upon us. Have we not cause for rejoicing, ay, and for a firm resolve to show ourselves in some degree worthy of such singular mercies? Brethren, my heart is too full to speak further save to One. Let us pray."

Up rose the old men, the grave and bearded men, the matronly women whose eyes ran over with the memories the elder had invoked; up rose the young men, rejoicing in their strength, yet reverent of their sires, and of the story they had learned in childhood and would not forget in age; the lads, the maidens, the little children, all rose, and stood with bowed heads and hushed breath to listen to the tremulous voice of that aged servant of God as, forgetting all save Him to whom he spoke, he poured forth one of those fervent and trustful appeals whose eloquent power are matter of history. And as he raised his hands in benediction, calling down a special blessing upon the new town and each and every one of its homes, a plume of smoke rose from Burying Hill far to the south, and the sunset gun boomed out its solemn detonation.

"Plymouth says Amen!" whispered Priscilla Alden in Betty's ear; and the girl silently pointed to Lora Standish, upon whose head the last sunbeam had laid a finger, lighting the pale gold of her hair to the nimbus of a saint. Priscilla looked, and suddenly clasped her own child close to her side; but neither spoke.

CHAPTER XXIII.

"LOREA STANDISH IS MY NAME."

"Lora! Aunt Bab! What do you think? Bessie Partridge has a sweetheart, and he's going to be a minister, and his father is one of the old sort that we're bound to hate; but the parson don't care and has given his consent, and they're to be married out of hand. There, now!"

"But, Betty, dear child, do catch your breath and sit down and put back your hair all blown over your face"—

"I know, Aunt Bab, I know; but I just put Jo's saddle on the colt and cantered him over here at his best speed, and of course my hair is blown about. Lora, I could shake you, you provoking girl, with your hair like new carded flax, and your fresh kirtle and wimple, and your stitchery in your hand"—

"The sampler is well-nigh done," interrupted the mother proudly, "and I think she hath done it fairly enough, don't you, Betty Alden?"

"Certainly I do, auntie, and I know as well as though you said it I shall never be a patch on Lora for delicate needlework; but then there are so many of us, and mother has no time for her needle, and the boys and father do wear out their hosen most unmercifully, and keep me darning or knitting all the time. I've a stocking in my pocket here for Jonathan; but first let me have a good view of the sampler, Lora."

"Wait but till I cut off my silk at the end of 'name,'" said Lora, busily fastening her thread at the back of the canvas. "There, now I've the needle safe! You know you lost one for me last time you were here, and mother and I hunted an hour for it."

"I know," replied Betty penitently, "and if you had not found it mother was going to send John and Jo over to the governor to see if he had some in store."

"He had some direct from Whitechapel by the Lyon," remarked Barbara, "but the price is advanced to fivepence each, and we must be careful."

"You see I have still the flourishing at the end to do," said Lora, handing Betty the frame in which a long and narrow piece of linen was tightly stretched and nearly covered with parallel lines of embroidery done in various colored silks. Near the lower end came a verse, or at least some rhymes running thus:—

"Lorea Standish is my name.

Lord, guide my heart that I may do Thy will;

Also fill my hands with such convenient skill

As will conduce to virtue void of shame,

And I will give the glory to Thy name."

The letters forming these words were characterized by a noble independence and freedom from any slavish adherence to custom, some of them being capitals and some small, some little and some big, and the *D's* turning their backs or their faces to their comrades as a vagrant fancy dictated. Such as it was, however, this sampler was in Betty Alden's eyes a work of art commanding her respectful admiration, mingled with a warmer feeling rising from her very sincere love for the artist.

"Oh, Lora!" cried she, throwing an arm around the girl's slender neck and kissing her heartily, "one can see that you come of gentle blood, and are fitter for silken embroidery than for the milking-stool which is my usual workbench."

"Nay, I would love to milk, and churn, and cook, and knit gray hosen, but father will not have it so," said Lora a little wearily. "I may spin, and sew, and do my tent-stitch, and help mother make syllabubs and the like, but it angers him if I soil my hands or wear a homespun kirtle such as is fit for rough work"—

"Rough work and Lora are droll ideas to bring together, aren't they, auntie?" interrupted Betty with another hug and kiss to her friend, whose sweet face had grown a little flushed and worried as she spoke.

"But come, dear, I want you to go with me to see Bessie and ask her if this wonderful news is sooth. She may come, mayn't she, auntie?"

"Yes, child, so that you're both back for supper. Father can't abide finding Lora's seat empty at table."

"We'll be sure to come. Now, Loly, where's your hood?"

"Put on your sleeves and your cape, Lora. You'll get burned else."

"Yes, mother," replied the girl patiently, and passing into her own bedroom returned presently with a cape covering her bare neck, and buttoning some loose sleeves to her shoulders, for in that day a gown with high neck and long sleeves was a vestment unknown, and when age or cold weather or out-of-door excursions demanded a covering for shoulders and arms it was supplied, as in Lora's case, by temporary expedients. A little white linen hood tied under the chin completed the girl's preparation, and with a gentle kiss upon her mother's cheek she joined Betty impatiently waiting upon the doorstep.

"Lora, I should think it would weary you to be such a cosset!" cried she, as the girls struck into a path leading northward through the captain's lands to Eagle's Creek, where hard by a clump of aged oaks stood the cottage where in the summer season Elder Brewster lived with his sons Love and Wrestling and the young wife of the former. Still trending north, the path led past Jonathan Brewster's comfortable cottage near the Eagle's Tree to Harden Hill, where a little way from the edge of the bluff stood a small and low building rudely put together of rough timber and hewn planks, with a thatched roof and windows of oiled cloth, and neither foundations nor chimney, the former unneeded because the colonists hoped at no distant day to replace this their one public edifice with something more elaborate and permanent, and the latter undreamed of as yet even in the mother-church of Plymouth, where the Rev. John Rayner and his colleague Charles Chauncey, both graduates of Cambridge, England, and bred in such luxury as England then knew, took turns in preaching, in overcoats and woolen gloves, sermons of two hours' duration to a congregation the weaklings of which kept themselves alive by the use of foot-stoves and hot bricks in their laps, while the stronger members grimly endured sitting three and four hours in an atmosphere considerably more chill than the outdoor winter air.

Following this example, Duxbury built no chimneys to her first meeting-houses, and Elder Brewster in the beginning, with Ralph Partridge and John Holmes to succeed him, preached and prayed with only the fire of their own zeal to keep them warm.

A little way from the meeting-house stood a cottage owned by William Bassett, but at present occupied by the Rev. Mr. Partridge, who waited for his formal installation as pastor of the new-formed town before settling himself in a house of his own, and still lingered in The Nook, although he had already bought of William Latham a house whose magnificence has descended upon the pages of history for our admiring contemplation; a house, and not a cottage, for it boasted a second story with a garret overhead, and a roof sweeping majestically in the rear, from the roof-tree to the ground.

But the Partridges had not yet removed to their new nest, and it was in the vicinity of the little hired cottage on Harden Hill that Betty and Lora found their friend Bessie demurely watering and turning a web of fine linen laid to bleach upon the grass. As they approached she started and turned round, a rosy, sonsy lassie, plump as her name, and overflowing with health and spirits.

"Oh, Bess, is it true?" began Betty, laying a hand upon each of her friend's shoulders and scrutinizing her face with its flaming blushes.

"Good-even, Betty, good-even, Lora! Is what true? What does she mean, Lora? Let me finish wetting my linen, you runagate!"

"*Your* linen! Aha! How many smocks and petticoats will it make? Or is it for sheets and pillowbers? And must we all come and help you sew it, or is there time a plenty?"

"Nay, Betty, there's some one coming!" whispered Lora, as the figure of a tall young man of a decidedly clerical cut appeared from the front of the house, and Betty, all at once as demure as a kitten, seized one end of the linen, saying,—

"Certainly I'll help you turn it, Bessie; and how is your mother to-night?"

"Mother's well, and— Master Thacher, let me bring you acquainted with Mistress Alden and Mistress Standish, two of the chief of my friends."

"And so right welcome in mine eyes," replied the young man heartily, as he lightly kissed the cheek of first one and then the other girl, a ceremony no more remarkable then than shaking hands is to-day.

"My uncle Anthony has gone with Mr. Partridge to pay his respects to Captain Standish," added he pleasantly. "All men delight to do honor to the Captain of Plymouth Colony."

"You are very courteous to say so, sir," replied Lora, with her pretty little air of dignity and reserve; "and your uncle will be right welcome."

"'Tis strange we did not meet them in the way," said Betty, whose brown eyes had not yet lost the gleam of merriment lighted by Bessie's blushes.

"Oh, they went by Master Alden's to see him as well; and look, there they all are now,—the captain and father and Master Thacher!" cried Bessie. "They must have come to your house just as you left it, Lora."

"Nay, father was at work with Alick and Josias in the great field beside the road, and I doubt if the gentlemen went to the house at all," said Lora, her face becoming radiant as her eyes met those of her father, now close at hand. Beside the captain strode the tall, gaunt figure of Ralph Partridge, a man whose many trials and persecutions had set their stamp upon a face naturally rugged, and bowed a form intended to be sturdy; at Standish's other side walked a man younger in years than the dominie, but bearing upon his face much the same expression of strong endurance and unforgotten experiences,—a man with a story, as any one accustomed to reading faces would say, especially when, as now, the broad-leafed hat was removed, displaying the hair, thick as that of a youth, but white as that of a grandsire.

"Here, Thomas!" cried this last comer, as the elders approached the little group of young people; "come hither, lad, and let me present you to the notice of Captain Myles Standish, whose name I have so often heard upon your lips."

"Doubtless 'twas for love of that poor old soldier that you have come hither, Master Thomas," said the captain merrily, and under cover of the little jest the awkwardness of the meeting was overpast, and a blithe half hour ensued. At last, while the shadows lengthened, and the clouds took on their evening glory, and the sweet breath of evening primroses and lowing kine filled the sunset hour, Myles and Lora strolled home along the footpath, hand in hand, while Betty Alden, light as a deer, ran along in front of them, impatient to reach home before her mother needed her.

Arrived at the house, father and daughter paused to look across the bay at Plymouth peacefully sleeping in the westering light, with Manomet purple against the golden sky, and the wide stretch of water smooth as a mirror, save where it fawned against the point of the beach and the foot of the bluff where they stood.

"A fair scene, a goodly scene, daughter," said the captain; "but not your home for very long."

CHAPTER XXIV.

AVERY'S FALL AND THACHER'S WOE.

Two hundred and fifty years ago, even as to-day, the betrothal of a young couple was cause of rejoicing and festivity among their friends, and three days after Lora and Betty had made what we may call their engagement call upon Bessie Partridge, the minister's family with its guests, and Elder Brewster and the Aldens, were invited to supper at the captain's. Not to afternoon tea, mind you; nay, not even to that old-fashioned tea-time still popular in the rural districts, where the guests sit down to a table loaded with hot bread and toast and all manner of sweets, with the choice of tea or coffee to wash down the heavy meal.

But Barbara Standish had never even heard the names of tea or coffee, and honestly called the last meal of the day "supper," setting it at about seven o'clock, when the labors of the day were over and all men at leisure for social enjoyment. At that hour, therefore, the guests sat down to a feast which I dare not describe because I have already described so many, but content myself with saying that it in no wise discredited Mistress Standish's housewifery, and that when Dame Partridge asked for the "resait" of the frosted cake, the hostess proudly replied that Lora had so improved upon the old formula that it was left in her hands altogether, and Lora modestly added that she should be more than glad to run over and show Mrs. Partridge exactly how she made it.

"I'm obliged to you, dear," responded the parson's wife; "for," with a sly glance at the betrothed pair sitting very stiffly and formally at the right hand of their hostess, "I expect we shall have to be making up some cake pretty soon."

But our concern is not so much with the feast, of which these friends partook with frank and honest appetites, as with the conversation that came after, while the women gossiped together in the house over a drop of mulled wine, and the men, pipes in mouth and tankards of sound ale at hand, sat under the trees carefully preserved upon the edge of the bluff when the land was cleared for building.

Two wooden armchairs, the only approach to luxurious seats to be found in the captain's cottage, had been set forth for the elder and Parson Partridge, and the next best given to Anthony Thacher, while the host, with Alden and Jonathan Brewster, sat upon a rude bench formed between two beech-trees. Hobomok, never far from his beloved hero, lay upon the grass solemnly smoking, and the younger men, Wrestling Brewster, commonly called Ras, as a diminutive of 'Rastling, John and Joseph Alden, Alick Standish, and Thomas Thacher hung about the door and windows of the great south room where Bessie, Betty, and Lora flitted around their mothers like pretty kittens around sober Tabitha.

Then it was that Myles, after a moment's thought and a dubious clearing of his throat, said tentatively,—

"Master Thacher, when I heard that you were to be sent deputy from your new town of Yarmouth to our court at Plymouth, I resolved within myself, if opportunity should offer, and your own mind prove toward the matter, that I would ask you to give me a particular account of your famous shipwreck upon the island men now call Thacher's Woe from that disaster. Would it offend you if I now urge that petition?"

But even as the words left his mouth the captain regretted their utterance, for the man addressed cringed and started in his chair, as one who feels a touch upon a new wound, while the pallor of his singularly colorless face turned to ashen gray, and his light blue eyes dilated and wandered as those of one who sees a vision of terror.

"Nay"—resumed Myles hastily; but as hastily Thacher took the word out of his mouth.

"Not nay, but ay, good friend!" exclaimed he with an attempted smile. "I know well that the terror of those fearful hours has left its mark not only upon my outer man, but upon the forces of my mind, which are no longer altogether under mine own control, but, like a horse once well terrified at a certain spot, will still swerve and start in passing it, despite of his driver's voice and rein. Albeit, even as it is well that the unruly steed should be often taken past the bugbear, which he will at last cease to dread, so it is well for me to talk of that day from time to time, and to tell its story as occasion shall befall, to friends who can enter into its solemnity."

"You are right, my son," said Elder Brewster quietly. "The unruly heart of man needs long and bitter discipline before it becomes truly meek."

"Ne'ertheless, Master Thacher, I do withdraw my petition, and beg you instead of that story to tell us how you like our fashion of holding court by deputies rather than *pro coram publico* as hath been our wont until this year."

"Nay, Captain Standish, one matter at a time an't please you, and I have no mind to be balked of the glory of mine adventure. What say you, friends? Shall not I tell you of the shipwreck?"

"It would give me singular pleasure to hear it, Brother Thacher," replied the parson, while the elder smiled approval, Jonathan Brewster murmured "Ay!" and the captain, lifting his shaggy beard and taking the pipe from his mouth, said with a merry gesture,—

"It were churlish to refuse to listen to a man who fain would tell his own adventures, so I will e'en put all scruples in my pocket and hearken with the rest of you."

"Well spoke, mine host, and I can comfort you by saying truthfully that the qualm hath passed and I would rather tell the tale than be silent.

"You men of Plymouth have not forgotten the great storm of August in the year of grace 1635, for it was then that the French villain D'Aulney seized upon your rich trading-post at Castine which they now call Bragaduce, and turned John Willet adrift with only a shallop and a worthless due-bill. The terrific storm that wrecked Willet's shallop and also the armed ship Angel Gabriel, bound to Boston in the Bay, overtook the humbler craft in which my cousin Dominie John Avery, his wife and six children, and I with my wife and four children, nine mariners, and other persons were making the voyage from Ipswich to Marblehead."

"It was a bark of Isaac Allerton's in which you voyaged, was it not?" asked Standish.

"Ay, he was owner, but not master."

"Never mind who played master, if Allerton was owner, the boat was sure of ill luck," growled Standish; but the Elder interposed serenely,—

"Your speech savors of superstition as well as uncharity, Captain Standish, and I had held you singularly free from both those vices."

"I crave your pardon, Elder. I had clean forgot that Allerton was for a while your son-in-law. Go on an' it please you, Master Thacher."

But again the power of those memories he had so resolutely evoked overmastered the speaker, and it was in a hurried and broken voice and with a furtive gesture of the hand across the eyes that he again began:—

"I fain would tell you, but I cannot, what John Avery was, not to me alone who loved him better than David could love Jonathan, better than mine own brother who yet was dear to me, but to all the world; a man so good, so holy, so devout, that he seemed sent hither to remind us of the Man of Nazareth whose humble follower he was; and withal so keen of wit, and so sound of judgment, and so ready to help with heart and hand wherever he saw need, that I leaned upon him and yearned toward him in all difficulties as a little child with his mother. Verily I believe it was for the chastisement of mine own overweening love that this thing hath befallen."

"Belike rather the God he served saw him fit for heaven, and so took him even as He did Elijah," said the Elder reverently.

"It may be, venerable sir, it may be; but I cannot forget mine own arrogancy when John told me that the church at Marblehead had invited him, and he was fain to go, and I said, 'Well and good, John, but you sha'n't be rid of me, for I'll go too, and naught but death shall part us.' Ah me! Naught but death, says I, and verily 't was naught but death!"

"Did it storm when you set forth?" asked Jonathan Brewster's clear and somewhat cold voice; and Thacher, recalling himself with a start, replied in much the same tone:—

"No, although the weather looked threatening, and our master was in haste to sail, hoping to weather Cape Ann before the wind changed as he foreboded it would. But it was just off the Cape that it fell calm, and then all in a moment the storm burst, and the wind, veering to every point of the compass, caught us as if in a whirlpool, so that before the sailors could trim their sails they were torn from their hands, torn from the masts, or if they clung, only helped to tear the masts from the hull and the rudder from the stern. I am not shipman enough to tell you how it all befell, but this I know: that when the morning of Saturday, the 15th day of August in 1635, broke in such fury of wind and rain and raging waves as I never beheld before or since, our bark drove furiously upon a reef, and in the shock went all to pieces, carrying ten souls into eternity before one could cry God have mercy upon them! One of these was Peter Avery, a fine lad, who had gone aft to fetch a rope whereby to bind his mother to the stump of the foremast, and in that act of filial charity he died."

"And his reward is with God," murmured the Elder.

"We who survived," continued Thacher, "speedily made our way from the crumbling wreck to the rock between whose horns our bows were jammed; and hardly were we all off when the last timber splintered beneath the hammer of the surge, and we were left, thirteen poor shivering wretches, two of them little babes in their mothers' arms, clinging desperately to that naked rock, the helpless prey of white-headed waves that like wild beasts ran raging along the sides of our poor hold, and now and again with a victorious howl leaped up and seized first one and then another of those poor little ones whom neither a father's arms nor a mother's piteous embrace sufficed to save. One by one they went, those darlings of our lives, and as her infant was torn from her arms, Mary Avery, with a cry I shall never forget, grasped after it, and was carried away with it. Then my friend, who had followed them but that I held him back, struggled to his knees and prayed aloud. O my friends! when I remember those words, when I remember that face, drenched with the storm, blanched by the blow that brake his heart, yet luminous as was Stephen's in his martyrdom, I feel like Paul who, being caught up to heaven, saw and heard what it is not lawful—nay, what it is not possible—for a man to repeat."

"Nay, we would not have you try, my son," whispered the Elder, while the captain folded his arms and grimly set his lips, and John Alden wept without disguise.

"The next thing I recall," pursued Thacher softly, "is holding my cousin's hand and saying over and over, 'You shall not leave me, John, you shall not leave me! We will die together or we will live together!' and I see once more amid the whirl and torment of the storm the smile wherewith he looked me in the face and said,—

"'We will die together, Anthony, and please God we will live together!' And then, while some loving cry to God rose afresh from his lips, came a giant wave and tore us asunder, and I knew no more until I was struggling in the waves with mine arm around my poor wife, and she clinging senseless to me.

"Then all His waves and storms went over me, and I yielded up my spirit to Him who gave it; but it was not yet purified enough to go where my friend was gone before, and God in mercy granted me yet another season of probation. When the Lord's Day broke, it found me with my poor wife stretched like two corpses upon the strand of a little islet hard by the rock I have named Avery's Fall, and beside us a poor goat, who all unaided or uncared for had come safe to land. My poor wife! when she recovered her senses and looked about her and knew our piteous case, who can blame her that she cried,—

"'A wretched goat saved, and my four sweet babies drowned! Doth God then care for oxen?'"

"The Father of us all can forgive the misery of a mother's heart," said the Elder, but Jonathan Alden gravely turned away his head and looked out toward the sea.

"Not only the milch goat, but a cheese and a rundlet of beer were washed ashore," pursued Thacher, "and oh, piteous sight! the cradle whence my wife had snatched her babe came floating safe ashore, with the covering wrought by my sister in England for our first darling, safe in the bottom. Like Noah's ark with the dove flown to return no more, it seemed to us, and as I dragged the cradle ashore and my poor wife sank beside it and buried her head in that pretty covering, her mad despair gave way in gracious tears, and she wept until she was able to pray.

"Thus, then, our Lord's Day passed, but with the Monday came rescue, and we two with our empty cradle and its fair-wrought spread, and the poor goat whose life had hung in the balance, were all brought first to Boston, and then to Yarmouth."

"But Thomas was not with you, was he?" asked Partridge at last, breaking his intent silence.

"Nay, and there is a matter wherein the Elder may hold me as superstitious as the captain," replied Thacher, forcing a smile; "but it has seemed to me that the Lord, not ready to take him, and not willing to try him by the sharp discipline vouchsafed to me, interposed with a special Providence in his behalf.

"Only the night before we were to sail, Thomas had a dream, and, like Belshazzar of old, he could not in waking remember its tenure, but only its terror. Of one thing, however, he seemed fully assured, and that was that he must not sail upon our voyage; and so strong and terrible was his dread that he would not so much as come to see us off, but as we went our way to the shore he struck into the forest and made the fifteen miles or so afoot."

"And has he never recalled the dream?" asked Mr. Partridge, with a look askance at his prospective son-in-law just then trying to snatch a rose from his sweetheart's hand.

"No; that is, he has always seemed so ill at ease in talking of the matter that we have let it drop. It runs in my mind that it is as much a puzzlement to him as it can be to others."

"'There be more things in heaven and earth, than are dreamt of in your philosophy' or in mine, quoth my old gossip Will Shakespeare," said the captain, and Anthony Thacher heartily replied,—

"And spake the truth as fairly as though he had worn gown and bands. A great student of men was that same gossip of yours, Captain."

"Ay, and a rollicking good fellow. I knew him well, and something more than well, in the time I was in England after the peace of 1609, and in certain of his plays there's many a quip and quirk shot at me and my poor achievements. Didst ever see a play called 'Henry the Fourth'?"

"Nay, Captain, I was never in a playhouse in my life."

"More's your loss, friend. Well, in that play there's a bit runs like this, or something so:—

—'I remember, when the fight was done,

When I was dry with rage, and desprit toil,

Breathless and faint, leaning upon my sword,

Came there a certain lord, neat, trimly dressed,

Fresh as a bridegroom'—

Well, I'll not give you the whole, if I remember it, and 'tis years since I thought on't, but a little later it goes forward:—

'I then, a'l smarting, with my wounds being cold,

To be so pestered with a popinjay,

Out of my grief and my impatience,

Answered full carelessly, I know not what;

He should or he should not; for 't made me mad

To see him shine so brisk, and smell so sweet,

And talk so like a waiting gentlewoman

Of guns, and drums, and wounds, (God save the mark!)

And telling me the sovereign'st thing on earth

Was parmaceti for an inward bruise;

And that it was great pity, so it was,

That villainous saltpetre should be digged

Out of the bowels of the harmless earth,

Which many a good tall fellow had destroyed

So cowardly; and but for these vile guns,

He would himself have been a soldier.'

Oh, well, well, but I must laugh, and laugh again as I mind me of the day when Will Shakespeare first mouthed those lines at me, and I stood staring like a stuck pig to hear mine own words so bedded in his poesy, like flies in amber in very sooth, for 'twas a story I had told him of a matter that happened to myself in the Low Countries"—

"Alas, my son," interposed the Elder, raising his hand, "such memories suit but ill with the lives of 'pilgrims and strangers' like ourselves."

"And for that very reason, Elder," replied Standish a little hotly, "when you and Master Partridge and the rest besiege me to become a church-member, I will listen to naught of it. The old leaven is still a-working by fits and starts, and I'll do no such despite to the saints as to count myself into their company. 'Nay, nay, mine ancient,' says Will to me one time when we stood side by side in Paul's Walk, and saw a grand procession pass us by, ''tis better to watch the lightning than to handle it.'"

With a mischievous glance at the Rev. Ralph Partridge, Standish resumed his pipe, and the parson wisely remained silent.

CHAPTER XXV.

JEPHTHAH'S DAUGHTER.

St. Martin's summer was in the land; that lovely parting smile of the year, so full of love, so full of reminiscence and of promise, so full of pathos and of that vague yearning that lies at the core of every heart, and which I fancy Bossuet means when he speaks of "the inexorable weariness which lurks at the foundations of all our lives."

The door of Standish's cottage stood wide, and between it and the lattice opening upon the sea, letting in the sweet breath of marigolds and thyme basking in the southern sun, Barbara stepped lightly back and forth, spinning from her great wheel the fine yarn that would be woven or knit into the winter garments of the household.

A shadow across the floor made her turn, quick yet fearless as a bird building in a tree above a house whose inmates never have threatened it.

A tall, good-looking young man stood in the doorway, and with his eyes searched the room before he said,—

"Good-morrow, dame. Is Lora somewhere at hand?"

"Oh, good-morrow, Ras! Lora has gone to the top of the hill for a breath of evening air. It has been so warm to-day."

"Yes, Hobomok calls it the Indian's summer because it comes just before winter," replied Wrestling Brewster absently; and then after another moment of hesitation he pulled off his wide hat, and coming close to the spinner's side fixed his eyes upon hers with a shy appeal while he asked,—

"Do you think, dame, I might ask her?"

"Ask her what, Ras?"

"Oh, Dame Barbara, you know full well what I fain would ask."

"There'll be an apple-bee at your house or at Jonathan's this week, will there not?"

"Ay, at Jonathan's on the Thursday, and Lucretia bade me invite you all."

"Well, then, you foolish boy, sure that is your errand to Lora, and you'll find her on the hill, most like at what she calls her sunset seat."

"'Twas I that made it for her," said Wrestling eagerly, and Barbara, smiling in the way matrons smile at transparent youth, replied,—

"Then you know where it is. Go, and God go with you."

"My grateful duty to you, dame," murmured the young fellow, and went like an arrow from a bow.

A half hour later Barbara, setting her wheel aside, stepped to the door to look toward the hill, and to judge by the position of the sun how near the hour might be to supper time.

Coming up from the shore she saw her husband, and at the first glance knew that he was ill-pleased; with this conviction came a foreboding that made her turn her eyes again toward the hill, but now it was the daughter, and not the sun, for which she looked.

"Where's Lora, wife?" inquired the captain so soon as he was within speaking distance.

"She went out an hour or so agone for a stroll," replied the mother mildly. "She has been so steadily stitching at your new shirts, Myles, that I sent her to get a breath of fresh air."

"Belike it's she I saw upon the hill; 'twas a white gown, at all events."

"And like you no longer to see her in white?" asked Barbara, apparently in great surprise. "Why, 'tis to please you she wears it, though it makes a mort of washing for poor Hepsey. But where hast been thyself, goodman?"

"To Plymouth, and Alice Bradford sends you a clutch of eggs from her new brought fowls."

"Nay, but that's more than kind!" cried Barbara. "And how fares she, and is it true that Prissie Wright will marry Manasses Kempton? And did you get the grist ground, and what said Miller Jenney of not having it yesterday?"

"Come, come, dame, 'tis not for naught your tongue wags like Priscilla Alden's all of a sudden. Tell me what man is on the hill with our Lora, and what 'tis you're keeping from me,—or would if you could. Out with it, Bab! who's the man I saw up there?"

"Nay, Myles, that's no tone for you to take towards me! 'Tis not one of the children nor one of the servants you're speaking to."

"What! ruffling her feathers like a Dame Partlet if you try to steal the chickens from under her! Nay, wife, that mood's as strange to you as the chattering one, and both are but put on to turn my mind from its course; but 'tis no use, Bab, no use at all. Come, now, stop these manœuvres and ambushes and false sallies and all your simple strategy, and meet me in the open field. Was it Wrestling Brewster that I saw sitting with Lora on her sunset seat?"

"I know not what you saw, Myles, but I know that Wrestling Brewster went up there to find Lora something like a half hour ago."

"And you knew it?"

"I sent him."

"You sent him! And for what?"

"For naught more than to find her, but I can guess his errand though he told it not."

"Oh! And might the father of the maid venture so much as to ask what this errand might be?"

"Nay, Myles, be not so bitter! If I cannot go with you in this matter, 'tis because I love my child even more than you can love her."

"Love your child! Love your own way and your own will, as you ever have done! Woman, do you defy me?"

"Oh, Myles, Myles!" And fearlessly approaching the angry man, Barbara laid a hand upon his arm and looked straight into his face with all her brave and noble soul shining out of those eyes whose wonderful charm time had not clouded in the least. The captain met them, and the terror of his frown subsided into an angry laugh.

"Well—you should not thwart me if you would not see me thwarted. But honestly, Barbara, have you forgotten or do you despise my constant wish for Lora's future? Must I mind you once more of my contract with my cousin Ralph whereby his eldest son is to marry our daughter, and so to her and her children shall be restored the fair domain which his grandsire stole from mine? Know you not that naught in all this world sits nearer to my heart than this scheme, and that only last month I wrote to Ralph and told him that Lora was now turned eighteen, and if his boy was ready to fulfill the contract I would come to England with the maid, and see her seated at Standish Hall? Mind you all that, Mistress Barbara?"

"Ay, Myles, I mind it well, and I mind too that you did not tell me of that letter till 'twas gone."

"Haply not, but what of that? Is a man bound to lay all his business before his wife, or to ask her leave to write to his own kinsman?"

"'Tis my kinsman in the same degree, mind you, husband. And because I too am born of Standish I have a right to speak, I have a right to know, and to decide in this matter,—yes, as good a right as yours, Myles."

"Oho! 'Tis a cartel of battle, is it? Partlet against Chanticleer, eh? Well, our cousins the Standishes of Duxbury carry a gamecock for their crest, and I'll e'en borrow his spurs."

"Oh, Myles, Myles! This over-weening ambition of thine hath turned thy brain! When till now didst ever treat me thus?"

"Nay, I'll not be wheedled with soft touch, nor tearful eyen, nor broken voice. There, there, let go mine arm and wipe thy tears away! Why, thou foolish lass, dost not know I'd liever face a tribe of Pequods than see thee weep? Tut, tut, silly wench, give me a kiss and be done with it. What chance hath Samson when Delilah cries?"

"But, dear my lord, listen now that your mood is somewhat softened. How can you be so sure that this great marriage will make our dear maid happy? You know how tender and how sensitive she is; you know how she clings to love, and seems to draw her life from us as the flowers do from the sun; sure am I, as sure as of to-day's breath, that parted from home and father and mother and brothers and friends and all she has ever loved and clung to, our Lora would droop and die just as that sea-bird did that the boys caught and tried to tame."

"And if she did!" cried the captain, flaming again into sudden wrath, the reflex perhaps of a stinging pain driven through his heart by his wife's last words. "Had not she better die as mistress of Standish Hall and be buried with her ancestors in the tomb of the Standishes than to vegetate here as the wife of Wrestling Brewster and fill a nameless grave in these wilds?"

"Since God has forsaken you and the Evil One seized upon your mind, I have naught more to say," returned Barbara, thoroughly angry on her own side; and as she turned into the house Standish, with a black frown darkening his whole presence, strode away toward the hill.

Almost an hour earlier Wrestling Brewster, making his way softly over the fallen leaves and ripe mosses of the hillside path, had stolen unawares upon as fair a picture as Captain's Hill has ever seen, or ever shall while time and earth endure.

Very nearly where the monument stands to-day, there then grew a clump of oaks, and between two of them had been fixed a commodious bench, with a back quaintly carved and ornamented with a border of red cedar. From this vantage-point could be seen a fairer view than that of to-day, for man had not yet conquered Nature, nor substituted his uncouth and commonplace works for her perfection.

Clark's Island, still covered with its primeval cedars and with its northern headland unwasted and majestic, lay like a bower upon the great field of flowing water, and matched Saquish, still an island, but beginning to throw out tentative arms toward the Gurnet's Head, where six hundred years before Thorwald, brother of Leif, wounded unto death by the savages, desired to be buried, with a cross at his head and another at his feet, directing that the headland should thenceforth be known as Krossness. Toward these yearned the loving arm thrown out by Manomet toward the Duxbury shore,—that arm now reduced to a barren sandspit, but then a green and fruit-laden peninsula; and within it glittered in the evening light the harbor, deep enough at that day to float not only the Mayflower, but Captain Pierce's Lyon, which now lay snugly anchored there, while the governor's barge rowed away toward the town, bearing Bradford and Winslow home with the jolly mariner as their guest. Blue smoke-wreaths floating idly upward from Plymouth cottages told of housewives busy with the evening meal, and upon the crest of Burying Hill a twinkling gleam now and again showed that Lieutenant Holmes did not suffer the brasswork of the colony's guns to grow dim now that they had come under his care.

But closer at hand than these things stretched the marshes, the beautiful Duxbury marshes with their grasses full grown and ripe, reposing under the sunset light like a fair garden, where great masses of color lay in harmonious contrast, and the heavy heads of seed bent, and rippled, and rustled to the evening breeze, murmuring sweet secrets that he carried straight out to sea and buried there.

O man, man! Lay out your modern gardens, and mass your pelargoniums and calceolarias and begonias and salvias and the rest, in beds of contrasting color, and then, if you would note your improvement upon ancient methods, go in the autumn and look at the marshes of the Old Colony, laid out by Mother Nature before Thorwald selected Krossness first as his chosen home, and then his chosen grave.

So fair, so wonderful, so entrancing, lay the view that evening at the foot of Captain's Hill, yet Wrestling Brewster, albeit a man of singular delicacy of perception, never saw it; saw nothing, in fact, but the lissome form of a young maid clothed in white samite, with pale golden hair wound around her head and held by quaint silver pins with crystal heads that now and again caught the light and sent it flashing back like the aureole of a saint. The great gray eyes, wide open beneath their level brows, were steadfastly fixed upon some point far out at sea, the vanishing point of earth's curve, the point where the straightforward look of human eyes glides off the surface of the globe and penetrates the ether beyond. What vision arose before the maiden's eyes in that dim horizon realm? What thought or what dream parted the soft mouth, and tinged the pure pallor of the cheek? What meant the sigh that just stirred the flower at her throat?

So asked the heart of the young man standing motionless and devout in the edge of the little grove, until with the feeling of one who intrudes upon sacred mysteries he withdrew his gaze, and rustled the twigs of the shrub beside him. The girl turned quickly, and as she met his eyes smiled gently.

"Oh, is it you, Ras? I'm glad you came."

"Are you, Lora? Are you glad I came? And I am glad that you are glad."

"'Tis so fair, so heavenly a scene that I would all I love might enjoy it as well as I."

"Lora! All you love, say you? Oh, Lora, do you love me?"

"Ras! Nay, let us not speak of just ourselves; we are so little and the sky is so great."

"The sky, dear? But the sky and the sea and the forest, they are always here, and we may look at them all our lives long,—all our lives, Lora, our two lives that might be one."

The gray eyes, still full of dreams, still questioning the far-off depths of the skies beyond the sea, reluctantly turned and rested fearlessly upon the eager and troubled face of the young man.

"What is it, Ras dear? Why are you so—so troubled is it? Why don't you sit down here beside me and look as we have looked so often upon all this beauty? It was so good of you, Ras, to make this seat for me. It is the happiest place I know in all the world."

"Then make it happiest to me, darling, by letting it be the place of our betrothal. Oh, Lora, I thought you knew,—I thought you understood, and—and—yes, I even dared to hope that you, just in some far-off maidenly, saintly fashion, felt somewhat the love that devours me like death until I know for certain that it is returned, and then indeed shall I pass from death unto life. Speak, Lora,—speak for God's dear sake, speak to me."

"But why are you so moved, Ras, and why after all these years of love and friendliness do you beg me as if I were some stranger to say that I love you?"

"Lora! Lora! You break my heart!"

"Oh, Ras, dear dear Ras! Don't look so, don't speak so! There are very tears in your eyes, and see, they call the tears to mine! Why truly, dear Ras, I love you, I love you dearly, as well as I love Alick or Josias,—as well as I love Betty Alden, who is the dearest friend I have, as well as"—

"Stop, stop, for pity's sake! I thought I suffered before, but oh, Lora, you have given me my deathblow."

"Nay, what is it, what is it I have done? What a wicked wretch I am to grieve you so, but how is it, dear? Indeed I do love you, Ras, I do indeed!"

"Yes, you love me as a child loves, as an angel loves, as you loved me years ago when I, already come to man's estate, watched you growing to womanhood like a sweet flower, and vowed that you, and none but you, should be my wife; and for the sake of that vow and for love of you,—yes, an ever growing love of you, mine own sweet love,—I have never looked upon a maiden's face save as a woman might. I have cared so little for their company that they flout me"—

"Yes, they call you the old bachelor," interrupted Lora, half merrily and half penitently. "But I never once dreamed it was for love of me you held yourself so strange to all the others. But now I do know, Ras, it seems no more than honest that you should have what you have waited for, and if you want me for your wife, and my father and my mother make no objection, why I will please you thus far."

"You will—you will be my wife!" exclaimed Wrestling. "Oh, Lora, do you mean it? Do you really, really mean that you will be my wife?"

"It seems to me, young man, that I have somewhat to say in this matter," broke in a strident voice, and Lora looked up in dismay at her father's face, very angry, very ominous, yet not turned upon her. At a later day Myles Standish was glad to remember that even in this extremity he never spoke one angry word, or cast one angry look to the child who was the idol of his life.

"Oh—Captain Standish!" stammered Wrestling, springing to his feet.

"Yes, Master Brewster, Captain Standish at your service, who ventures to suggest that you might have done better to ask his leave before urging his daughter to defy his wishes."

"Oh, father!" And Lora, rising to her slender height, stepped forward and fearlessly slid a soft little hand into the captain's brawny half-closed fist. "Defy you, father!" murmured she, looking into his face with eyes of loving reproach, "nay, I never could do that."

"I know it, my pet, I know it; but there, make you home as soon as ever you may—mother is waiting for you—run away, child, run."

"Nay, father, but I fain would know first why you are so angry with my dear friend Ras. He says he loves me very much, and he wants me to be his wife, and I love him too, and if you please to have it so, I said I would marry him"—

"As you might have said you would take a sail with him!" exclaimed the captain with angry fondness in his tone; but the fondness died away as his eyes turned from the fair face of his daughter to the flushed and anxious one of her suitor, while he said,—

"You may see for yourself, Wrestling Brewster, that this child knows not the meaning of marriage love. She is no fonder of you than of—say Betty Alden, or mayhap her pet cat"—

"Nay, nay, father, I must not let that go unsaid! Not love Ras better than I do Moppet! Oh, but I do!"

"Lora, if you will stay here, do not speak again until I speak to you," commanded the father sternly.

"I would not be harsh upon you, young sir, for you are son of mine honored friend, Elder Brewster, and I believe a worthy son, but you did amiss, yes, shrewdly amiss, in speaking to my daughter before you did to me."

Wrestling's lips opened and closed again. He was about to say that Lora's mother knew of his suit, but in the captain's mood, that plea might only have brought down wrath upon his wife's head.

"I have not found it fitting to tell all my affairs to all my neighbors," pursued Standish haughtily. "But I have mine own intent with regard to my daughter, and that intent is not to marry her in this colony. Let that be answer enough for you, Master Wrestling, and if you like, you may advertise any other aspiring youth that designs to honor my daughter with an offer that it is but needless mortification, for my answer will be to all as it is to you,—nay, nay, nay!"

And with the last word Myles placed his daughter's hand under his arm and led her down the hill, leaving Wrestling to cast himself prone upon the sunset seat, his face hidden upon the back of it, and his eyes smarting with the tears his manhood refused to allow to flow.

Almost at home, Standish, looking with anxious love into the lily face at his shoulder, said,—

"Poppet, you're not over-sorry, are you? Why don't you speak to me?"

"You bade me not speak until you spoke to me, father dear. Nay, but I am sorry, heartily sorry, you should have chided Ras so hardly. Poor lad! He was fit to cry when we left him."

"But you do not really care for him, dear child? You are not set upon becoming his—his wife?"

"Nay, father, I do not care to be any man's wife. I would far fainer stay at home with you and mother, but Ras seemed so keen upon the matter and declared I loved him not, that to make him content I said yes; for indeed I do love him, father, more than I love any man after you and the boys."

"Ha, ha! My little lass, there'll come a day when the boys, and haply your poor old dad as well, will fly down the wind like thistledown before the love that still lieth sound asleep in my maid's pure heart."

"Nay, father, not asleep, but too dear and too holy to be spoken of," murmured Lora, a soft flush upon her cheek, a tender light in her eyes as she raised them to her father's face.

"What! what!" stammered he, half affrighted lest the girl had lost her senses. "You love some one already!"

"Oh, father, so much, so dearly! 'Tis for that I love to go and sit all alone there upon the brow of the hill, where I may see the beauty He has made and gaze away and away into the heavens where He lives. Sure the hills of Judah were not so lovely as this place, and who can tell but some day He may descend and stand visibly upon them"—

"Aha!" breathed the captain, stopping short and gazing appalled upon the face of the girl, set seaward, with a half smile upon its lips and a look of yearning love in the unfathomable eyes. But as he gazed she turned, and throwing an arm around his neck hid her face upon his breast with a sobbing sigh.

"Oh, father dear, I'm sorry I tried to speak about what no words can tell. Don't talk to mother or to any one, will you, dear, and please do not ask me again. 'Tis so precious and so wonderful, and 'tis all the love I ever want beyond my home loves. You won't talk about it, daddy dear, will you?"

"One word, Lora. You mean that your love is given to God alone?"

"To Him who loved me and gave Himself for me—to Him who is chief among ten thousand and altogether lovely—to the King in his beauty in the land that is very far off."

"My child, my child!" groaned the father, drawing the girl's form close to his thickly beating heart and pressing his lips upon her brow, while Jephthah's agony turned him sick and white, and his eyes rose with an almost angry protest to the skies.

CHAPTER XXVI.

GILLIAN.

The apple-bee at Jonathan Brewster's house by the Eagle's Tree, where The Nook merges into Harden Hill, was in full tide, and one could hear the merry voices of men and maidens, and the cheerful shrilling of matrons talking above the din, before one reached the house. Beneath a clump of trees surrounding the great cedar known as the Eagle's Tree a number of horses were tied with comfortable measures of corn and trusses of hay before them, and in the little cove lay half a dozen or so boats uneasily tumbling upon the incoming tide. These conveyances had brought the remoter dwellers in the new town of Duxbury and its neighborhood: the Aldens from Eagle Tree Pond, the De la Noyes from Stony Brook, the Soules from Powder Point, the Constant Southworths from North River, the Howlands from Island Creek, the Bassetts from Beaver Pond, and the Abraham Samsons from Bluefish River where they lived neighbors to the Aldens and intermarried with them.

Of The Nook people who came on foot, the Standishes, and Brewsters, and Pabodies, and Prences, and Colliers, and Doctor Comfort Starr, the new physician, with his family, and the Partridges, and Wadsworths, and others, had mustered strong and in every variety of condition, age, and sex; for our ancestors, having far fewer opportunities of amusement than we have, made a great deal more of each one as it came along, and not only sucked the juice from their orange, but ate every bit of the pulp. The apple-bee was but a prelude to the evening's entertainment, and for weeks before, every young girl in the colony had planned her dress and simple ornaments, and dreamed of some face or voice that should belong to her own especial Robin Adair, or of the games and the songs and haply the contradances that might be permitted when the church-members had withdrawn; and Lucretia Brewster, with her daughter Mary and Love's wife Sarah, and such fantastic aid as Gillian had chosen to bestow, had been for a week busy in preparing the house and a big shed just finished, for the reception of the expected guests and their steeds.

Gillian! Well, Gillian! And when one has said her name the subject widens until it becomes impossible to handle. Niece of Lucretia Brewster, whose sister had married a Spaniard, this Gillian, left a deserted orphan in some foreign port, had drifted back to England, and thence to New England, where a year or so before the apple-bee she had arrived by hand of Captain William Pierce, consigned along with a present of kersey and Hollands linen to Jonathan Brewster by a cousin who claimed that, as Lucretia was the girl's nearest relative, her maintenance should fall upon Lucretia's husband. At first the charge was joyfully accepted, for Gillian was just the age of Mary, Jonathan's only daughter, and would be a sister to her, as they said. But as the weeks and months went on both Mary and her mother grew silent upon the subject of the new sister, while Jonathan, and his sons William and Jonathan and Benjamin, never ceased to congratulate the women and each other upon the joy and delight of her presence; the father especially often calling upon his wife to recognize how in this case virtue had brought its own reward, and their benevolence to the orphan received a blessing of singular richness almost in the first moments of its exercise.

To these pious thanksgivings Lucretia Brewster, who was a very discreet woman, never offered any contradiction; but when next her husband found some little matter essential to his comfort neglected, or some detail of the rigid family rule calmly set aside, the gentle explanation was, "I left it to Gillian to do;" or, "It was Gillian who chose to do it in spite of all I said."

On these occasions Gillian sometimes came by a little reprimand, not half as severe, so Mary jealously remarked, as was administered to her very lightest offense, but apparently more than Gillian could bear, for before it was half over she would fall into such a passion of tears and sobs as seemed fit to rend her white throat asunder, and either crouch moaning upon the floor in some corner like a wounded creature, or rush headlong from the house to the woods, where she would hide all day long, and once all night long, although Brewster and his three sons searched and called for her till sunrise, when she appeared on the edge of a thicket, her wonderful deep red hair hanging all matted and tangled, with briers around her shoulders, her great passionate Spanish eyes dilated and full of gloomy fire, and her mouth, that bewildering, tempting, ripe red mouth, with its myriad expressions and suggestions, its curves and dimples, and its little laughing teeth, all drawn and pale.

Is it to be wondered at that, after the first few times, the uncle and guardian ceased to attempt even the discipline of a reproof, especially as for days after one of these passions the girl would shrink out of his presence with every mark of terror, and if he spoke to her, reply in hurried, timorous accents, with the air of one who dreads to give offense, and fears unmerited blame or misunderstanding.

So at last it came to pass that Gillian did what she would, and left undone what she chose, and quietly setting at naught all Lucretia's admonitions or attempts at control, was ever bright and charming to her uncle, and remained a wonder and a fascination to the boys, who were all wildly in love with her, a condition shared by nearly every unmarried man in the Old Colony.

As for Mary, good, homely, ungraceful, slow moulded Mary Brewster, she wore herself thin and peevish in struggling against the innate depravity of her own heart which continually urged her to hate Gillian with a bitter hatred, more especially when John Turner, of Scituate, came a-wooing, and Gillian, having contemplated his courtship during a few visits, picked him up as a kitten might a great lumbering beetle, tossed him hither and yon, patted him with her velvet paws, suddenly thrust sharp claws through the velvet, gave him one or two contemptuous buffets to this side and to that, and finally walked away, purring serene indifference.

John Turner was perhaps the only man at the apple-bee who saw nothing to admire in Gillian, and Mary never looked her way. But Betty liked her, and now, as the girl flitted into the great kitchen where around the baskets and piles of apples, brought together from all the neighborhood for Lucretia Brewster to dry in her own superlative fashion, crowded the maids and matrons, who pared and cored, and quartered or sliced, the rosy fruit, it was Betty Alden who cried,—

"Oh, Jill, is that you? Come help me string these slices. These are our own apples, and mother wants to keep them separate from the rest, so Sally and Ruthy and I are doing them."

"Did your brother Jo pick them?" asked Gillian, sinking down in her peculiar and graceful fashion upon the floor, beside Betty, but not offering to take the needle threaded with coarse flax that Sally held toward her.

"Jo and David picked them, you naughty girl, and talked of naught but you while they did it."

"Betty, Betty, here's Alick Standish coming this way, and don't you blush; now mind you, Betty, don't you blush! Fie! but you do! What makes her hate Alick so, Sally?" asked Gillian maliciously.

"Who hates Alick?" asked the cheery voice of the good-looking "heir apparent" of Myles Standish, who had obeyed a glance of Gillian's eyes and joined the group.

"Who but the one who colors red as fire with vexation when he draws nigh," replied the girl coolly; and Standish, curiously regarding the faces of the three, perceived that both Betty's and Sally's faces were aflame, while Gillian's cream-white skin looked cool as a calla lily.

"Are you paring the apples I picked, Gillian?" asked another voice as David Alden joined the group.

"Nay, for 'twas Satan who first plucked an apple for a woman," replied Jill, with a mocking little laugh; and Alick whispered in her ear, "There's ne'er a son of Adam would refuse if you offered him the apple, Gillian."

"What! not if he lost Paradise thereby?"

"The paradise of your love would"—

"Oh, Master Pabodie, do come and reason with these terrible blasphemers who are talking of Satan and nobody can tell what else. Say to Master Pabodie what you were saying to me, Alick!"

Thus dared, the young man looked half of mind to accept the challenge, but John Pabodie, shrewdly glancing at the audacious girl, replied, "Nay, mistress, I'm twenty years too old and haply twenty years too young to cope with such a matter. But here's my son William just come home from Boston and farther, and I'll leave him to fill the place of Paris, if one may quote the old mythologies in a Christian land."

"Surely, when such a Helen rises before one's eyes," added a sonorous young voice, as Gillian suddenly stood up, her sinuous and suggestive figure displayed in a gown of creamy mull clinging to every curve, and covering yet not concealing the exquisite roundness of arms and shoulders white with that peculiar *mat* whiteness never seen save in persons of Latin blood.

"Who was Helen?" asked Gillian very slowly, while the velvety darkness of her eyes rested with infantile confidence upon the handsome face of William Pabodie, who, after the pause of an instant, said significantly,—

"The handsomest woman that ever lived."

A little silence ensued, and all eyes turned upon Gillian, who, nothing daunted, softly replied,—

"She must have been well pleased when Paris told her so."

"Welcome home, William Pabodie!" cried Lucretia Brewster's wholesome voice, scattering as with a puff of west wind the strained and bewildering atmosphere that seemed stifling the little group around the Spanish girl. "You know all these lads and lasses, your old neighbors, and I see that you have already made acquaintance with my niece Gillian,—Gillian Brewster, as we call her"—

"My name is Gillian de Cavalcanti," interposed Gillian quietly, but Lucretia, flushing angrily, continued without looking at her, "If you will come with me, Will, I will take you to Mary and some other friends, Lora Standish and her guest, Mercy Bradford from Plymouth."

"My sister Anice well-nigh raves over Mistress Lora Standish," replied the young man, following his hostess, but even as he did so turning to look once more at Gillian, whose eyes, soft and dewy as a chidden child's, followed him with a vague appeal that sent a tremor through the young man's heart.

"Can it be that her aunt does not treat her well?" asked he of himself, and his next reply to Lucretia was so cold that she turned and looked at him, and then remembering said to herself,—

"The poison works quickly."

The apples were pared, cored, quartered, or sliced, and, threaded upon twine, hung in festoons upon a frame erected for the purpose on the south side of the house; the cores and skins and smaller apples were heaped into the cider-press, which on the morrow would begin its work of reducing them to the cheerful and wholesome beverage as essential to our forefathers' comfort as tea and coffee are to ours; the bountiful supper had been eaten and merrily cleared away by a committee of bustling matrons, and at last the great houseplace, the shed, and a platform extending for some distance from the house were "sided off" and swept, to make room for the frolics which to the young people were the true meaning of the whole affair. "Kissing games" were in that day not more objectionable than round dances are now, and perhaps that visitor from Jupiter to whom we sometimes refer for impartial judgment would have found them less so. Both classes of amusement depend very much upon who indulges in them, and when Gillian's soft warm lips frankly pressed William Pabodie's mouth a quick flush mounted to the young man's temples, and he cast a startled glance into the dark eyes upraised to his with a look of fathomless meaning. Lucretia Brewster saw that look, and her own matronly cheek colored angrily. Later in the evening she sat herself down beside her sister-in-law, with whom she was on very affectionate terms.

"Tired, 'Cretia?" asked Mistress Love Brewster with a pleasant smile.

"No, not to say tired, Sally, but a good deal worked up."

"About what?"

"Well, one thing and another. You know my Mary's to be married Thanksgiving Day, and John Turner joins hands with her in begging me to go to Scituate along with them and set her off in her housekeeping. You know, being the only girl, she never's quite let go of mammy's apron string; and for that matter, I'm as loath to part with her as ever she can be with me."

"Then, why not go?" asked Sarah sympathetically. "I'm sure the change will be good for you, and you've had a mort of work and worry lately."

"Yes, I know, but—well, I'll tell you, Sally. I don't want to go away and leave Jonathan and the boys with nobody to do for them."

"Why, there's Jill and your Indian woman Quoy."

"Yes, Quoy knows all about the house, and can get the meals and all that as well if I was away as if I was here; but Gillian"—

"Why—yes, I suppose I know what you mean, 'Cretia. You'd be just as well content if Gillian wasn't here, eh?"

"Full as well," replied Lucretia with emphasis, and gazed full in her sister's face. Then both turned and looked at the girl who, crying, "Button, button, who's got the button?" was daintily trying to pry open the stalwart fist of Josias Standish, while Mary Dingley looked uneasily on.

"Yes," said Sarah softly, as if answering some unspoken appeal. "And you don't want to take her?"

"Take her, no! I believe Mary wouldn't be married at all if it was to carry that girl along with her."

"Well, 'Cretia, I'll take her, for a while at least. You know the Elder is with us more than he is at Plymouth, and I'll lay she won't carry on lightly under his eyes. I never knew any man like Father Brewster in my life! He'd make the Old Boy behave himself, I believe, and never say a hard word to him neither; and my boys are but boys, and I'll risk Love."

"Oh, it isn't Jonathan I'm afraid of," said Jonathan's wife quickly. "But"—

"Oh, don't you say a word," interrupted Sarah with a little laugh. "I know all about it, and it's just as it should be; but it would be main lonesome for a young maid here with none but men for company, and I'll ask her to come and make me a visit."

"Will you? Now that's comfortable of you, Sally, right comfortable and friendly," replied Lucretia, rising to attend her summons, but with a face so relieved from care and worry that Jonathan, meeting her, whispered softly,—

"I'd liever look at thee than any of the young lasses, sweetheart."

CHAPTER XXVII.

DONNA MARIA DE LOS DOLORES.

The weeks and the months gliding along with their exasperating illustration of the *festina lente* principle brought a morning of early spring, chill but bright, with a merry sun contending in the sky against some unseen adversary who continually pelted him with great white snowballs of cloud, which he either evaded or melted with the fervor of his breath. In the farmhouse built by the Elder for himself and Love, but not passing into the possession of Love and Love's wife, a great fire of cedar logs burned fragrantly upon the hearth of the sitting-room, and flashed its light upon the silver tankard and cup burnished to their utmost brightness, and modestly boasting themselves upon the little mahogany elbow-table in the nook beside the fire, conveniently at hand to the leathern easy-chair, so inharmonious with our ideas of ease, which with a footstool in front was the Elder's seat of an evening, or in the brief repose he in these latter days allowed himself after dinner, or when in the short and stormy winter days he could do nothing but sit beside the fire and delight his soul with study.

In this blithe March morning, however, the old man was out with his son and the oxen breaking up fallow ground, and chanting half aloud brave verses of Holy Writ as he guided the team while Love's mighty arms held down the ploughshare.

"'O let the earth bless the Lord; yea, let it praise Him, and magnify Him forever!

"'O all ye green things upon the earth, bless ye the Lord; praise Him, and magnify Him forever!

"'O ye seas and floods, bless ye the Lord; praise Him, and magnify Him forever!

"'O ye children of men, bless ye the Lord; praise Him, and magnify Him forever!

"'O let Israel bless the Lord; praise Him, and magnify Him forever!'"

"Wow! but this new colter is heavy; let us rest a minute, father," cried Love, feigning to pant and wipe his brow, but really appalled at the look of his father's face, and fearing to see him rapt out of his sight as was Elijah from that of Elisha.

"Rest? Ay, ay, I should have sooner remembered you, my boy. Yes, yes, rest if you need it, lad, rest and don't strain your young muscles till they're seasoned like mine."

But reverent son though he was, Love, as he turned to lift the yoke and pat his oxen a bit, did not deny himself a slow smile of sober amusement.

In the sunny sitting-room, Gillian, with the firelight in her ruddy hair, moved around, dusting and arranging the place, and especially ordering the chair and footstool dedicated to her best friend. But why, when she had wiped away the last grain of dust, and placed the stool at just the best angle, and even drawn the wolfskin mat a trifle out of the centre that it might reach the front legs of the chair, why did she all at once cross her arms upon the high back, and, bowing her head upon them, sob as though her heart would break, and suffer a few great tears like the first drops of a tropic thunder-shower to roll down the leathern back and under the comfortless cushion? Lora Standish, coming noiselessly through the door from the kitchen, stood a moment wondering in the doorway, then half timidly exclaimed,—

"Why, Gillian, what's the matter?"

"Oh! It's you, is it, or is't a ghost that it looks like? Let's try it!" And with a sudden gliding motion, too much like that of a snake for beauty, Gillian seized her visitor by the arm, inflicting such a nip with her cruel slender fingers as left its mark for many a day. The blood flew for a moment to Lora's cheek, but it was the blood of warriors, and she only said as she drew back a step,—

"I am looking for Mistress Brewster. Do you know where she is?"

"Yes, gone over to John Alden's to help Priscilla in some mystery of housecraft; but come you in and sit down for a minute or so, or I'll think, you proud peat, that you mean to slight me."

"Why should I want to slight you, Gillian?" replied Lora with the angelic smile that distinguished her, as, throwing aside the little white scarf around her head and shoulders, she came forward to the fire, and leaning against the high mantelpiece put a foot upon the fender, looking frankly the while into the sombre face of the other girl.

"Oh, well,—oh, well!" muttered Gillian after a moment. "'Tis well you're angel-like, since so soon you'll see them."

"What say you, Gillian? 'Tis well I'm what, said you?"

"Nay, sit you down, maiden,—sit you here in the Elder's chair and put your feet to the fire, upon his footstool. There, now, be biddable and meek, as fits your face."

"Why, Jill, 'twas but yesterday that you almost smote Betty Alden to the ground because she would have sat in that chair; and after all, 'tis not half so comfortable as mother's splint chair."

"Oh, ay," replied Gillian, as she turned toward the bookcase and began brushing the books with a wild turkey's wing, "that's different,—that's different. I wouldn't have let you sit there but for what I saw a minute gone by."

"What you saw!" echoed Lora, not overmuch moved, for Gillian's vagaries had long since been voted insoluble by the simple folk of The Nook. "And what was't you saw?"

"Now, now! Can you read, Lora?"

"Yes. Father taught me when I was but a little trot. I learned as fast as the boys, he said."

"Well, a priest taught me just as a man of the outside world would have taught a parrot or an ape. All the people who have done me any good have done it for their pleasure or their pride, and I'm naught beholden to them. But these books!—I often spell out their titles when I'm dull, and tired of laughing at men and women. Now hark you, Lora, here's some of 'em:

A Toyle for 2 legged Foxes.

A Cordiall for Comfort.

Burton wearing His Spur.

Memorable Conceits.

Jacob's Ladder.

The Review of Rome.

Troubles of ye Church of Amsterdam.

A Garland of Vertuous Dames.

Romances of Brittannia.

"There, heard you ever the like? It ever seems to me as if these writer folk hetcheled their brains to find some title for their books that will prick curiosity to the quick and force a man to buy, that he may certify himself what 'A Toyle for 2 Legged Foxes' may truly mean. Is't not so?"

"Haply. I'll get father to beg the Elder to lend him that 'Romance of Brittannia,' for it sounds right relishing in mine ears."

"And you love to read?"

"Dearly well."

"Then you should have been a nun. They made much of me at Los Dolores, because I could, when I would, read the 'Life of Teresa de Jesus' to them."

"And when you would not, could you not?" asked Lora mischievously.

"Indeed I couldn't. I miscalled the words, I gabbled, I lost my place, I dropped the book, I doubled the corners and broke the parchment,—oh, they were glad enough to let me off, the poor nuns, the poor nuns!"

"And did you like the convent, Gillian?" asked Lora, so wistfully that the other paused a moment as if struck with a new idea; then throwing down her turkey's wing she crouched upon the wolfskin, and nursing a knee between her clasped hands looked up into the pale face clearly defined against the dark leather of the chair-back, as she slowly said,—

"Why, what a nun you'd make, Lora Standish! Passing strange I never thought of it before."

"Methinks 'twould be a happy life," replied Lora, stifling a sigh.

"Happy! Well, for you it may be. Your father is of the old religion, is he not?"

"I do not know, для he says naught and will hear naught about it. You know he will not join the church here, although mother belongs to it, and when we all were christened he said lay baptism was better than none; but he goes to meeting as we all do, and gives as much as any man to the support of the minister. He knows best, doubtless, and mother and I do not much care to know all his mind."

"Oh, ay!" replied Gillian, who had listened attentively, and now shook her head as if discarding some plan. Then lowering her gaze from Lora's face to the fire, now crumbling into caverns, and vistas, and toppling turrets, and fantastic feathery piles of ashes, she slowly said,—

"'Tis out of possibility, but I would well have liked to see you a sister of Donna Maria de los Dolores. It would have been a heaven on earth to you, and the guimpe and coif and barb ought to suit you as jewels do me.

"Oh 'twas so fair there betimes!" continued she with sudden passion. "I mind me of one even just before my father fetched me away to see my mother die, one even in deep midsummer, and after vespers we walked in the garden, the sisters and another girl and I. Such a garden, Lora, oh, such a garden as you never dreamed of in these hateful northern solitudes! Closed all round with a high gray stone wall covered with passion flowers and jessamine and gay trumpet flowers, a bank of bloom and greenery that seemed to us the end of the world, for the banana-trees no more than reached the top of it, and inside, smooth green walks bordered with every flower that grows, and more especially all that are sweet and bewildering of perfume; for, Lora, when a woman puts on a nun's robes she does not cease to be a woman, and while with the one hand she flings her flask of essences and her pomander box into the fire, with the other she plants a bed of pinks, to flaunt their color and send up their spicy odors for her delight."

"Who cared for the garden at Los Dolores?" asked Lora, vaguely uneasy at the other's tone.

"Oh, the sisters one and another. 'Twas rare recreation for them, and never permitted to those in penitence. They even mowed the lawns, and shaved the paths, and rolled the gravel, for it was a great and wide garden, with room in it for one to get away alone and entertain the blue devils in solitude."

"Nay, Gillian, but could devils, blue or black, ever overpass that high wall you told of?"

"Could they? Oh, well—at least they never would have found you when they searched for prey, so much I believe, maid Lora."

"But tell me more of the garden."

"Well, as I say, 'twas wide and fair and perfectly ordered, and there was a fountain where a poor ball still was tossed up and down, up and down upon the current, till I used by times to snatch it off in very pity and toss it into a posy-bed to rest awhile, but Sister Marina always found it and put it back. Then there were bosquets, where the sun never came; and there were bordered walks, and benches under some great cork-trees at the foot of the garden; and there were, in their time, Annunciation lilies as fair and sweet as that Señor Don Gabriel laid at the feet of Madonna Mary, and roses like those among which she laid her little Jesu to sleep; and there were incense trees where the berries and gums and bark grew that the sisters gathered so solemnly, and dried and brayed in a special mortar, and that smelt so sweet when the sister thurifer swung her censer up and down, and this way and that, to keep it alight till the priest who said mass on the great days was ready to take it from her.

"And there were goldfish in the fountain and birds in the trees,—oh, such glorious birds, and some of them so sweet of song! and there was a pond where the nuns fattened great fishes for Friday dinners, and feasted better on them than on the flesh of other days.

"But I was going to tell you of a time, one of the last times I ever walked in that garden or slept in my little whitewashed cell at Dolores. Ah, now, mayhap I had been a better girl had they left me there. Well, we walked up and down the wide grassy middle alley, the sisters, and Inez de Soza and I, and all of us were merry, for the Mother Superior was in a good temper and the prioress had got on her talking-cap, and we girls and the novices asked no better than to laugh at all our elders' jests and cry Oh, marvelous! to all their stories, when all at once the sister portress came down the old mossy steps from the house, and kneeling to the Superior, who bade her rise, for it was recreation time and all rules were relaxed, she told her that a Dominican friar was at the gate with a comrade and asked lodging in the priest's chamber outside the wall.

"'But surely! When did we refuse hospitality to a holy man, Sister Juana?' replied the mother. 'Have him in with his comrade and give him supper in the sacristy; when he has refreshed himself I will see him there.'

"'But he also begs permission to preach to the sisters,' persisted old Juana, who was as obstinate as a mule; and as the Mother paused upon her reply, Inez and I who held her hands cried,—

"'Oh, do, reverend Mother, oh, do let us hear a sermon!' and she laughing said:—

"'Well, yes, perhaps 'twill turn your hearts from the world to religion as I have not been able to do.'

"So we walked another turn or so and then went into the chapel, which was full of that soft purple shadow that fills such places as the night falls without. The wide door to the garden stood open, and I placed myself at the end of the bench so that I could well look out and see and smell and listen to the world while the friar should talk of religion.

"Oh, maiden, 'twas as strange an hour and as sweet as ever I knew or shall know! Outside was that fair garden, with the last rays of the sun touching the crests of the trees, the palms and cork-trees and acacias, and the fountain vainly leaping up to reach the sunlight, and the birds at their vespers, and the blinding sweets of the posy-beds, and just outside the door a great banana-tree that swayed and rustled in the breeze, and threw its long green leaves like wooing arms in at the door as if to drag me out, wooed me so strangely that if I looked and listened too long I must have yielded and leaped out to its embrace. And inside there was the dusky chapel with the pictures of the saints glimmering from the walls, and the white Christ upon his cross with his eyes downbent to mine, and such a passion of pleading in them as seemed to drag the heart from my breast, and the sisters in their white robes and rosaries, tinkling beads, and the blue cross sewed upon the breast of each fading into the white, and their pure profiles downcast as they listened; and there above us all in the dim obscurity of the place the pulpit, of some black wood, and rising out of it that gaunt gray figure of the friar, his face pale and worn, his eyes ablaze with the fervor of his thought, his emaciated hands upraised, and his air now that of an angel of mercy, now a minister of vengeance and wrath.

"Oh, how he preached, that man! How his words poured out like a river in spring and carried all before them like that river in a freshet! Long ere he was done I was on my knees crying my heart out, and bowing myself to God in a life of sanctity and religion,—had he given me the chance, I would have dedicated myself as a novice that very night; and before he was done I had whispered to Inez,—

"'Take your vows with me to-morrow,' but she replied,—

"'Yon comrade of the friar is no monk!' And looking where she looked I saw close by the door where the Dominican had placed him a man in a friar's robe and cowl to be sure, but with bold black eyes that gazed like those of a caged bird at all around, resting most often upon Inez and me, who were the only ones who wore not the sisters' livery, but our own white school frocks and little caps. Somehow the sight of that face and the regard of those bold eyes scattered all my holy mood as the sun scorches up the dew and— But there, there, I'll say naught to shock you, pale saint. 'Twas a fair picture, though, was't not?"

"Yes, passing fair," replied Lora dreamily, "and I were well content to spend my life in such a blessed retreat."

"Your life, maiden! Nay, you have faith in God?"

"Why surely, Gillian! Who has not?" And Lora's clear gray eyes rested in a sort of alarm upon the sombre face of the girl at her feet, who only shook her head, murmuring,—

"And God will care for his own."

CHAPTER XXVIII.

A SALT-FISH DINNER.

"Nay, Betty, flout me not! 'Tis an honest word I've said to you, and I look to have it answered honestly."

"I know not what you call honest, Master Alexander Standish"—

"There, now! You can't even speak without a gibe at my high-sounding name. I count it right down unkind, Betty"—

"Then if I don't please you, there's the road home. Isn't your name Alexander in very sooth, or is that a by-name your mother calls you for short?"

"It seems to me, Mistress Alden, that your humor is a little shrewish."

"There, that will do! Never speak to me again so long as you've breath to speak at all."

"Nay, Betty, I crave your pardon. 'Twas rude of me, but you put me past my patience."

"Which is such a straitened foothold the least jostle will drive you from it."

"Betty, I love you. Will you be my wife?"

"Trust a modest man for impudence, when once he makes a start."

"Betty, I pray you lay aside this mood, and answer me seriously. 'Tis my just due, maiden, and John Alden's daughter should be honest."

"Well, then, Alick, in all sadness I will answer you—no."

"Do you mean it, Betty?"

"As I mean to be saved."

"And will you so far humor your oldest friend as to tell him why?"

"You do not love me as the man I wed must love, nor do I love you save as a dear friend of childhood, and as such I shall ever love you. As such and no more."

"I do not love you, say you, lass?"

"No. You fain would marry some one out of hand, because Gillian has fooled you, and you're longing to show her that you care as little as she."

"What—who—did she say such a thing, Betty?"

"Nay. Oh, Alick, I must laugh,—you look so red and so befogged!—like the sun rising on a misty morning."

"Who told you—what puts it in your head that I care for Gillian?"

"I said not you cared for her; I said she'd fooled you; and 'twas mine own eyes and mother wit told me, and no one else. She's played with you as my Tabby does with a mouse, only at the last she let you slip from under her claws, not quite killed, and you ran to your old gossip to have the wound salved; that's all!"

"And do you believe it was all put on? Do you truly think she cared nothing at all for me?"

"No more than she did for your brother Josias, or my brothers David and Joseph, or Constant Southworth, or, or—the rest"—

"The rest! Oh, you mean Will Pabodie, don't you? You've noted how of late she's all eyes and ears for him."

"Nay, I've noted naught." The words were few and the voice was cold, but something in the tone made Alick Standish look keenly into the face of his old friend. It was scarlet, and the brave brown eyes were full of tears; but as Betty caught his look she returned it with one of right royal defiance.

"Poor David!" said she, steadying her voice with a mighty effort, "he has not got over Tabby's love-pats yet. He's worse off than you, Alick. But here we are at home. Come in and have a mug of cider or a noggin of milk after your walk, won't you, lad?"

"I'll have the milk and thank you kindly. Isn't that Sally peeping out of the dairy window?"

"Yes, she's dairy-maid this week, and will give you the milk. You'll catch her in her short gown and petticoat."

"Won't she be vexed?" asked the young man, with a smile anything but heart-broken.

"She'll not eat you if she is. Open the door of a sudden and catch her at work," whispered Betty; and Alick, the smile broadening into mischief, sharply pushed back the cleated door, revealing the figure of a tall girl, who, with arms bare to the shoulders, was at that moment tossing a great mass of yellow butter high into the air, her lithe form well displayed as she leaned back and held up her hands to catch her ponderous plaything. A linen cloth pinned around the forehead just above the brows formed a piquant frame for the rosy, dimpling Greuze face, with its sweet blue eyes and pure but tender lips; a lovely innocent maiden, and as Alick Standish looked at her as if for the first time, while she, suffering the butterball to drop upon the stone slab in front of her, would fain have pulled her kirtle straight, but dared not touch it with her moist hands, and half cried in her pretty confusion, he knew as by a revelation that all his other fancies had been but dreams and follies, and here before him stood the woman, whom out of all the world he would choose to be his wife,—the woman whom he could love, and love to the end.

But while the man's heart leaped up within him, like his who, searching for mica, suddenly comes upon diamonds, all that rose to the lips was a little laugh, and the prosaic petition,—

"Might I have a noggin of milk?"

"Surely. Betty shall give it you— Nay, she's gone. Well, wait but till I wash my hands and put my butter down in the cellar hole. Mayhap you'll lift up the trap for me."

"Of course I will! Where is it?"

"Just here." And tapping with one foot, Sally Alden showed an iron ring set into the floor, and evidently intended to raise a big trap door in the middle of the dairy. Throwing it back so that it rested upon the floor, Alick looked down the steep steps into the little deep and cool cellar, which in those days imperfectly forestalled the refrigerator of to-day.

"Let me carry down the butter for you, Sally," said he. "'Tis too steep."

"'Tis no steeper than it was last week, or will be next," laughed Sally in a sweet tremor of bashful joy; for Alick was her hero, and hitherto had only treated her as one of the children. "But if you like, you may hand me the dish after I am down."

"Yes, indeed. It looks like the head of John Baptist on a charger, as 'tis seen in the Elder's big Bible."

"And so it does," replied the girl, glancing with a new interest at the great ball of butter in the middle of the pewter platter, which Alexander held aloft in mimicry of the picture both had seen as children.

Then presently, the butter deposited, the trap door closed, and the noggin of milk presented and quaffed, the two came through the long passage dividing the dairy from the kitchen, and were met by the mistress of the house, our Priscilla, a little older, but still as charming as when we first knew her, and showing among her daughters like the rose among its buds, the glorious fulfillment of a gracious promise.

"Good-morrow to you, Alick. Go into the sitting-room, you and Betty,—or no; Sally, you've been busy while Betty was on her travels, you go and make Alick miserable till dinner's dished"—

"Nay, dame, I'm beholden to you, but I must go"—

"Surely you must go, but not without your dinner, my lad. 'Tis Saturday and salt-fish dinner, you know, and I'll warrant me your mother's 'll be no better than I shall give you."

"My mother'd be the first to say she's no match for Mistress Alden in delicate cookery."

"There, there, go say your pretty things to the girls, Sally or Betty, it matters not which, but don't whet your wit on an old woman like me. Be off with you!"

Laughing and well pleased that fortune so favored his half-formed wishes, Alick followed Sally through the sitting-room to the front door, standing wide open to the summer; and then, sitting on the threshold, their feet upon the great natural doorstone which their children's and their children's children's feet should press, the man and the maid entered into that fairyland we all pass through once in our lives.

"And some give thanks, and some blaspheme,

And most forget, but either way,

That and the child's forgotten dream

Are all the light of all our day."

"Alick! Sally! Come to dinner!" cried Betty's blithe voice; but as the young man arose and turned his glowing face toward her, she stared at it for a moment in astonishment, and then turned sharply away to hide the smile that would in her own despite curl her lips.

"They're stronger than we women in some ways, but they're wondrously weak in others," was the thought beneath that smile.

In the great airy kitchen, where no fire was made in the warm weather, a table was spread large enough to accommodate, besides the heads of the family, their eight children, and the two men and a woman who lived in the house really as "help," and not servants.

A fourteenth seat was now placed for the guest between Betty and her brother Joseph, still his mother's true lover and helper, but Alick noted with pleasure that Sally sat opposite, and gave him the opportunity to study her face, which he seemed never to have seen before.

The long grace ended, and the clatter of chairs and feet upon the bare floor a little subsided, John Alden, viewing with satisfaction the great codfish lying at full length upon the platter yet longer than itself, said,—

"George Soule has had more than ordinary luck with his dunfish this season; don't they say so at your house, Alick?"

"Yes, sir, a small share, if you please."

Alden stared, and his wife interposed:—

"He says he'll have some, father. Did you know that George Soule had set up as dry-salter for the town, Alick?"

"Yes, I heard so. Indeed, father bought a quintal of dun and another of white fish of him," replied Alick, wondering what Betty and Sally were laughing about.

"Now I don't see why the captain portioned them that fashion," mused John Alden, rapidly distributing the fish into fourteen empty trenchers. "For doubtless he knows as well as I, or rather your mother knows as well as our housewife here, that the only way to cook your fish aright is to bind a good dunfish carefully between two whitefish, and steep the three all night in lukewarm water; then in the morning to cast out that water and put in fresh, and again steep it so nigh the fire that it ever tries to boil yet never makes out. Finally, when all else is ready, master dunfish is released from his bondage, and carefully laid upon a platter unbroken, while his bedfellows the whitefish are thrown to the ducks or the pigs"—

"Or made into a mince wherein no man can tell the white from the dun fish," interposed Priscilla. "Why, father, I should suppose you'd been ship's cook all your youth, and major-domo ever since. I never mistrusted you knew how a salt codfish should be cooked."

"I see a mort of things I don't talk about," retorted Alden quietly, "and if you knew not more than most women, I could tell you just how master tomcod should be served."

"Try it, father!" cried Betty, who was her father's darling and might say what she liked, because she never liked to say anything amiss. "Tell us now without looking around the board, tell us what should lie on it to be eaten with salt codfish."

"Well, there must be a white sauce, compounded of cream and wheaten flour and butter; and there must be pork-scraps cut in dice and fried of a dainty brown; and there must be beets boiled tender, but not cut to let out the color; and there must be parsnips and turnips and onions; and there must be brown bread and white bread; and there must be sallet oil and mustard; and above all, there must be a good flagon of cider, and another to back it."

"Right, right! Here's every one of the things you told about and more, for here's a dish of those roots John Howland got in Boston of the sloop trading to the Carolinas. Molly begged so hard for them that mother cooked some, but I doubt if they will suit with salt fish."

"Father told of eating some in Boston, but we've had none as yet," said Alick, and Sally, taking up one of the sweet potatoes, broke it in two and handed a piece across the table to Alick, who, eating it skin and all, as if it were a fruit, declared it with sincerity to be the most delicious morsel he had ever tasted.

"I've an apple pasty to follow," announced Priscilla, as her husband pushed away his plate. "Rachel, you and Timothy may take away the trenchers and bring some fresh ones; and Sally, have you a jug of cream and a morsel of cheese for us in your dairy?"

"Yes, indeed, mother," and Sally, glad to escape Alick's scrutiny, jumped up and retreated to the dairy.

"While John Howland was in Boston he saw Ras Brewster," said Joseph to keep up the conversation, which rather lagged through Betty's preoccupation and her mother's housewifely cares.

"He has been at Kennebec all this time, hasn't he?" asked Alick with somewhat languid interest.

"Yes, but Master Winslow sent for him to company him to England. Will they make any stay there, father?"

"The Lord only knows, my son," returned Alden with a ponderous sigh. "The Bay people, that is to say the authorities, have to my mind done an ill-advised thing in tolling Edward Winslow away from us. They say he has a skillful tongue and good acquaintance with the ways of courts; and so he hath, so he hath, but also he has a home, and comrades of old time who look to him for comfort and aid, the more that so many of the old stock are removed by death or distance. It is not well done of the Bay people, and much do I hope that Winslow will not deeply engage himself in their concerns."

"And Wrastle has gone with him?" asked Alick in a low voice of Joseph, who nodded assent, adding presently, as his father lapsed into silence,—

"He'll be writer and keep the papers,—a secretary, Master Winslow called it; and Ras said there was no knowing when he might come back."

"Now here's the pie, and the cheese, and the cream, and some fresh nutcakes, and some metheglin; so cease your lament, John, and be merry while you may!" cried Priscilla, cutting the pie, which was baked in a great iron basin, and was more of a pudding than a pie, as it needed to be, since fourteen hungry mouths were to feed upon it.

CHAPTER XXIX.

TOO LATE! TOO LATE!

The Thursday evening lecture was over, and Barbara Standish, with her son Josias and some of the neighbors, strayed homeward along the footpath leading from Harden Hill to the Brewster and Standish farms; but Lora lingered with her father, who spoke of English politics with Kenelm Winslow, who had just received a letter from his brother Edward now at the English court.

"One moment, Captain," said the Elder's grave and friendly voice, as Winslow bade good-night, and Standish turned to look after Lora who had strayed down toward the water. "One moment before you summon the little maid. I have letters from England"—

"And I too, God save the mark!" growled Standish, who all the evening had worn the face of a thundercloud.

"Ill news, I fear," said his friend gently.

"Not more ill than one who has known the world for half a century should look for; naught more novel than falsehood, and treachery, and covetousness, and wrong."

"Nay, friend Myles, nay, my brother; 'Charity suffereth long and is kind'"—

"Suffereth long, but opens her eyes at last. However, I will not burden you with mine own griefs, Elder; you had somewhat to say to me."

"Yes, but I fear me 'tis in an ill-chosen time. Your spirit is much disturbed."

"Not so much that I cannot heed my duty, sir."

"Nay, Myles, take not so stern a tone with your ancient friend and constant well-wisher. I fain would touch the tender spot that well I know lies deep within your heart. I would speak of our children, Captain."

"Ah! and you have heard from Rastle?"

"Yes. A long letter, the full outpouring of his heart, and still the song has but one refrain, the story but one theme. Can you guess it, friend?"

"Ay, I can guess it."

"And fain would hear no more on't?"

"I know not, Elder, I know not; of a truth my soul is vexed within me, and shapes of wrath and bloodshed that I had thought buried with the old life have wakened and are thundering at the gate of my will. Had I that man here on this convenient sod, and I with Gideon in mine hand"—

The grating of strong teeth, set all unconsciously, closed the sentence, and in the soft gray of the twilight hour the Elder examined the face of his companion with anxious scrutiny, then sternly spoke:—

"Man! Satan is at your shoulder and whispering in your ear! I can all but see and hear him."

"All but!" laughed Standish. "There is no peradventure about it to me."

"Call that pure maid to your side, and the Evil One will flee."

"Nay. Tell me what your boy says. Haply 'tis a better time than you could guess."

The old man once more examined the face Standish would neither avert nor soften, and then, unable to comprehend, yet following meekly the intuitions that guide faithful souls in such matters, he drew from his breast a folded sheet of the coarse rough paper Spielmann had in England taught the men of Dartford to manufacture at a cost which would terrify Marcus Ward to-day, and slowly unfolding it said,—

"I will read you my lad's own words. The first page doth but tell of his voyage and his situation in fair lodgings with Edward Winslow, who is as a father to him, and then he goes on:—

> "'There are many fair ladies at the court who kindly notice me as Master Winslow's associate; but, father, you know how it is with my heart, for I fully laid it open to you before I went away, sore hurt by what Captain Standish said to me the day you wot of; nor have I seen the lady of my love since that day, nor shall I, as I think, while we two abide below. And yet, sir, her image is more present to mine eyes than are the faces of these dames, or even your own, though there is naught so dear to me in this world as yourself,—that is to say, if you will bear with my fantasy, there's naught outside of me so dear as my father; but Lora is within, the life of my life and essence of my being, and how should a man say his own being is dear to him, for to what should his own being belong save to itself and the God who gave it? Honored father, I feel that I should crave pardon of your dignity for thus claiming its indulgence of a lover's fond imaginings; but, sir, you know

how since my mother's death left me a little lonely child, your tenderness and care have filled both a father's and mother's room in my life, and to-day I speak to you as I might to her had she been alive; and as I dream of laying my head in her lap and feeling her hand upon my hair and her half-remembered voice in mine ears, so now I come to you and say, I love this maid. I love her with all the power of loving God hath given me. I love her as Jacob did Rachel, as Isaac did Rebecca, ay, my father, as you did my mother, and life will never reach its fullness for me except I may mingle it with her pure life. Father, is there no hope? Is there no seven years' or fourteen years' probation that may for me pass as a few days for love of her? Will not you speak once again to the captain for me? I know not how she feels concerning me. When I spoke to her on that fair eve it was like arousing a child from its dreams of heaven; she knew not what I meant, nor how far her own heart could respond to a love whose face and voice as yet were strange to her; but with all her tender innocence she hath a singular aptness of mind, and a delicate discrimination that will ere now have spoken to her heart many a homily drawn from the text I gave her in that sweet hour. I cannot tell, I dare not think, but something within me dares to hope that Lora loves me. Oh, how fair those words look set down on paper, LORA LOVES ME! Nay, father, I have spent a good half hour in staring at those three words as if they were some new gospel of hope. Father! I dare not ask your indulgence, and yet I know I have it, and well do you know when I thus unveil what some men would call my weakness to your eyes, that my reverence never was greater or more profound; but as I writ before, 'tis to my mother in you that I dare tell all these the deepest secrets of my heart. And now I will say no more, lest repetition weaken what hath already been said. But you will speak to the captain, will you not? Tell him—nay, you shall, if you see fit and find him in the mood, you shall show him this letter; for though 'twas written for no eyes but my father's and mother's, 'tis the truth as I would speak it before God, and if all went as I would have it, Lora's father should be my father too,—not like you, mine own father, but in some sort; and well do I know how dear he loves mine own sweet maid. Mayhap that love in him will answer to this cry of love from me, since both are fixed upon the same dear object. But there! I will stop at this word, for should I go on all night and all to-morrow, my pen could only trace again and again the words it hath so often writ. I love her, I love her, I love her!

"'On this other slip of paper I have copied out some verses lent me by a lady of the court, Countess of Pembroke she is called, and a right sweet and fair dame she is; but still I must speak of her as Sir Henry Wotton, who wrote the verses, saith to all other ladies as compared with his sovereign lady, the English princess whom he served after she became queen of Bohemia,—

"What's your praise,

When Philomel her voice doth raise!"

"'And so with my humble duty and constant affection, I am, dear sir,

Your humble and obedient son,
WRESTLING BREWSTER.

"'P. S. The copy of verses is meant for Mistress Lora's own hand, if her father makes no objection.

W. B.'"

"And here are the verses," said the Elder, as the captain took the letter and immediately gave it back, while conflicting emotions strove eloquently upon his face. Then accepting the second paper, and turning his shoulder to the failing light, he read half aloud:—

"'Ye meaner beauties of the night,

That poorly satisfy our eyes

More by your number than your light,

You common people of the skies,

What are you when the sun shall rise!

"'You curious chanters of the wood

That warble forth Dame Nature's lays,

Thinking your meaning understood

By your weak accents, what's your praise

When Philomel her voice doth raise!

"'Ye violets that first appear,

By your pure purple mantles known,

Like the proud virgins of the year

As if the spring were all your own,

What are you when the rose is blown!

"'So when my mistress shall be seen

In form and beauty of her mind,

By virtue first, then choice a queen,

Tell me, is she not one designed

The Eclipse and Glory of her kind?'"

Folding the verses, Standish held out his hand for the letter, and placed the one carefully within the other, his deliberate movements betraying the preoccupation of his mind; then raising his gloomy eyes to the Elder's face, he said,—

"Your son speaks of Rebecca. When Isaac's ambassador asked her from her kinsfolk they made answer, 'We will call the damsel, and inquire at her mouth.' So say I to you, Elder."

"What! if Lora consent, you will not refuse her to my son?"

"We will call the damsel, and inquire at her mouth. Oh, no, we will not startle her again, as your son confesses that he did on that ill-starred night. Give me the letter if you will, and I will bid her read and ponder it through the night, and to-morrow I will come and tell you; or no,—if it be as you wish, she shall come herself and tell you."

"I felt that my boy's words must move a father's heart," replied the Elder with a loving complacency, which sank abashed before the fierce glance of the captain's eyes, as he strode away, muttering,—

"Had not they suited my purpose, his mops and mows had been my scoff."

Down near the edge of the bluff that finishes Harden Hill stood Lora, leaning lightly against a birch, whose silver bark seemed some quaint ornament of her white samite robe, like the gauzy scarf thrown around her head and shoulders. One slender foot in its silver-buckled shoe showed beneath the hem of her robe as if about to follow the earnest gaze bent seaward. So profound was the maiden's meditation that she did not hear her father's step, and was only roused by his sombre voice asking,—

"Of what are you dreaming, Lora?"

"Oh! Is it time to go home, father?"

"Of what are you dreaming, child?"

"Nay, father dear, my dreams are not worth the telling." And with a pretty air of coaxing the girl turned and laid a hand upon her father's arm; but he, withdrawing a step, almost sternly persisted,—

"But yet I will know them, Lora. Tell me truly, of what or of whom were you thinking, and why did you look so earnestly over the sea?"

"The moon is rising, father," stammered the young girl with a piteous attempt at unconcern. "I was looking at her."

"'Tis not like you, my maid, to trifle and palter in your replies. Will you tell me of what or of whom you thought?"

"Nay, father, if you insist I must obey, but mayhap you'll be vexed at my thought."

"Mayhap 'tis my own thought, child. Mayhap I've come to wish what you were wishing as you looked over the sea."

"Oh, no, no, father, and no indeed!" cried Lora with a horror-stricken look upon her face. "'Tis not your wish, and yet perhaps 'twill be what—and it may be but mine own foolish fancy, but I was thinking, father dear, that if the time comes soon, I would well like to lie just here under this loving tree that seems bending to clip me in its arms; just here, father, on this little slope, with the sea singing lullaby at my feet, and the fair moon making a silver road from earth to heaven, and the whispering leaves of the birch,— to lie down still and dreamless, with this my robe of white samite folded close around my feet, and my hair, so far too heavy now, uncoiled and unbraided, and my two hands clasped upon my breast, and some of mother's fair white posies beneath them"—

"Lora! Lora! For Christ's sweet sake, look at me! Look at me, darling, and change that smile for one that I dare to meet! Change it for tears, mine own, tears rather than such a smile; but no, no—see, here is a letter, a letter full of this world's love, and life, and a man's honest human longing to make my maid his wife. Wrestling wants to marry you, my bird, my flower, my little Lora! Oh, Lora, Lora darling, understand me, and take that awful smile from your lips! Wrestling would marry you, and I give my full and free consent; yes, freely and gladly, dear. See, here's the letter, and some pretty poesy, and such honey-sweet words,—take it, darling, and read it; or no,—'tis gruesome here among the graves; come home to mother, and read it sitting in her lap. Come, pussy, come! You love him, don't you, my lass? That's all that ails you, isn't it? Oh, say you love him and will be his wife, and we'll build you such a fair little home close beside father's, my poppet; and there'll be little children by and by to call me granddad, and make a hobby-horse of Gideon— Nay, nay, she hears not a word! Lora! Lora! Speak to me!"

"This letter, father! Did it come from Ras? Did he write it with his own hand?"

"Yes, my darling. Come home and read"—

"I am reading it now, and more—and more."

"Nay, dear, you have not opened it." And Myles, pale and trembling, tried to take the letter from between Lora's folded hands. But she, drawing away, held it firmly, and gazing fixedly out to sea murmured,—

"He loves me so! Dear lad! He loves me so, and thinks of all it may cost him, and yet—brave Ras! brave and noble heart! She clings to him, and he will not push her aside! Oh, poor woman, how she writhes in her agony, and clings and clings; and now he has carried her into the hovel and laid her down, and one says, ''Tis the plague, and yon poor gentleman must die for his charity,' and he turns away and whispers, 'Lora!' Yes, darling, yes! I know now that I love you, dear,—wait—nay, he cannot wait, but goes before, and I—will come—yes, dear heart, I will"—

And before her father could grasp her she slid from his hands, and lay there beneath the birch-tree, the moon shining upon her white robe, and her face as white, and the hands clasping the letter to her breast.

CHAPTER XXX.

PEEPING TOM AND HIS BROTHER.

Dame Alice Bradford sat alone in her fair bedroom, its latticed windows swinging wide to admit the flower-laden breeze that, young and fresh as when we saw it peeping in at the council of the fathers and the stitching of the little maids, peeped now at the still figure of the matron, sitting for once quite idle, her hands folded listlessly upon her lap. She was thinking, as it chanced, of that very morning, long ago, when the green footstool cover was finished, and her little Mercy and Desire Howland had admired it so much, and each begun one like it; and now Mercy, her one daughter, her little ewe lamb as she called her in thought, was Mistress Vermayes, with a home in Boston and a grand future before her, and Desire Howland was married to John Gorham; and although her two boys William and Joseph were as good sons as a mother need ask, they were sons, and not daughters, nor was Dame Alice in haste to see them bring daughters home to her.

A few slow, meek tears gathered in her eyes and overflowed just as the door opened and the governor came in with a letter in his hand. A glance at his wife showed him her case, and he said tenderly,—

"Is it the empty nest, sweetheart, that grieves you?"

"Nay, Will, how can I be lonesome while you are left to me?"

"Well and bravely said, my wife, and yet I blame thee not, I blame thee not. I miss the dear maid myself oftener than I would like to say. But you know how oft we've spoke of your sister Mary Carpenter in her lonely estate since her mother died"—

"And my mother as well as hers," suggested Alice with a little sob.

"Why surely, dear heart, and I know well that you grieve for her; but now I've written to Mary, bidding her come and make her home with us, and offering to pay the charges of her voyage, since she is left in such straitened case, and here's the letter all ready to send by Kenelm Winslow, who is summoned by his brother to England to receive some instructions. Kenelm will go to Bristol and see Mary, but I have bidden her not to wait for his escort back, but to come so soon as she can light of safe company, since you need her here."

"Oh, Will dear, which shall I praise first, your tender thought for me, or your goodness to my sister?"

"Well, for that matter, dame, I fancy it all comes under one head, for if it were not to pleasure you I know not that I should urge Mistress Carpenter across the seas to bear me company."

"There's a young gentlewoman below asking to see our dame," said the voice of Tabitha Rowse at the door, and Alice, with a gentle look of love and thanks in her husband's face, followed the girl downstairs, and entering the new parlor said pleasantly,—

"Oh, it is you, Mistress Gillian, is it? I should think Tabitha would have remembered you."

"I have not been in Plymouth more than once or twice since the dear Elder's funeral," said Gillian sorrowfully.

"The dear Elder, yes," replied Dame Alice. "He's been mourned but once among us, for the first mourning hath not ceased, nor will it soon with those who knew and loved him."

"Yet none loved him like me, for he was the best friend, the only friend I had in all the world!" And in a burst of emotion honest enough, and yet more uncontrolled than the emotions of most persons of that place and time, Gillian sobbed and cried, and hid her face upon the cushion of the great chair beside which she had sunk, until the dame, laying a hand upon the round shoulder whence the cape had slipped, said kindly yet reprovingly,—

"Nay, Gillian, 'tis not meet to give way to even the worthiest grief in such fashion as this. Dry up your eyes now, while I go to fetch you some orange-flower water, and when you have drunk it we will speak of other matters."

"Nay, dear lady, I want no orange-flower water, nor to keep you longer than need be, but I have come to you a beggar, and would fain make my petition ere my courage fails."

"A petition, maiden? Well, now, what is it? Something that I can grant, I hope, for I love to pleasure young maids for my dear daughter's sake."

"Ah, sweet Dame Alice, if I might come and be a daughter to you! There's my petition all in one word,—that I may come and live with you. Am I overbold?"

"To live with me, Gillian? Why, how do you mean, child?"

"Let me come and be in the place of a daughter and yet not claim a daughter's love or rights, unless, indeed, I serve you so well that you cannot but love me a little, and so comfort your own heart. I have no home, and I know no one with whom I am so fain to live as with you, dear dame."

"But your aunt, Lucretia Brewster"—

"They are going to Connecticut as soon as may be, and my aunt says she needs me not, if I can find another home, and Love Brewster and his wife treat me ill, and since the dear, dear old Elder died I have no one left to say one kind or careful word to me; and oh, dame, I do wish, and more than once or twice, that I lay beside my mother"—

"Poor child, poor orphan child!" murmured Alice Bradford, laying a hand upon the girl's silken tresses as the head rested against her knee in all the abandonment of grief. "Yes, you shall come and stay with us for a while, at least, if the governor consent, as I am sure he will, and if your kinsfolk make no objection. Love and Sarah are here to-day, are they not?"

"Yes; Sarah's father, Master Prence, is removing his chattels left in the house he used while he was governor, and Love and Sarah came to help him." And Gillian, her end attained, rose gracefully to her feet, straightened her dress and smoothed back her ruddy hair, while Dame Alice, gazing out of the window toward the harbor, sadly thought of the bereavement Plymouth that day was suffering; for a colony of some of her best men, headed by Thomas Prence, with Nicholas Snow and his wife, once Constance Hopkins, Cook, Doane, Bangs, and others, were embarking with all their cattle and household goods for Nauset on the Cape, there to found the town of Eastham, fondly dreaming it should become the successor of Plymouth, which by successive emigrations, deaths, and shrinkage of values seemed threatened with extinction, dull and lifeless. As Bradford himself wrote that day in the journal so invaluable to us all,—

"Thus was this poor church left like an ancient mother, grown old and forsaken of her children, until she that had made many rich herself became poor."

Fighting against the depression of spirits and want of interest in what remained that assailed his spirit, the governor gladly consented to accept Gillian Brewster, as everybody called her, as an inmate of his house, and a few days later she was installed in the pretty bedroom first occupied by Priscilla Carpenter, now a portly and sedate matron, wife of John Cooper, of Barnstable, and at a later date by Mercy Bradford, lately become Mistress Vermayes. Nor did her new patrons regret their generosity for some time to come, since the girl, warned perhaps by late misadventures, restrained the "wicked lightnings of her eyes" to such flashes of summer lightning as only served to startle and amuse the beholder, or at most to suggest electrical forces beneath the surface, and to arouse a certain interest in the nature that concealed them. Sometimes, to be sure, the governor's serious and intent gaze would rest upon the girl's face until she turned uneasily away, and sometimes Dame Alice would speak in her gentle and pure-toned voice of the beauty of modesty and reserve in a maiden's character; but William and Joseph noticed her hardly more than they did their mother's kitten, and when occasionally she tried some little coquetries upon them, William would look bored and absent-minded, and Joseph laugh in a satirical fashion hard for Gillian's hot temper to endure. One word between the brothers may explain much that to the girl herself never was explained. It was spoken in the first days of Gillian's sojourn under their father's roof, when the two young men, gun on shoulder, were traversing the hills about Murdock's Pond in search of birds to tempt their mother's languid appetite. It was Joseph who said, wiping his brow and resting his "piece" upon a crotched tree, for the day was warm,—

"Bill, this maid Gillian is the one David Alden spoke of last harvest, isn't she?"

"Ay, is she. And mind you, Joe, what he said of her?"

"That she would wile a bird off a bough; yes, that's what Dave said, and Betty Alden, she puts in, 'Allowing 'twas a male bird, so she would.'"

"Ay, Betty's keen as a needle, and as straight. Well, Joe, if she's made a fool of a score, there's no call for us to make it two-and-twenty, is there?"

"Indeed there's not, and I wouldn't vex the dear mother for a cargo of red-gold heads like hers."

"Nor for any other. So, that's settled, Joe, and you're breathed by now. Come on."

An hour later the young men, worn, weary, and sore athirst, welcomed the sound of rushing waters, heard but not seen through the thick foliage, and Joseph, in the advance as usual, cried out,—

"Hullo! Here's Jenney's Mill close at hand. We've got enough birds for a famous stew, so let's stop and rest awhile, and speak with the miller's folk."

"'Folk' standing for Abby and Sally and Sue Jenney," said William provokingly.

"And Sam and his new wife, who was a great friend of yours, Master Bill, while she was called Nanny Lettice, and the Widow Jenney, who to my mind is better company than the girls."

"Ho! Ho! Well, there's naught like a sober mind to recommend a young fellow, and I'm glad to see it cropping up in your field, Father Joseph. Well, we'll make a neighborly call upon the widow, and while you talk about

Parson Chauncey's notions of immersion and Mr. Ainsworth's psalmody I'll e'en say a word of a lighter sort to the young gentlewomen."

"Have your jest, Will, have your jest," returned the younger brother coolly, "but I know somewhat you don't."

"Think you do, I dare say! A wise man in his own conceit is Joe Bradford."

But seeing that his brother, instead of being teased, was holding himself very quiet and peeping through the branches of the young maples crowding down to the brink of the little river Plymouth modestly calls The Town Brook, William stepped softly behind him, and with something of the guilty joy of Actæon, looked upon almost as fair a sight as he did.

No prettier spot was then, or until very lately, to be found in the dear old town which is mother of us all, than Holmes's Dam, or as it then was called Jenney's Mill, where in the midst of a dense wood The Town Brook, rushing toward the sea, found itself at a very early date impeded by a dam, more or less artificial and effectual according to the owner, but always sufficient to turn the big wheel of the gristmill first erected by Stephen Dean, husband of that Betty Ring who inherited so little of her mother's great estate, and afterward carried on by burly John Jenney, who sat as Assistant at the council board when Duxbury wrung consent for separate identity from the mother town. And now John slept, although *not* with his English fathers, and his widow jointly with her son Samuel administered the mill and ground the grain not only of Plymouth, but of Duxbury, Sandwich, and several other towns. With so wide a custom the miller's was a flourishing business, and might have been still more so had it been more carefully carried on, but alas! John Jenney was a shipowner, and aspired to setting up salt-works at Clark's Island, and in fact had a soul above the pottles of meal by which he was supposed to live; and when his widow succeeded to his estate the customers complained that they were forced to share their grain with rats and mice, and that the miller's widow was too easy tempered to be very efficient. Now, however, that the oldest son was married and the daughters were grown up, things went better, and the mill became a popular resort for the young people, especially in hot weather.

But all this time the governor's sons are peeping through the boscage, and we peeping with them see four young girls, their kirtles of blue and white homespun linen drawn about their knees, while with bare feet they comfortably paddle in a little pool formed by a bend of the stream, floored with beach sand and bordered by a grassy bank, whereon the four damsels sit, and chat with all the sweet volubility of blackbirds. The rays of the morning sun sifting through the branches of the young oaks overhead dance merrily upon heads of gold and brown, and the flaxen locks that curl around Susan Jenney's head, while her eyes, blue as the blossom of the flax, gleam beneath as she says,—

"We wouldn't do this to-night, girls, would we?"

"I dare say the lads wouldn't say nay, if we asked them to a wading match," replied her sister Sally with a twinkling laugh, while Abby, older than the rest, looked sharply among the bushes, saying,—

"Who knows but we're spied upon! I feel a creep up my back."

"'Tis Harry Wood, be sure on't!" cried Susan with a little flirt of her white toes that sent the water into her sister's face, while William Bradford, softly pulling Joseph backward, whispered in his lowest tones,—

"Betty Alden's there, and she'd never forgive us if she knew we'd spied on them."

"Here goes, then!" and Joseph, laughing silently, pointed his gun at the sky and pulled the trigger, then hastily turned back to his post of observation, clinging to Will's arm and shaking with an earthquake of suppressed merriment, as if he would go to pieces.

"'Tis like a plump of white ducks that hear the shot pattering around them," whispered William; but Joe was beyond speech, and could only gasp and shake with laughter as he watched the girls, who with little shrieks and screams and exclamations clung to each other, staring wildly around, and then gathering their feet up under their skirts wriggled backward in some mysterious feminine fashion, until gaining the shelter of the undergrowth they stood up and looked around them in timid defiance for a moment, and then, no foe presenting himself, Abby, as oldest and bravest, darted out, and seizing the shoes and stockings lying in a heap, bore them triumphantly under shelter.

Some fifteen minutes later, William and Joseph Bradford, dignified and grave as two young parsons, arrived at the door of the mill and were received by Abby and Sally Jenney, demure and self-possessed as possible, but with eyes on the alert for any indication that these were the peeping Toms whom they suspected.

"We've a surprise for you, William," remarked Abby, as steps were heard descending the stairs. "Who do you suppose is visiting us from out of town?"

"Is anybody visiting you? I had not heard of it."

"Well, here she is. Betty, you did not think we'd have company so soon to bid you welcome, did you, now?"

"Nay, Betty, heed her not," exclaimed William, rising to claim the privilege of a salute. "'Tis no company, but only two of your old playmates. Why, you're looking fresh as the morning, Betty, isn't she, Joe?" And both young men gravely surveyed the blushing girl from head to foot, noticing especially the white thread hose and dainty buckled shoes that covered the feet but now so rosy white in the water of the little pool.

"How long is it since I saw you, Betty?" demanded Joseph presently, and William paused in a speech to Sally to hear the reply.

"I really do not know, Joe; don't you?"

"I can't say, Betty, can't say at all;" and Betty, casting a hasty glance at his face, was met by so serene a smile that she comfortably assured herself, "It was not they, or they didn't see."

"We're going to have a little company to-night, and some games in the old mill," said Abby presently. "Will you both come? And if the young gentlewoman at your house would like to make one of the guests, we're more than happy to have her."

"My mother is beholden to you for remembering her companion, but I doubt if Gillian Brewster can be spared," said William a little hastily, and perhaps a little haughtily, for he shrank from seeing the siren who had wrought such mischief among some of his friends introduced to others under shelter of his mother's name. But Joseph, heedless of his brother's tone and only half hearing his words, replied almost in the same breath,—

"You're very thoughtful, Abby, and I doubt not Gillian will like to come. I'll bring her in my boat."

"Gillian Brewster!" murmured Betty in a tone of dismay that drew William Bradford's attention to her face, suddenly pale and disturbed, and going close to the girl who had been to him almost a sister for the first ten years of their lives, he whispered, "Shall I prevent it, Betty?"

"No, no, Will! Why should I care? She's naught to me."

"Nay, I thought"—

"'Tis a poor custom, Will; better break it off while you can."

"The custom of thinking?"

"Ay. How is Mercy, and when did your mother hear from her last?"

Half an hour soon ran away, and so did the great stone pitcher of cider which the miller's wife insisted upon producing, and the young men took leave, promising to be ready at an early hour for the evening's frolic.

CHAPTER XXXI.

JENNEY'S MILL BY MOONLIGHT.

"For 'tis the twenty-first of June,

The merriest day in all the year,"

sang Jack Jenney, the younger brother of the mill and the miller, as to amuse his sister's visitors he threw the great wheel into gear and set the machinery in motion. "Put in a grist, you young idiot, and don't grind off the face of the stones," growled Samuel, standing by, and not so hospitable as to forget business.

"Well, here's Squire Pabodie's Indian waiting—English, too, but that wants daylight. Here, bear a hand, Sam, with the Indian." And the two young men poured the two bushels of gold-colored maize into the hopper, while little Hope Howland, bending over to see it drawn down the vortex of the cruel stones, cried,—

"Poor Indian! Do you know, Jack, one of those Englishmen that came from Boston to see the Rock where our fathers first landed was at the governor's to dinner, and father was there, and Master Bradford said he must have some more Indian ground, and the man made great eyes and said,—

"'But does your excellency chastise the savages in such fashion as that?' He thought, poor gentleman, that we ground up the Indians!"

"And doubtless he feared our governor next would roar,—

'Fee, fie, faw, fum!

I smell the blood of an Englishman!

And be he alive, or be he dead,

I'll grind his bones to make my bread!'"

And John Howland junior put his great hands upon his sister's shoulders to draw her back, saying, "But we won't have you ground this grist, Hope; so don't tumble in. Mother wouldn't like it."

"Oh, John, how you tease!" cried Hope, pouting, yet clinging to the arm of her stalwart brother, a fine young fellow, who at a later date calmly incurred judicial censure and a heavy fine for the sake of warning some Quakers, in whose belief he had no share, that they were about to be arrested and imprisoned. And from that day to our own the stout Howland blood has held its own, foremost in that Army of Occupation which the departing Pilgrims left to hold the land their prowess had won.

But while this little scene was enacted around the hopper, William Pabodie, who, bringing his father's corn to mill late in the afternoon, had accepted an invitation to spend the evening and join the merrymaking, wandered out of the house, and standing beside the pool, idly broke the branch of lilac that some one had given him into little bits and cast them upon the waters.

"Nay, don't spoil the pretty posy so," cooed a dulcet voice at his elbow. "If you don't want it, give it to me."

"And welcome, Mistress Gillian," replied the young man coldly, as he held out the flowering branch.

"Oh, but 'tis all torn and ragged," remonstrated the girl, touching it, then drawing back as if it wounded her. "Trim it for me with your knife, good Master William. Nay, then, I'll not borrow your unfriendly tone. A scant two months agone 'twas Jill and Willy"—

"I ever hated the name of Willy since I was a baby!" exclaimed the young man petulantly, yet taking the branch and trimming it as he was bid, while Gillian, pressing close to his side, watched the operation as if it were some rare and fascinating sight.

"But why are you so changed to me?" murmured she, scorning the side issue, and like a true woman keeping to the point of personal interest.

"Changed? Am I changed?" asked the man helplessly.

"Oh, Will! Think of the night you took me in your sledge to ride across the snow."

"'Twas a great while ago," muttered Pabodie awkwardly.

"Ah, yes, a great while ago; and all that is fair and sweet and worthy to be had in remembrance of all my life is a great while ago," said the girl bitterly, and as she raised her great dark eyes to the moon, whose light mingled with that of dying day, Pabodie could not but see that they were full of tears, and that the ripe mouth quivered piteously. What man ever yet saw such a sight unmoved, especially when the face was so wondrous fair, the June air so full of fragrance, the moon so softly bright.

"Nay, Gillian, I never meant to be unkind to you!" murmured William Pabodie, half unconsciously taking the hand whose finger-tips grazed his palm, and at the least invitation nestled so confidingly into it.

"Gillian," said a clear, cool voice just beside the pair. "I am sent to call you both to a game,—a game for all of us to play together."

And Betty Alden, whose light footfall had not been heard through the sound of the falling waters, quietly looked into William Pabodie's face, superbly glanced over Gillian's, let her eyes rest for a moment upon the branch of lilac which Gillian had seized, although Pabodie all unconsciously still held it, and then, with one of those smiles upon her lips which most women remember to have smiled, and most men shiver in remembering to have seen, she turned and climbed the little path to the mill door.

"And now you'll never speak to me again, lest Betty Alden should chide," cried Gillian, turning sharply aside, and with a gesture of inimitable grace resting her folded arms against a tree-trunk, and laying her forehead upon them, while a storm of unfeigned sobs and tears shook the very tree she leaned on. William Pabodie, flinging the lilac branch to the ground, would have passed her by, but she made no movement to detain him, and so he lingered, looked at her in sore perplexity for a moment, then said in a voice of contemptuous kindness,—

"It distresses me to see you so, Gillian, and in very truth there's no call for it; I'm not your lover, and that you know"—

"Oh, yes, I know it, I know it! Poor me, there's none to love me, and those I could love to the death care less for me than for another's frown."

"Nay, mistress, I'm one that fears no woman's frown, nor change my friends to suit any fancy but mine own."

"But alas, Gillian's not one of those friends!"

"Why, yes you are, Gillian, yes you are as much my friend as—as ever."

"I'm your friend? Ay, but are you mine, Will?"

"Yes—that is to say"—

"That is to say, so far as Betty Alden permits," cried Gillian, honestly losing control of herself, and flashing into the young man's eyes a look that made him start back as Julio did when Lamia suddenly revealed herself a serpent. Without a word he strode past her and up the hill, where seeking out his friend, Will Bradford, he drew him aside and said, "Would you do me a kindness, Will?"

"You know I would, man. What is it?"

"Take Gillian Brewster away as soon as may be."

"Oho! What has she done now?"

"That's what I can't tell you, Bill, but you'll trust me that it's no discourtesy that I can help, to make such a petition."

"I know that, Bill Pabodie."

"Well, then"—

"I'll manage it, but not of a sudden."

"No, no; only so that I may get a quiet word with Betty before I leave."

"Ay, it's in that quarter the storm is brewing, is it? Well, in an hour or so I'll manage it."

But before the hour was over Gillian herself, for after all she was as yet but a young maid, and not seasoned in such matters as another ten years might have seasoned her, came to William, and resting on his arm said plaintively,—

"I'm very weary, Will. When might we be leaving?"

"They're just going to supper, and while they sit down we can slip away if you like, and in sooth you do look weary," said Bradford not unkindly, and Gillian, in a little impulse of womanliness, replied with a wan smile,—

"Nay, I'll not take you from your supper. There's a roast pig and apple-sauce, I hear."

"Oh, that's naught, that's naught," protested the young man; but his healthy appetite so rose up in approval of the roasted suckling that it looked out at his eyes, and Gillian, laughing a little, scoffingly said,—

"If it's naught to you, it's something to me, and I'll not stir till I've had roast pig and seed-cake and a glass of sweet wine, and mayhap a little taste of arrack punch. May I sit by you, Will, and sip out of your glass?"

"Yes, that will be fine," cried Will, seeing a happy compromise open before him. "If you'll sit by me and look at no other fellow but me, I'll stay; but if you're going to tease me, I'll not."

"I'll look at none but you," promised Gillian gently, but her active brain was already shaping the query, "What does he know? What has he heard?"

and then replying to itself, "What matter! Fools all of them, and I the worst fool of all."

So amidst the frank, possibly unrefined, certainly hearty merriment of the time and place the roast pig and roasted russet apples were eaten, and the loaf of seed-cake and another of fruit-cake were cut in great wedges and passed around, and a choice comfiture of wild cranberries with candied lemon peel and plenty of sugar was served on little wooden trenchers, carved in the winter evenings by Samuel Jenney as a present to his bride; and there was plenty of beer and cider, which to our hardy sires were no more injurious than cold water to us, who have bred nerves in place of their muscles and brawn; and there was sweet Spanish wine for the ladies, passed from hand to hand in a little pewter wine-cup, burnished like silver; and there was a good joram of punch for every man; and the girls with little gasps and chokings put their lips to the edge of the rummers, while Gillian, nestling close to William Bradford's side, was gentle and quiet as a chidden child, and spoke to none but him, eating the while as a bird might, and no more, until in his heart the young man felt that William Pabodie was after all something of a churl, and not over courteous to the governor's guest, and Pabodie forgetting them both watched Betty Alden, who now and again glanced at or spoke to him just as she did to Sam Jenney or John Howland, and was the brightest, the merriest, the most winsome lass of that gay circle of men and maids.

"And now we'll go, Will," whispered Gillian, as all rose from the table.

"Yes, poor little Jill, we'll go now," replied Bradford far more tenderly than ever he had spoken before; and Joseph, who heard it, turned sharply, and surveying his brother with astonishment whispered,—

"If there's a score, need we make it two-and-twenty, Bill?"

"Gillian is tired, and I am taking her home in the boat," answered William coldly. "Will you come with us, or on foot later?"

"Take care of yourself, man, and I'll give as good an account of myself," retorted Joe a little huffed, and presently the governor's boat glided down Town Brook, which glittered like a stream of silver under the full moon. In the stern, her elbow on the gunwale and her hand supporting a sorrowful face upturned to the sky, reclined Gillian, a dusky red shawl half covering her neck and arms, and throwing up in startling relief the exquisitely molded hand and wrist lying palm uppermost upon her knee.

Close beside her sat Bradford, silently dreaming a young man's vague sweet dreams of the wonder of womanhood, while the Indian boatman, erect and silent as a bronze automaton, guided the boat down the rapid stream, and far within the dewy covert of the wood a whippoorwill made his perpetual moan, echoed softly back from the breast of Dark Orchard Hill.

At the mill, the after-supper fun grew fast and furious, and who but Betty Alden to lead and queen it with a gay vivacity of invention and power of will that made itself felt by all within its reach, while William Pabodie, his own man once more now that the strange sorcery of Gillian's presence was withdrawn, calmly bided his time, and at last, when Giles Hopkins, over from Barnstable on a visit, was trolling a sea-song and all the rest joining in the chorus, he edged between Betty and the girl next to her, saying,—

"Come out to the doorstep, Betty; I've something to say to you before I go home."

"Then say it here, or leave it unsaid, for I've no mind for the doorstep," drawled Betty with would-be carelessness; but some instinct told the lover that here was a citadel whose half-hearted garrison might be taken by assault, and grasping her by the arm, he moved toward the door, exclaiming half laughingly,—

"You must come, Betty, for else I'll make such a noise that they'll all stop singing to turn and look at us."

"You're overbold, William Pabodie," replied Betty icily; but yielding to both force and argument she allowed herself to be led not only to the doorstep, but down the steep path, through the garden all odorous with pinks and roses, to the spot beside the pool where still lay the broken branch of lilac, and where upon the old willow-trunk still seemed to linger the perfume of Gillian's presence.

"Why do you bring me here?" asked Betty, a sob rising in her throat, but bravely choked back again.

"Because here where an hour or two ago you set me down as false and fickle, here have I brought you to hear me say that I love you, Betty; and, what is more, I never have loved any woman but you, and if I may not have you for my wife I'll go a bachelor to my grave. Betty, will you be my wife?"

"If you've naught else to recommend you, Master Pabodie, none can accuse you of want of courage," replied Betty quietly, and throwing aside the mask that in the last hours had smothered her true feelings, she stood before him pale, stern, and pitiless. The young fellow looked at her in dismay.

"Betty! Don't you believe me, Betty?"

"Believe you when, or at which time? I believed a year or so ago that you cared somewhat for me, at least you came as near to saying it as I would let you, till I could know mine own mind"—

"And then did your mind turn to me, Betty?" demanded the lover eagerly.

"There was no time for it to turn, unless it had been such a weather-cock as yours, for I had not well got to thinking of the matter before I saw that you had forgot it, and were running like a well-broke spaniel at Gillian Brewster's heel, so I thought no more on't, and was just as well content it should be so. And then Gillian went away, and you, just like our Neptune when father's from home, went questing round seeking a master, and seemed willing to have me for one; and partly because you plagued me so, I came here to stay awhile, and then when you came to-day, and whispered in mine ear that it was to see me you'd made the excuse to come, my silly vanity believed the tale, and I had well-nigh been fool enough to trust you, as I would one of my own brothers who know not how to lie; but happily for me, Gillian also came, and I found you toying with her, and giving flowers, and looking into her eyes, and—oh, I know not what all—it makes me sick, it does, and all I want is to go mine own way, and have you go yours, and let there be an end of all this folly here and now."

The words were no sharper than the voice was cold, and the lover had well-nigh accepted the dismissal and turned away hopeless and humiliated, but that as he looked gloomily down, the moonlight glinted upon the buckle of a little shoe, and he perceived that the foot was viciously, if silently, grinding a blossom of the poor lilac branch into the earth. Somehow, he could not have told how, that sight brought courage to the all but discouraged heart, and suddenly seizing both cold and repellent hands, the young man pressed them to his breast, crying,—

"No, Betty, no, and no again! I'll not believe you. I'll not take such an answer. I'll not give you up, nor turn to any way that is not your way! Betty, I love you. I never have loved any but you. I'll have you and none other for my wife. Betty, darling, can't you forgive a blind folly, a stupid, senseless blunder? I could say a good deal to excuse myself but for the duty every man owes to every woman, and that I'll not forego, even to defend myself to you"—

"Oh, I know well enough what *she* is," murmured Betty; the young man paused, but would not, could not speak the thoughts that arose in his mind. Perhaps Betty was, after all, not ill pleased, for let men say what they will of the jealousies of women, there is among them an *esprit de corps* that rises indignantly in every true woman's breast when she hears her own sex or any member of it scorned by man.

So an abrupt silence fell between the two,—an eloquent silence, for as his hands firmly grasped hers, and the strong throbbing of his pulses vibrated along her nerves, there was no need of words, until after a few wonderful moments, moments that life could never repeat, the young man drew his true love close, close to his heart, and their lips met in a betrothal kiss.

CHAPTER XXXII.

ROBED IN WHITE SAMITE.

There was company at the captain's house, the same dear friends whom we have seen with him on so many joyous occasions, the Aldens, the Howlands, the Brewsters, the Pabodies and Hatherleys, and Cudworths; and from Plymouth, the governor and his wife, the Hopkinses, and other of the captain's friends and associates of the old time now so long gone by, and yet so powerful in the ties then formed. Parson Rayner was there, too, and Ralph Partridge, but it was as friends and neighbors that they came, and the only official word the minister of Duxbury uttered was when he wrung the captain's hand and said, "'Be strong and of a good courage,' my friend," and Standish, lifting sombre eyes to the speaker's face, answered him never a word.

And in the midst lay Lora, very pale and still, with the golden lashes folded close upon the cheek hardly whiter now than it had always been, and the faint rose tint lingering in the lips just touched with that mysterious smile that seems the trace of a joy so divine, so all powerful, that it bursts even the icy fetters of death, and insists upon revealing itself, if ever so dimly, for the assurance of those who must see before they can believe. The pale golden hair that was the mother's pride and boast was released from all bands, and lay a shining and rippling mantle at either side of the slender figure which at her father's desire was clothed in the robe of white samite he had brought her from over seas, saying in his pride that thus the mistress of his ancestral home should be clothed. And now! Alas, poor father! it clothed her for her nuptials indeed, but she must cross a darker sea than the Atlantic to enter into her kingdom. The delicate hands lay folded upon the breast, and beneath them some snowdrops that Betty Pabodie had nurtured, watering them with her tears and foreseeing this day, of which indeed Lora had calmly and cheerfully spoken more than once.

"Put on her shoes, and fold the train of her robe around her feet," commanded the father. "She said it should be so." And wonderingly the mother obeyed, for in these awful hours none dared to intrude upon the darkness that clothed Standish more gloomily than the mantle the Angel of Death had lightly laid around the maiden.

Once in the middle of the night, Barbara, rising from her sleepless couch, sought him where he sat alone with Lora, and throwing herself upon her knees beside him, her arms around him, and her head upon his breast, she cried,—

"Oh, Myles, Myles, let us try to bear it together. Do not shut me out of your heart. Oh, Myles, my heart is breaking—comfort me!"

"Hush, wife, hush! What need of words or clamor? Let her rest, let her rest—and leave us alone, good wife, my maid and me—go!"

Then chilled, silenced, well-nigh affrighted, the mother crept away, and left the defeated soldier to his own bitter retrospect.

The brothers, working day and night, fashioned an oaken casket, not of the gruesome shape in use at a later date, but more like a dainty cradle, and the women had spread in it a couch of sweet herbs and the fragrant tips of the balsam fir and the blossoms of the immortelle which they called life-everlasting. A pillow of dried rose-leaves and lavender-blossoms and the hop-flowers that soothe to dreamless slumber was laid ready for the gentle head, and a sheet of fine linen was spread over all.

"The captain said when he brought home that bolt of Hollands linen from Antwerp, that it was for Lora's wedding clothes," sobbed Barbara, as she drew the shining folds from the chest that held her most valued household treasures, and Priscilla Alden, with an arm around her friend's neck, kissed her, and bit her tongue lest it should say in spite of her, "Had he let her marry Wrestling Brewster, she might have needed wedding clothes of another sort from these."

And now all have looked their last, and the mother's tears have dropped thick and fast upon those eyes that will weep no more, and the father, silent, stern, and tearless, has laid a hand upon that golden hair that no longer twines around his fingers, and Betty has gently drawn one of the snowdrops from between those resistless fingers, a snowdrop that she will press in her Bible over the words "for of such are the kingdom of heaven," the cover is laid gently over that fragrant cradle, and the brothers, with the Alden sons who have been Lora's playmates and dear friends, place it upon the bier and carry it along the field path her light feet have so often trod, past the Brewster homestead, where now only Love and his family remained, and so on to what to-day we call Harden Hill; here around the little church already outgrown, and soon to be superseded, the graves of some of those who thus far had passed away were made; others, indeed, had directed that their remains should rest upon Burying Hill in Plymouth, and some would lie within the radius of light from their own hearthstones; but a few were here, and the captain with his own hands marked out the spot where Lora had fallen on that night when she knew, months before the news came over seas, that Wrestling Brewster was dead. There they laid her, softly, gently, as still we lay down the loved ones whom rudest touch could not harm, or crash of thunders disturb, and her own kinsmen did the rest. A little heap of turfs was piled near, and as the others turned away

Alexander and Josiah began to lay them; but Hobomok, the faithful friend and long-time servitor of Standish, laid a finger upon Alick's arm, saying in his guttural voice,—

"Hobomok do something for the Moonlight-on-the-water. Hobomok put the green cover over her."

"He's right, Alick," said Josiah, with a friendly glance at the old Indian. "He's all but worshiped Lora ever since she was born. Let him lay the turf."

"We couldn't better show our friendship for you, Hobomok."

"Hob know all about it," replied the red man sententiously, and the brothers followed the long line of friends who scattered along the road toward their different homes.

Standish walked silently beside his wife until nearly at his own door he stopped, looking frowningly out across the sea, his teeth set hard upon his nether lip, as if fighting out some problem in his own mind; then falling back, he touched William Bradford upon the arm, and drew him a little aside.

"Send home the rest with your sons, Bradford, and stay here to-night."

"My good friend, many occasions call me to Plymouth"—

"No occasion greater than the choice of life and death; nay, if all they say be true, the choice of salvation or damnation,—nothing weightier than such a choice, is there, Will?"

"What ails you, old friend? Your grief has—has made you ill!"

And the governor, grasping his friend's arm, looked apprehensively at the deep color that suddenly had overspread the pallor of his face, and at the fierce light that some thought had kindled in the gloomy depths of his eyes, hollow and strained by vigils and unshed tears.

"Tush, man! I'm not gone mad. I'm not such a weakling as to let any grief master the man in me. It's only that I'm in a strait between God and the Enemy, and there's no man alive I'd choose for umpire but you."

"If you need me, Myles, I'm with you, whatever else betide."

And the two men grasped hands and looked into each other's eyes. Then with a voice more moved than any had heard from him in three days Standish said, "I thought I could count upon your kindness, Will, if you knew my need. Let all the rest go, and when darkness has fallen, we two will come back to my little maid's grave, and I'll tell you there."

And so it was. The funeral feast, almost a necessity where so many came from far, was served and eaten nearly in silence, and then the guests departed, Dame Bradford under charge of her two sons, and tenderly served by Gillian, whose volatile spirit was quenched in the abundant tears that meant so little from her eyes.

Night had fallen, and the waning moon was shining mournfully over the waters, when at a signal from his host Bradford followed him into the open air and, with a word or two, along the path the funeral procession had just trodden.

The young birch was in leaf, and a little west wind rustled and sighed among its branches, casting flickering shadows across the new-turfed mound, lined from west to east that the sleeper, obedient to the great call, might in upstanding face the rising of the Sun of Righteousness.

"Sit you down, Bradford. There's a rock she's often rested on. Don't speak until I gather my thoughts and know what 'tis I mean to say."

Without reply Bradford, drawing his cloak around him, for the spring night was chill, sat down upon the boulder, where indeed Lora had dreamed away many an hour, gazing across the sea that ever drew her with its vague, sad calling, and waited silently while Standish, with folded arms and head bent upon his breast, paced up and down, up and down, now standing upon the crumbling edge of the cliff near at hand, now pacing back to the little church a bow-shot from the shore.

At last, with sudden and hurried footsteps, as though fearing to linger over his decision, the soldier drew near, holding a folded paper in his hand, and exclaimed,—

"Bradford! You too have an only daughter. If a man insulted her bitterly, bitterly, what would you do to him?"

"Insulted her? How?"

"No matter how. What would you do to him?"

"It is not fair to ask me such a question in such a way, Myles, if you mean to find an augury for your own course in my reply. I cannot tell what I should do until I know all, and mayhap not then. But surely no man ever offered insult to the sweet maid who's gone?"

"'Tis all you know about it. Well, here's the story. When I was in England almost a score of years ago, I went to Standish Hall to talk with my kinsman now in authority there, and asked him if he would do me the justice his father denied to my father. He seemed a kindly man enough, or mayhap 'twas only that he was a smooth courtier, and cozened easily enough a rough soldier who has never learned to lie. At all odds, it ended in our making a solemn compact, that if the child my wife then looked for should be a girl, she was to become the wife of that man's son, then a child of two or three years old, and all that ought by right to have been mine should be settled upon her and her younger children. We did not set it down on parchment, nor call witnesses to our oaths; but we grasped hands upon it, and passed our word each to each as honest gentlemen, and there it rested. When I was in England ten years or so ago, I traveled down to Eton to see the boy, and give him a little compliment, small enough for the heir of Standish Hall, but large enough for my own pocket. I said naught to him about Lora, of course, though I let him know that I felt more than a kinsman's interest in him, and he seemed a brave lad, a trifle set up, but I could pardon that. Well, the time went on, and there was some talk of Wrestling Brewster and my girl. I dealt with that as seemed good to me, and then I wrote to my kinsman, and said the time had come to consider our contract, and that my girl was woman grown and his boy must be one and twenty, and I asked how and where we should meet to give them to each other. Almost a year went by, and my blood already began to stir at the delay, although I schooled myself to believe it no slight, when at the last a letter came, this letter. Wait till I read it out, for though there's no light, I can see every word as if 'twere printed off on mine own eyeballs. First a flummery of 'dear kinsman' and the like vapid compliment, and then:—

"'As touching what you call the contract of marriage between our children, I confess I had all but forgot that we two did hold some such discourse a matter of eighteen years ago; but what will you, cousin? These young folk must still take their own way, and my son before reaching his majority had set his fancy upon a young gentlewoman, one of the great Howard family, and with a very pretty estate tacked to her petticoat, marching well with our lands of Boisconge. So they were betrothed some months ago and will be married come Whitsuntide. Hoping the fair and worthy Mistress Lora, whose name so pleasantly recalls our family tree, will soon marry to please you as well as herself, I remain,' et cetera, et cetera.

"There, now, William Bradford, what would you have done to the man who so scorned your Mercy?"

"My faith, Standish!" cried the governor, springing to his feet, "I cannot blame your anger, for 'tis righteous. Your cousin is but a knave in spite of his fair words"—

"And what would you have done with him, had you been in my place?" persisted Standish coldly.

"Nay, what could be done?" faltered Bradford so lamely that Standish uttered a little bitter laugh of derision.

"There you see! You've studied Christian charity so long that you will not say Kill him! and your manhood will not let you say Forgive him! and you can find no middle way.

"But I, thank God, am not so hampered; and as I finished reading that letter my fist clenched on old Gideon's hilt, and I promised him that he should carry conviction to that false, proud heart. I would have gone at once, but I saw that my little maid was grievously ill, and I could not leave her; then I saw that she would die, and one day I drew Gideon from his scabbard and thrust his sharp tooth through that cartel,—see, here are the marks of him,—and I bade him hold fast till we could wet that paper in the red ink of my reply"— But here the governor interrupted him,—

"Myles! Man has no right to predetermine vengeance. In the heat of affront I too might have longed to combat to the death with one who had so lightlied my child, but I never could have stored up death for him like that."

"You were bred to the land and to books, Bradford, and I to arms," replied the soldier haughtily; and then in sudden revulsion of feeling, he grasped his friend's hand, saying hoarsely, "I never can be the man you are, Will, and you better deserved than I to have had that saint for a daughter. But come, now, I must e'en tell you the whole, as if 'twere to a father confessor, and, by my faith, I wish you were one, for the old practice rises up in a man's mind when trouble comes. But there! I won't rake up old disputes, but rather on with my shrift: I was fully purposed, then, so soon as my sweet maid was gone, to travel to England and seeking out Ralph Standish challenge him to mortal combat, and to thrust my brave old sword with that letter spitted upon its blade through his false heart and so avenge my girl. I was as fully purposed that way as ever I was to eat when I was hungry and saw victual before me, and I'm not more apt to change my purpose than a mastiff is to lose his grip.

"The night she died I went down by the edge of the water and tramped along the beach the night through, yearning to throw myself in and get to him. I was half mad, I think, and could I have reached that black heart then, I fear I should have shamed my manhood by not leaving the villain time to defend himself. The next night, that is, last night, I was calmer, for as I had not slept nor eaten, I was not so full of lustyhood, and sending the others away, I sat by my darling the night through, alone, save when the poor wife came and I would not let her stay. Poor Barbara! I've not remembered her grief as I should; but mine swallowed up all else, because it was so much bigger and stronger than all else. So sitting by her, and reading that gentle, subtle smile that mayhap you marked upon her pretty mouth— How can I tell you, Will? Didst ever grasp a handful of sea sand and try to hold it fast?"

"Ay, and felt it slip, grain by grain, between my fingers."

"Yes. You catch my meaning, as I knew you would. Even like those grains of sand, my fierce desire for that man's life slipped and slipped away, and what I had deemed a noble vengeance grew to seem only a brutal thirst for blood, and the thought of him and of his offense seemed to fade into the forgotten years whose record is closed. Perhaps I slept, perhaps I dreamed without sleeping, but all at once it seemed to me that my maid stood beside me, close, and yet so far away I dared not put out a hand to touch her; and that smile was on her lips, and someway it seemed to speak its meaning without words, and the meaning was, 'To him that overcometh'— That was all, and yet, something,—that dear spirit or mine own heart, or my memory of that Book she ever made me read to her all through the last year,—something told me that it was to him that overcometh his own self, to him who can trust his vengeance to the Lord and forego it for himself,— to such an one that the path lies open to the place where Lora has gone; but to the man of bloodshed and heady violence that path is no more to be traced than a highway through this wilderness.

"But when the daylight came, and I had eaten and slept, I began to think 't was all a fantasy bred of long watching and fasting, and that my first thought was the best, and even I fancied that I was growing old and my hardihood was on the wane, and the cold apathy of age was what held my hand; and so, tossed this way and that, and sore bestead with doubt and anguish, I turned to some other for calmer counsel and a juster view. In the old days I would have sought a priest, but now I turn to you, Will; give me your counsel,—tell me where is my right."

Throwing himself upon the ground, the soldier hid his face upon the fresh green mound and lay exhausted and passive. His friend stood many moments motionless, his eyes uplifted to the sky, where the little white clouds flying across the face of the waning moon gave her a look of hurry and perturbation, as if she too were sore beset by the doubts and temptations of the earthly atmosphere. At last he slowly spoke:—

"Old friend, I am no better or wiser man than you, and I can only speak as a fallible sinner may to one for whose welfare he yearns as for his own. It seems to me that God has already answered you through that dear child who has gone to Him. 'Vengeance is mine; I will repay,' saith He, and the promise to him that overcometh is as precious and as many-sided as' the white stone that he shall receive, and which commentators hold to mean the diamond"—

"Enough, enough, man!" cried Standish, starting to his feet. "I cannot listen to so many words. I care naught for commentators or texts. Tell me as man to man, may I go and kill mine enemy or no!"

"Well, then, no! You shall here and now kneel down and lay your revenge at the foot of Christ's cross and leave it there. Man! Has your enemy hurt you more than those who drove the spikes through his hands and feet, what time He prayed 'Father, forgive them; they know not what they do'? and bethink you how easy vengeance would have been to Him."

"Ay. Knew not what they did!" muttered Standish. "Knowing it or not, that man slew my child, for had it not been for the contract, I would have let her marry Brewster, and she might have been to-day a happy wife and mother."

"And if you will reckon in that fashion," replied Bradford sternly, "it was surely you who slew Wrestling Brewster, since it was because he might not have Lora that he went to England and found his death. Should not God and our dear Elder have required his blood at your hand?"

A great silence was the only answer, and presently Bradford spoke again, and now in the tone of assured conviction and well-grounded authority that in some moods the human soul yearns to hear, especially an ardent, impetuous, and loving soul like that of Standish; a nature that, while the impulse lasts, will dare heaven and hell and earth to achieve its purposes, and when the revulsion comes distrusts all that is within, and turns like a drowning man to some external authority. Such a man makes a good soldier, for as he says, "Go here, and go there!" to those beneath him, he is ready to add, "For I also am a man under authority."

And in this need, characterizing some of the strongest souls that animate humanity, masculine and feminine, lies the yearning for confession and guidance, absolution and penance, that has for centuries been the strongest weapon in the hand of the Catholic Church.

"No, my friend, you shall not carry this controversy away from this spot. It is Satan who buffets you so sorely, and if you will fight, it is with him the combat shall be. Which is the stronger, you, or that great dragon, that old serpent, whom Michael, of old, fought and conquered? Fight *him* in the name of the Lord, and with Gideon if you will, but here and now relinquish all, yes, every iota of the desire for your brother's blood. Destroy that letter,—yes, tear it in pieces here beside Lora's grave, and bury the remembrance of it as you have buried her. You have left it to me, Myles, and I have been given this to say to you. Take it, in the name of God who hears us."

"I take it as I took her message," replied Standish in a low voice, and rising to his knees, for he had been lying prone beside the grave, he sought about for a moment, and finding a bit of stick began carefully to remove one of the turfs at the foot of the new-made grave. Laying it at one side, he took the letter from under his knee, where he had held it, and quietly tore it into fragments, which he held in his left hand, while with the right he scooped a hollow in the loose loam beneath the sod; but in deepening the cavity his fingers encountered some foreign substance, and drawing it out, held up to the moonlight a little package enveloped in a strip of the cloth-like inner bark of the birch-tree, and bound around with cord twisted of fibres of the hackmatack.

"Some of Hobomok's work," murmured Standish, carefully unrolling the bark, and disclosing a curiously shaped and much worn stone of a peculiarly hard and dense quality, fashioned at one end into a neck by which it could be securely carried, and at the other sharpened to a curved edge capable of cutting wood.

"Why, 't is Hobomok's totem!" exclaimed Standish, turning it over and over. "He always wore it about his neck, and for all he calls himself a praying Indian, I sorely mistrusted he prayed as much to his totem as to any other god, nor would he ever let us see him use it, or take it in our hands, though the boys have urged him more than enough. The dear maid used to talk to him in her gentle way, and try to make a good Christian of him, just as she used to set up her dolls and play go to meeting with them, and with as great results. But now,—did he bury it here for a charm to keep away the afrits, or did he lay it at her feet to show that in her sweet patience of death she had conquered his unbelief even as she conquered that other savage, her father?"

"Ask him," suggested Bradford, but Standish, carefully replacing the totem in its covering, shook his head.

"No, no! Hobomok is too much of a gentleman to pry into what is not meant for him to know, and I should be ashamed to let him know that I had surprised what he fain would have held a secret.

"No, I'll lay the letter in first, and then the totem to keep it down, and my little maid will understand all that is meant by the one and the other. There! And now, friend, I thank you. We're growing old men, Will; 'it is toward evening, and the day is far spent,' but this night's work will stand both for you and for me when all else fails. Come, let us be going."

CHAPTER XXXIII.

A BOLD BUCCANEER.

"It's an ill wind, they say, that blows nobody good, and I believe this is that same wind."

"Tut, tut, man! 'Tis ill luck speaking against the wind. Wot you not who is the Prince of the Power of the Air?"

"Sathanas; and I verily believe he's in this smoky chimney."

"Well, then, Jacob Cooke, get you outside the house, and if Jack Jenney's afeard of the one he says makes it smoke, he'd as well go out with you."

"Thank you for nothing, Dame Damaris," retorted John Jenney, laughing as he rose to his feet. "I didn't look to be turned out of the house when I came to make a wedding visit, but mayhap 'tis so new to you to have a house that you haven't welly learned to govern it."

"That's the truth, Jack," interposed the master of the house, a little mortified; "so we'll e'en leave the shrewish dame to her own devices, and go out to find a warm corner beside a chimney that doesn't smoke, and a woman that doesn't scold."

"Go your ways. Your room is aye better than your company," responded the comely dame, whom as Damaris Hopkins we saw a baby on board the Mayflower, and who, lately married to the son of Francis Cooke, was one of the most stirring young matrons of the town.

The two men, laughing, and yet a little reluctant to turn out into the shrewd east wind, paused outside the house. This new home, built upon land inherited by Damaris from her father, Stephen Hopkins, was on the westerly edge of Training Green, and thus high enough to catch the full force of the wind rising steadily since noon.

"Phew!" whistled Jenney, dragging his hat over his brows, "'tis enough to take the curl out of a pig's tail. There'll be some wracks along the coast, if this holds all night."

"Come up the hill to the Fort, and ask Livetenant Holmes to give us a squint through the spy-glass."

"I'm with you. But Holmes isn't half the good fellow the captain was. The Fort don't seem the same place."

"No. And yet the captain could give a rough lick with his tongue, if one angered him."

"Yes. You, and Bart Allerton, and Peregrine White, and Giles Hopkins used to catch it once in a while when you meddled or made with the guns."

"Yes, and when he trained us in the manual exercise. But we're all beholden to him for knowing how to manage a piece man-fashion."

"Ay, we're all beholden to him, and sorry am I he's gone from the town, and they say is breaking in health and spirit."

"Since father went it seems as if the old settlers were passing away and we youngsters are to hold the helm." And Jacob sighed in a gruffly sentimental sort of fashion.

"You're right, Cooke, and I sore mistrust our fathers' chairs will prove too wide for us. I know mine is, and often enough I wish the old man back."

"Ha! That was a shrewd twist of the wind! It seemed to snatch my breath. Well, here we are." And raising the heavy iron latch, the two men precipitated themselves into the great lower room of the Fort, where once we saw the Pilgrims hold their fast when drought and famine were sore upon them, and once we assisted at the trial of John Oldhame.

The religious services of the town were still held in this place, although it had long been Pastor Rayner's urgent appeal to the people that they should build a suitable meeting-house for the worship of God, and no longer mingle ecclesiastical and secular pursuits in the same building. But since the removal of some of the colony's wealthiest and most influential townsmen to Duxbury, Scituate, Marshfield, and the Cape towns, poor Plymouth had become so destitute that her sons could barely provide food for the body, and had little money or energy to spare in suitably serving the soul's aliment.

And now help was to come, and from a most unexpected source.

Upon the platform at the top of the Fort the two visitors found Lieutenant Holmes, sheltered from the wind behind a sentry-box, and absorbed in the use of the spy-glass they had come to seek.

"Well, and what do you see, Livetenant?" demanded Cooke, ever ready with his tongue. The soldier, who after the manner of most men when absorbed in the use of one sense was slow to occupy himself with another (it being one of the privileges of womanhood to do two things at once and do both well), did not reply at once, and Jenney, screening his eyes with his hand, looked out to seaward for a long moment, and then cried,—

"Surely there's a sail in the scurry off the Gurnet! Isn't it so, Livetenant?"

"A sail, say you?" replied Holmes slowly, and in the mechanical tone of one whose eye is glued to a spy-glass. "Well, double it, and thribble it, and mayhap you'll hit closer to the bull's eye."

"Three sail!" exclaimed Cooke, fairly dancing with excitement. "Come, now, let's have a squint, Holmes, just a cast of the eye, and I'll give back the glass in a jiffy. Let's have it, there's a Christian!"

"Well, then, Jake, take your squint, and tell me what you make of it." And the lieutenant, laughing a little, rose to his feet, handed the glass to Cooke, and rubbed his eyes, which, in fact, had declined to serve any longer in that one-sided fashion.

"You're right, Holmes, you're right! 'Tis three sail, and sizable craft, too; brigantines, I should say."

"Come, come, Jake!" expostulated the lieutenant jealously. "A man's not going to tell a brigantine from a bark at this distance, and with such a spoor flying."

"Mabbe not, Livetenant, mabbe not; but I'll miss my guess if it's not a brigantine I've got in the field now, and laboring mightily she is. Take my word for it, Brown's Island'll be the death of her, unless they've got a skipper out of a thousand, and men of might to handle helm and canvas."

"Give me one peep before you take the glass," pleaded Jenney, and jolly Holmes consenting, the young fellow so availed himself of the privilege that Cooke, who was a trifle short-sighted, and found his own eyes useless, protested,—

"It's bad manners for any man to take so long a pull at the glass! Pass it around lively is the rule."

"My chance now," cried Holmes peremptorily; so the three men watched, turn and turn about, until Holmes after a long survey handed the glass to Cooke, saying,—

"It's time for me to go down and report to the governor. Stay you here and keep goal till I come back."

"All right. I'll do it," briefly replied Cooke, already absorbed in the sense of sight.

In the wide house under the hill, where Bradford and his early love were growing placidly old together, there was a guest of unusual degree, and Lieutenant Holmes, requesting to see the governor at once, was ushered into the dining-room, where with the master and mistress of the house, their two sons and Gillian, sat a priest in the strait garb of the Jesuit, and bearing upon his thin, shrewd face the traces of that cultivation and worldly facility generally marking the Order which has ruled the world, and yet failed to save itself. This was Father Drouillette, a Frenchman by birth, a cosmopolitan by training, visiting the New World, not, as we may be sure, without a purpose, and yet quite capable of allowing himself to be torn in little shreds without suffering that purpose to be discovered.

He had already been in Boston, and the fishing-smack that brought him from thence to Plymouth would with the morning's tide sail for Manhattan, so that four-and-twenty hours comprised his stay in Plymouth; but this brief sojourn was enough for the Jesuit to see and know that the soil of the Old Colony was not yet ripe for the seeds of the cinchona (then called Jesuit's Bark), and also to read Bradford's noble nature and courteous kindliness, to both of which he did full justice in his report, adding that as the day was Friday, the governor gave him an excellent dinner of fish.

After the fish came a delicate pudding, succeeded by a dessert, over which the family still sat when Lieutenant Holmes, entering the room, reported three large vessels in distress driving into the harbor, and already off Beach Point.

"Are the lives of the mariners in danger?" inquired the priest, crossing himself so unobtrusively that only Bradford perceived the gesture.

"I fear for them if they do not keep to the channel, for the tide is on the ebb, and 'tis but a crooked course," replied Holmes; and the governor, rising, said somewhat hurriedly,—

"If you will excuse me, sir, I will leave you with my wife for a little, and go to see that a pilot is sent out"—

"I told Doten to get his boat ready, and wait your Excellency's orders," interposed Holmes, resolute to give the governor his full honors before this stranger.

"That was well done, friend," replied Bradford gently, and would have left the room, but the priest, rising nimbly, and taking his cloak and hat from the deer's antlers where they hung, exclaimed, in his perfect although accented English, "Nay, I will not be left behind. There may be use for another pair of hands."

"And possibly for a turn of priest-craft," thought Bradford, smiling to himself; but Drouillette, catching the smile, returned it with a little shrug and arch of the eyebrows, saying in French,—

"And why not? Few mariners sail from Geneva."

"You are in your right, sir," returned the governor in the same tongue, and courteously motioning his guest to pass before him, while Gillian, to whom French was a mother tongue, listened with both ears, and resolved to by and by hold a private conversation with the priest, who already had perceived her knowledge of his language and taken the measure of her nature; that she would prove an easy proselyte, and quite enjoy the intrigue of covertly becoming a Catholic while openly remaining in a Protestant community, he had also perceived, but after a moment's thought had decided the facile victory to be at once valueless and dangerous, and during the rest of his stay opposed a bland stupidity to all the girl's ingenious advances.

The stout pilot boat, clumsy enough as contrasted with those that to-day skim across the waters of Plymouth harbor, but then a model of beauty and skill, lay ready beside the Rock, and at a word from the governor speeded forth under its close-reefed foresail, carrying three active fellows to the rescue of the foremost brigantine, which, warned by the sounding-lead of shoal water, and struggling against a current which insisted upon setting her ashore on the beach, was lying to and waiting for pilotage. Half an hour later the three vessels were anchored in the stream, and a procession of boats was bringing their officers and detachments of the crews ashore, discharging them at a rude stone pier and bulkhead extending a few feet beyond the Rock, which, as yet uninjured by patriotic zeal, lay calmly presiding over the modern commotions that had come to disturb its centuries of solitude.

In the place of honor in the first boat sat a very elegant gentleman, dressed in all the picturesque bravery of a cavalier: his broad hat covered with ostrich plumes, his doublet of Genoese velvet slashed with satin of Lyons in harmonious shades of cramoisie and murrey, his breeches of velvet adorned with a deep lace almost hidden by the wrinkled tops of boots of soft Cordovan leather. To correct the effeminacy of this costume, accented as it was by jewels, lace, and perfume in profusion, Captain Cromwell, prince and leader of the buccaneers soon to swarm the Spanish seas, carried so proud and warlike a countenance, curled his mustachios so fiercely, showed such strong white teeth set in so massive a jaw, and such broad shoulders and muscular limbs, that it must have been a rash man, indeed, who ventured to make criticism of whatever the captain might choose to wear, or to inquire how an officer under commission from the new

Commonwealth of England still displayed himself under the guise of a royalist cavalier. The explanation probably, had he chosen to give it, was that the Spanish seas were a long distance from England, that it was a long while since his letter-of-marque had left home, and that as the King was still at large, the fortune of war might at any moment replace him upon the throne, so that in view of all these circumstances a successful buccaneer must be in a great measure his own lawgiver. Nominally, Captain Cromwell was in religion and politics a Parliament man; at heart, he was a Roman Catholic and a cavalier, and at this distance from the central authority indulged himself in at least dressing to suit his own taste.

Springing ashore as the boat touched the pier, the commandant, without waiting for an introduction from Lieutenant Holmes, who escorted him, doffed his hat until the plumes swept the ground and bowed low, both to the governor and the priest, saying,—

"My respects to you, most noble Governor, and to you, reverend sir, and my thanks for the timely aid you have sent us. Allow me to present myself as Thomas Cromwell, in command of these three brigantines sent out by the English government to hold our country's foes, especially those of Spain, in check, and to make reprisals for certain offenses offered to the British flag in these waters. As it is long since I had news from England, I will not add 'God save the King!' nor yet 'God save the Parliament!' lest I should offend somebody's sensibilities, but content myself with simply exclaiming, 'God save old England!'"

"An aspiration we all may echo, Captain Cromwell," replied Bradford gravely, "and I am happy to assure you that by the latest advices from England the parliamentarians under whose authority you sail are still favored by Providence. For the rest, all honest Englishmen are welcome to such hospitality as our impoverished town can offer. There is an Ordinary at the head of this hill kept by James Cole, where very decent accommodation may be had for your men, and I shall be most happy to welcome you and your officers at mine own house, nearly opposite the tavern, as often as you are pleased to come. This gentleman, a guest like yourself, is called Father Drouillette, from France."

"My duty to you, father," responded Cromwell, bending his knee, and the Jesuit, keenly regarding him, made a slight motion of benediction, murmuring, "Bless you, my son."

"And now," continued Bradford, in a less formal manner, "let us at once seek the shelter of James Cole's roof and mine, and escape this biting wind, of which, Captain, you will already have had more than enough, as I opine."

The buccaneer assented, and speaking a rapid word or two among the men surrounding him, sent the mass of them to the tavern with a stern injunction to sobriety and decency; then calling the commanders of the three ships, he presented them to Bradford, who at once extended his invitation to them, and led the way to the house, where a merry fire and refreshments were found awaiting them, but nobody was to be seen.

"I wonder through which crevice that little schemer is peeping," said Father Drouillette to himself as he took snuff and presented his box to Cromwell, who took a pinch, and absorbing it delicately, said,—

"You must let me offer you a jar of Spanish mixture, prepared, as I hear, especially for the Archbishop of Toledo, who is curious in his tobacco. It is most agreeably scented with vanilla, and carries a certain odor of incense that arouses very devout reminiscences in the mind of a poor wanderer like myself."

"My poor nose would indeed feel itself honored by a pinch of such truly ecclesiastical snuff as you describe. But as I sail with the morning tide, I fear I shall not have the opportunity of trying it," replied the Jesuit; and Cromwell, after a moment's thought, suggested,—

"Unless, reverend sir, you would do me the honor of sleeping on board the Golden Fleece, as my ship is called. I can offer you a decent bed, and my fellows will doubtless purvey in this good town the material for a breakfast. Shall I have the honor of entertaining your reverence?"

"I shall be most happy to accept your hospitality, my son, if Governor Bradford will accept my humble excuses for cutting short my visit to him," began the priest; but before he could finish, a door at the end of the room quietly opened, and Gillian, with downcast eyes and air of timid modesty, glided to Bradford's side, murmuring:

"Our dame fain would know how many beds we shall prepare. She says there are plenty for all the gentlemen."

"St. Anthony befriend us! Is that the daughter of our worthy host?" whispered Cromwell to the priest, who only shook his head, and rising from his chair said in English,—

"Master Bradford, will you hold me excused if I accept this gentleman's invitation to pass the night aboard his vessel? It may be more convenient for my early embarkation, and less disturbance to your household."

"You shall perfectly suit your own convenience, sir," replied Bradford in his calm and gentle fashion, although the murmured colloquies of priest and buccaneer had rather annoyed him; "but you will all take your supper with us, I trust. Gillian, you may tell the mistress that these five gentlemen will sup with us, but prefer to sleep on board ship."

That night Captain Cromwell transferred a curious chronicle of the misdoings of a year past from his own conscience to the custody of the priest, and received some very sensible and practical advice. But at the end of all, the penitent, with a gesture of deference, declared,—

"You're right, father, doubtless right, both as priest and man of the world; but I feel it in my marrow that yon lass is my fate, and 'tis useless striving against it. Those eyes of hers pierced my heart to the core when first they met mine own, and when at supper she served me with meat and drink, no nectar or ambrosia was ever more Olympian."

"Well, well, my son," answered the priest indulgently, "I say not you shall not marry the maid if she will have you; but I forebode it will be a marriage of haste, most vainly repented of at leisure. I spoke with the governor about her, and find she is a penniless orphan, although connected with the family of their late teacher, Elder Brewster, as they called him; and Mistress Gillian is under the austere protection of the governor and his most sweet and gracious lady. Your wooing, if you persist in this mad intention, must be wholly honorable and worthy. Remember that, my son!" and the priest's voice assumed a stern and authoritative accent, which the penitent accepted with a bend of his head while he replied,—

"Most positively so, father. The homeless maid shall become Mistress Cromwell, with all the pomp and ceremony"—

"Of Master Bradford's office," interposed the Jesuit. "For these poor rebels to our dear Mother's authority are only married by civil process, and scorn the church's benediction."

"Is that the way of it!" exclaimed Cromwell, a little dismayed. "Well, I will bring my bride to Manhattan or to Virginia, where you tell me you are to found a college, and our nuptials shall be blessed there. The civil rite binds us so far as law is concerned."

"Man's law, yes," replied the priest dryly; "and I will trust your word to fulfill this promise, if indeed you carry out your most rash resolve."

"I shall carry it out, father," asserted the buccaneer quietly. "'Tis my way."

The next morning Father Drouillette, the richer by a gloriously illuminated missal, a gold crucifix set with five great rubies, and half a dozen jars of the Archbishop of Toledo's snuff, embarked on board the fisherman, while Cromwell took up his quarters at Cole's tavern, which woke to such thriving business as it had never known before. Examination of the brigantines showed two of them to be in need of extensive repairs in consequence not only of the storm which had driven them into Plymouth, but of the long cruise preceding it; and as this cruise had been exceedingly prosperous, the mariners, who during the next month pervaded the town and made acquaintance with most of its inhabitants, scattered their money and precious commodities of various sorts in such profusion that Governor Winthrop, of Boston, in chronicling this visit, attributes the storm that drove the buccaneer into Plymouth to a divine interposition intended for the maintenance of the impoverished town, threatened with utter desertion and destruction.

Nor was the leader less generous and profuse than his more reckless followers, so that not only were the governor's family overwhelmed with as many rich gifts as he could be prevailed on to allow them to accept, but nearly every one of the poorer families was so substantially relieved as to give all new hope and energy to help themselves.

Not a week from the day of his arrival had elapsed before Cromwell sought an interview with the governor, and, without mentioning that he already had obtained her full consent to his proposals, offered himself as a suitor for Mistress Gillian's hand. Bradford, utterly amazed at the idea, would at the first have absolutely set it aside, declaring that such a sudden fancy could have no substantial foundation, and was unworthy of discussion; but when next the governor was closeted with his wife, he discovered that in her mind this marriage was a scheme to be encouraged as much as possible, and at the last, a little impatient of masculine density, the wife exclaimed,—

"'Tis an honorable and safe way out of the moil we have been stirring in, since first we made Gillian one of our family; and so that she desires it, and he hath means and will to care for her, all that remains, if she has Love Brewster's consent, is for me to make up the piece of brocade Cromwell hath given her into a wedding gown, and for you to bind them fast in matrimony."

"Say you so, Elsie, say you so?" demanded the governor, pausing in the perilous operation of shaving his chin to stare into the mirror at his wife, who was settling her cap at one corner. "Why, I fancied you prized Gillian's company and daughterly service above all things."

"I can spare it," briefly replied Alice Bradford with an inscrutable smile.

"But hasn't the child won a place in your affections, wife?"

"She has in yours and Will's and Joseph's, and that's three parts of the family."

"Surely, Alice, you've not turned jealous?"

"You lightly me, William, when you ask if I am jealous of—of Gillian."

"I do not comprehend," murmured the governor, resuming his razor, but presently suspending it to demand with considerable energy,—

"You really mean, then, that as honest and Godfearing guardians of this child we should give her in marriage to this stranger?"

"Yes, I do. When all is said, she is almost as much a stranger as he, and I know not why they should not suit each other well."

"So be it. I will tell the man, and do you speak as a mother should to the maid. 'Tis not like you, Alice, to be bitter."

"I shall not love her the better, if you are to chide me on her account, Will."

"Nay, chide thee, sweetheart! 'Twould ill befit me to chide the better half of mine own life."

So the suitor received permission to woo his bride openly, and Gillian presently so shone with jewels, and so rustled about in gorgeous raiment, that matrons and maids suspended their work to run to the doors and watch her as she passed by.

CHAPTER XXXIV.

THE HILT OF A RAPIER.

"Voysye! Hold on, man! Here, come along back!"

"Belay your jaw, you landlubber! I'm bound to overhaul that clipper before she gets away! Cast off your grapnel, or"—

And twisting his arm away from Francis Billington, with whom he had been drinking until both men had had more than enough, Richard Voysye, seaman of the Golden Fleece, set out to overtake the female figure which had just flitted past them in the twilight. Billington, not so tipsy as the sailor, lunged forward in pursuit, and once more grasping his arm exclaimed,—

"'Tis the young dame your captain is going to marry, I tell you, and 'twill go hard with the man that affronts her"—

"Hang the captain, and you too! There, then, you fool—take that!"

Delivering, as he spoke, a cruel blow in the face of his opponent, Voysye felled him to the ground, and pursuing Gillian, who hearing the scuffle had paused to look behind her, threw a rude arm around her waist, crying,—

"Come, now, I'll have one kiss, if I die for't."

But Gillian, lithe as a cat, struggled and fought after her kind, so successfully that the ruffian had not been able to snatch his kiss before a heavy foot reached him with a kick, and a furious voice roared in his ear,—

"Avast there, you"—but the epithets are not writable, and in these days no man, however angry, would use them in a woman's presence. They were, however, effectual, for with an oath quite as furious and quite as unmentionable, Voysye quitted his hold upon the girl's waist and, turning, aimed at Cromwell's face a buffet which, however, only reached his shoulder. Angered, not so much at the assault as the insubordination, the captain seized his sheathed rapier, and dealt with the hilt a blow upon the sailor's head which prostrated him, bleeding and senseless, at Gillian's feet.

"You've killed him, and they'll hang you for murder!" cried she. "Hide him, and get away with your vessels before it's found out."

"And would you go with me?" demanded Cromwell, gazing curiously in the girl's fierce, flushed face.

"Yes—no—yes, if you could get clear, and save your neck and your money," returned Gillian with cynical frankness.

"Ay, I thought as much, Mistress," retorted the sailor, "and I'm a fool to care for such a woman; but still I do, and when I go you shall go too, or if I'm hung you shall have the price of a soul. Thirty pieces satisfied Judas, didn't it?"

"Here's another man coming," replied Gillian coldly, and with no more words she walked away, while Cromwell, turning to the new-comer, said,—

"Well, Higgins, I'm beholden to you for setting me on his track, and here he is. He lifted his hand on me, and I felled him with a tap of my cutlass hilt. See if he's hurt."

Higgins, a man of few words, stared for a moment into his captain's face, looked after the retreating figure of Gillian, and then kneeling beside his comrade fingered the wound awhile, mumbling, "Hurt, I should say! 'Tis a shrewd wound i'faith! A parlous cut! 'Tis life and death, and nigher death than life, to my mind."

"Nonsense, man," replied Cromwell a little uneasily. "A great hulking fellow like that don't die of a tap on his numskull. Run you into the village and fetch a surgeon. Hasten, now, and when you've sent him, see about some sort of litter, that we may take him to Cole's tavern."

"'Tis no use," grumbled Higgins, but still scrambled to his feet, and set off at such good speed that in half an hour Doctor Matthew Fuller, nephew and successor of our old friend Doctor Samuel, was on the spot and encouraging the wounded man's efforts toward consciousness. But so soon as he could sit up and speak, Voysye, true to his nature, paid his surgeon's bill with a curse, responded to his captain's rough expressions of amity with sulky silence, and scorning the litter, or even the support of a friendly arm, staggered off toward the shore, and as soon as possible got aboard ship and comforted his wound with as much Santa Cruz rum as he could obtain, seasoning it with dire threats of vengeance against Higgins, who prudently kept out of his way.

"'Tis an ill wind blown over," reported Cromwell to his sweetheart that night; and so it might have proved but that Voysye, waking next morning in the dispositions natural to a man who has a fevered wound across his head, and has gone to bed very drunk, insisted upon going ashore to find and fight with Higgins, who had, as he knew, reported him to the captain. In the captain's absence all discipline had fallen into such disrepute that nobody opposed the half-delirious movements of the wounded man, who went ashore, roved around for a while, and finally, just as he had discovered Higgins and was pointing a pistol at his head, was seized with convulsions, and twenty-four hours later lay a dead man in an upper chamber of Cole's tavern.

So serious a matter as this could not be suffered to pass unnoticed by the authorities, and with some grave expressions of regret and an assurance of honorable treatment, Captain Cromwell was placed under arrest and lodged in the strong-room of the Fort under guardianship of Lieutenant Holmes, while a messenger was dispatched to Captain's Hill to summon Standish to a conference with the governor and the others of his council; for the sailor had requested to be tried by a court martial, and who but the General Officer of all the Colonies could organize and head it? With the great captain came Lieutenant Nash, and Ensign-bearer Constant Southworth, with Hatherley, Alden, Willett, Cudworth, and other of the Duxbury men, so that for some days Plymouth assumed the air of a garrisoned place in time of war, much to the delight of Gillian, and perhaps some other of the lonely maids of the almost deserted town.

The court martial, formal and dignified in its proceedings and absolutely just in its dealings, lasted for a whole day, and much testimony to Cromwell's generous and humane treatment of his men was rendered, as well as a good deal most unfavorable to the character of the dead man, who seems to have been a very drunken and brutal fellow. The only possible testimony as to the rencontre was that of Gillian, and this she was most anxious to be permitted to give in person before the court; but here both Bradford and Brewster interposed, and insisted that a written affidavit made and sworn before the governor should be accepted, a course indorsed by Standish with great alacrity.

In the end Cromwell was acquitted, but not without an exhortation from Parson Rayner, the Chaplain of the Commission, to greater reverence and tenderness for human life, to which the prisoner listened respectfully, but Standish with a covert smile playing around the sadness of his mouth, as he recalled a similar reproach long ago made to him by John Robinson, now many years gone to his rest.

Perhaps as a mark of respect to the court martial that had tried and acquitted him, possibly as a late testimony to his tenderness for human life, Cromwell's first act as a free man was to order a military funeral for Voysye, and to request the presence of the train band of Plymouth, to every member of which he presented a piece of black taffeta to make a mourning cloak.

"And now I will marry you," said Gillian, when next she saw her lover alone; but he, with a queer smile, replied,—

"Think better of it, my dear! my money is well-nigh spent, and I feel it in my bones that the next court martial will order me to be shot. You'll make a poor bargain, and that's not to your mind."

"A poor bargain indeed!" retorted Gillian, her temper flaming up; and as John Alden's boat was over from Duxbury she begged a passage in it, and an hour later was on her way to visit Betty Pabodie, as she pretended, but really to torment Sarah Brewster, who felt that she had no right to refuse her willful kinswoman shelter whenever she claimed it.

A few days later Cromwell sailed for Boston, where he remained for some months, presented Governor Winthrop with an elegant sedan-chair, taken out of one of his prizes, and was much admired and petted. Whether Gillian joined him there and was openly married to him, or whether the innate romance pervasive of the sea moved Cromwell to plan and execute an elopement for the girl, whose relatives would have been only too glad to give her to any worthy husband, we cannot tell; but that in some way they at last came together is evident, and also that they were married, since she was allowed to inherit his property. The manner of his death was one of those marvels which men then regarded as a direct judgment from heaven, but which we moderns are content to call a strange coincidence.

It was in the late autumn, and Cromwell, after a merry feast at the house of a boon companion in Dorchester, was riding rapidly homeward, when his horse slipped upon an icy slope, and threw his rider violently over his head. The night passed, and in the morning a wayfarer found the faithful beast standing pensive and patient beside his master's prostrate body, now cold and stiff; and when he was brought into the town and carried to his lodgings a wild-eyed woman rushed to meet him, and staring at the wound whence his lifeblood had drained away, shrieked, "'Tis Voysye's hurt over again," and fell in a swoon across the body.

John Higgins, who had followed his captain's body home, started in terror at that word, and coming forward drew away the hair from the wound, stared at it as Gillian had done, and hoarsely asked,—

"Was't Voysye's spook did it?"

"Nay, man," impatiently answered the man who had found him. "See you not that 'twas the hilt of the poor gentleman's own rapier did it? When I came upon him, the brass was bedded in the wound, and you may see the blood and hairs upon it now. See!"

"Ay, I see," replied Higgins heavily. "And well do I know, without seeing, whose hand it was that urged the hilt to just that spot upon my poor captain's head. Wow! But I wish I might have seen the tussle that befell when the old man got free of his carcase and fell upon Voysye man to man; nay, spook to spook. Would they still be at it, think you?"

In a month or so more, Gillian, a very wealthy young widow, sailed for England, where she married a pious and passing rich old Covenanter, whom she also survived, and became one of the gayest and least prejudiced ladies of the Court of Charles the Second, where we will leave her.

CHAPTER XXXV.

CANARY WINE AND SEED-CAKE.

It was in what Captain William Pierce called the ebb of the afternoon; that dreamy, quiet leisure hour that falls in country places when the heavy work and heavy feeding of the day are over, and the evening milking and bedding the cattle and providing the pleasant meal called supper still lie in the middle distance.

Priscilla, our own Priscilla, not forgotten or unloved, although unmentioned and a little hidden behind the throng of new-comers,— Priscilla Alden stood in the thrifty orchard of pear and apple trees, planted twenty years before by her goodman, trees whose lineal descendants may to-day be found in the place of the old ones, just as Aldens still till the Aldens' farm.

At the edge of the orchard a row of lime-trees shaded the well and the southern door of the comfortable house, and beneath these trees were set the beehives, whose dainty denizens loved the golden blossoms so well that from morning until night they swarmed up and down their fragrant pasture, making a sound like the surf upon a pebbly shore. Priscilla is gone, those trees, those bees are gone, and you and I are going, but the bees of to-day swarm just as vigorously through this lime-tree at my window as those did then, and as the bees of two or three centuries hence will through the trees whose seeds are not yet planted. Only man is ephemeral and changeable: the bees and the trees are conservative.

Some such idea, but too vague to be recognized by an unspeculative brain, floated through Priscilla's mind as, leaning against the trunk of her favorite pear-tree, she gazed up into the yellow lime blossoms, listened to the bees, and remembered the years when she and John had planted the trees, while their little children looked on and asked questions.

"Ah well, ah well!" murmured she at last. "'Tis their nature to swarm—the children and the bees, both; and Betty shall have the best hive as soon as they're settled. Ah me!"

Then with one of her old impetuous motions Priscilla dashed her hands across her eyes and cleared them of the coming tears. Good, kindly, honest eyes still, if not so bright or so brown as they were once, and as Betty's are now; and a comely matron face, albeit the colors are somewhat ripened; and the chestnut hair, lined with a silver thread here and there, is put back under a matron's coif, but the mobile lips still disclose perfect teeth, and

John Alden still holds it a delight to take a kiss from those lips, and put his finger under that smooth, round chin. 'Tis no more than later summer yet, and the frosts of autumn are as yet far distant.

"Ah well, ah well!" said Priscilla once more, and restlessly plucked a rose or two from the tall bush beside the door, those old-fashioned, sweet white roses now almost forgotten. As she pinned them in the kerchief covering her bosom, the matron paused, and with eye and ear questioned the grassy path leading from the new-made highway to the front of their own house. Yes, a horse was heavily trotting up the path, and, going around the corner of the house, Priscilla was just in time to meet Mistress Standish, mounted upon a pillion, with John Haward in the saddle.

"And glad am I to see you, Barbara," cried she, embracing and kissing her friend with more vivacity than most mothers of her day ventured to show. "'Tis a sight for sore eyes to look upon you. Where have you been keeping yourself?"

"Where housewives must—at home," replied Barbara pleasantly. "John, you can lift the saddle and cool the mare's back, but I shall not tarry over an hour, so hold you within call."

"Nay, you'll stay supper," remonstrated Priscilla as the two women went into the house, and the hostess removed her guest's riding gear. "There's a moon, you know."

"Ay, and there's a goodman at home," retorted Barbara, and then, her face suddenly losing its somewhat artificial air of cheerfulness, she looked piteously in her friend's eyes and said with a catch in her voice,—

"'Tis about him, about Myles, that I've come to see you, Priscilla."

"Why, what is the matter, dear? Is the captain ailing more than usual?"

"No, though he's far from well, and naught angers him so quick as saying so; but that's not the worst. 'Tis his soul that's sick, Priscilla."

"But how? Has the parson been at him again to join the church?"

"Nay, I'm afraid Master Partridge will never look over the things Myles said the last time he urged him so vehemently, and the captain gave way to the ache in his back, that he says is ever with him, and let out a strange oath or two about meddling parsons and I know not what. To be sure't was in Dutch, but I think parson spelled out enough of it to anger him, and"—

"And serve him right, plaguing a sick man with the catechism," broke in Priscilla. "But if not that, what is it ails the captain?"

"Why, it's not so much the captain that's ailing as Josiah, poor boy."

"Josiah ailing!"

"Yes, with a sore and sharp disease called love-sickness, Priscilla. You know he's sweethearted Mary Dingley these five years or more, and a dear, pretty, loving little maid she is."

"Yes, and what's come across their courting?"

"Why, there's where Myles is distraught. Before our Lora went, you know she and Mary Dingley were closer than sisters, and while my poor girl lay sick Mary was ever at her side, and helped us dress her for her burying"—

"Ah, the sweet saint, how pure and holy she looked when we had done!" murmured Priscilla, but Barbara hurriedly raised her hand.

"Nay, talk not on 't, or I shall lose sight of all else. 'Tis only by times I dare to speak of her. You know when our Alick married your Sally, his father would fain have had them come home to live; but Sally had liever keep her own house, and Alick felt himself old enough to be goodman,—and, well, never mind all that, but Josiah talked to me—you know he was ever my own boy—at that time, and he said when he and his Molly got wed, 'twould be his wish and will and her pleasure to come home to us, and be the stay of our old age, and so 'twas settled; but then my poor maid took sick, and there was no thought of aught but her in the house, and when she was gone, Josiah, who loved her tenderly, said not a word until the year came round and more, and then, man fashion, he spoke out more honestly than shrewdly to his father and me together, and said 't was time now that he was wed, and he would fain bring his wife to us to fill the place of her that was gone. Mayhap 'twas just the word 'fill the place' that angered Lora's father; perhaps he forgot that he was young himself once, and that God lightens the burdens that he lays upon young hearts lest they should be broken before they're used, while to us that have well-nigh done our work he lets grief crush out this world's life that we may be ready for the next. But, however that may be, the captain took mortal offense at the thought of any young woman filling Lora's place at the hearth or in the love of those who mourned her and should ever mourn her, and he said things that no temper but one so sweet as my Josiah's could have brooked. If it had been Myles, he would have broke out at his father and given as good as he got, and when o' stormy nights I think of my poor sailor lad at sea, I comfort myself with the thought that he's safe from breaking the fifth commandment. But there, 'tis not of son Myles I'm speaking, but of poor Josiah."

"And he took his father's rating in brave patience as he ever does,—so Alick says," said Alick's mother-in-law.

"Yes. Then Alick has told you of our trouble?" demanded Barbara almost jealously, but Priscilla hastened to reply,—

"Oh, no. Only he loves to magnify his brother, who is more than dear to him. But go on, Bab, with your story."

"Well, dear, I tried to talk with the captain when we were alone, but the wound was too deep and too angry to bear much handling, and so I e'en left it to nature and to grace. But at the end he consented that Josiah should marry, and he would talk with John Dingley about setting up the young folks, and he promised never to say another bitter word to Josiah about it; but on the other hand he would not go to the marriage, and he bade me tell the poor lad that he was not to bring his lass to the house either before or after they were married, for no, not for one half hour should Lora's place be filled, nor should any woman call him father so long as he lived."

"He bade Alick tell Sally as much as that, and she hasn't been anigh your house since," interposed Sally's mother indignantly; but Barbara raised her shadowy blue eyes so piteously, and looked so imploringly into her friend's face, that a misty softness suddenly filled Priscilla's own eyes, and petting the other's hand she said,—

"There, there, gossip, 'tis all right! Go on, go on."

And Barbara, smiling faintly as one well used to control her own feelings, and to make allowance for the impetuosity of others, went on: "So I told Josiah, and he told Mary, and she her father and mother, and not one of them would hearken to any marriage so shadowed, nor could I blame them. All that was a year ago, and Josiah has been as good a son as ever man could ask ever since; but a week apast or so, he spoke to me, and said his youth was going, and Mary was of full age, and 'twas not right that he should ask her to wait in her father's house till her younger sisters were married over her head, and he had made up his mind to go to Connecticut and make a home whereto he might carry his wife. John Haward could manage the farm, and Hobomok the fishing and boats, and perhaps his brother Myles after this voyage would settle down awhile at home. Oh, Priscilla, when I heard that word I felt as if the end had come, and I must e'en lay down under the burthen that I could not carry. Alick gone, and Myles gone, and my one sweet maid gone, and my two dear little fellows left over on Burying Hill at Plymouth, and now Josiah, the one whom, God forgive me, I haply loved the best"—

"No, no, it sha'n't be, it can't be," interrupted Priscilla impulsively. "Myles shall listen to reason; he shall see that what he calls grief has grown into cruel selfishness. I'll tell him so; I'll talk to him"—

"'Twas what I came to ask of you, dear Pris! Well do I know, that from the days before I came until now, Myles has held you in singular tenderness, and you may say to him things that no one else dare, and that I will not say lest he mistake it for chiding, or for want of love, or—well, now, how can I say it, Priscilla, but you know as well as I, that when a woman has once made her husband ashamed of himself, she has lost what she never will recover in his eyes. Our masters love not to be mastered by a woman, and she the one sworn to obedience."

"And so you'd put me in that place and make sure that hereafter Myles shall not love me too well!" exclaimed Priscilla petulantly, and in the same breath added, "No, no, that was but a peevish jest, and you know it, Bab. Wait, now, till I take counsel with myself, for there's a thought lurking somewhere in the back of my head that I'd fain catch and look in's face before I say more."

And jumping up, Priscilla went to a cupboard, and taking out a decanter of canary wine and a loaf of seed-cake, placed them before her guest with a napkin and a sheath-knife. Then, lifting a forefinger to silence Barbara's acknowledgments, she went to the open door, and stood plucking some withered leaves and faded flowers from the white rosebush with automatic tidiness, but with a mind altogether unconscious of the body's occupation.

A few moments of summer silence followed, that living silence of summer so different from the deadly silence of winter, and then, suddenly flinging her handful of leaves and roses upon the ground, Priscilla turned, and coming back into the room cried triumphantly, "I have it now, Barbara! 'Tis Betty!"

"Betty!" echoed Barbara dropping the morsel of cake from between her fingers. "What about Betty?"

"She's the one to speak to Myles about Josiah and Mary Dingley."

"Betty!"

"Yes, Betty. See here, now, woman; 'tisn't that I'm afeard of Myles,—the dear knows that I never yet quailed before the face of man; but, Bab, you've hit on one sad truth about our masters, and I'll give you another. They ill brook to be taught by their wives, say you, and I will add, they still love a fair young face better than one whereon they've watched the wrinkles come and the bloom fade out. Some thirty years ago I was a comely lass enough, and our gallant captain thought me so; but he's seen me at least five times a sennight ever since, and I could tell you well-nigh the day he stared long and shrewdly in my face and said in his heart, 'She's lost her comeliness'"—

"Nay, nay, Pris, he's said more than once that Sally's not a patch upon her mother."

"Upon what her mother was once, was what he meant, gossip, no matter what he said. Oh, don't tell me, Bab! If I know naught else in this world, I know Priscilla Alden, and I can spell out a page or so of Myles Standish. But pass all that, and come to Betty.

"It's not only that she's far comelier than ever her mother was, but she's fresh and new in her matronhood; as a maid she held her tongue before her elders as a maid should do, and I'll lay you a pretty penny that the captain don't guess she has a tongue, and a headpiece to keep it in, that'll match any man in the colony, if once she starts out. Now what I say is, that she shall go in boldly, as Esther did to Ahasuerus, and speak her mind, and as Esther said, If she die, she dies. Thank goodness, the captain can't kill her outright, and she can stand a strange word or two in Dutch better than poor Parson Partridge did."

"Well, 'tis an idea to think on," replied Barbara slowly, and Priscilla, knowing that the matter was settled, smiled the smile of a contented diplomat, and brushing the cake crumbs into the napkin, shook them out of the door before she quietly clenched the matter by saying,—

"I'm going over to Betty's in the morning, and I'll speak to her."

CHAPTER XXXVI.

BETTY BEARDS THE LION.

It was perhaps a week later, but as fair and peaceful a summer evening as that when Priscilla Alden showed herself more worldly-wise than vain, that Myles Standish, according to his constant custom, climbed the Captain's Hill to sit upon the sunset seat, and with sad eyes fixed upon the horizon line to muse in lonely bitterness upon the sorrow he endured but did not accept. Half an hour of solitude no more than sufficed to deaden the physical pain, aggravated by the steep climb, against which the soldier in his latter years fought in the grim silence of hopelessness, and with a long breath of relief he leaned back against one of the trees supporting the seat and wiped his forehead. The sound of a light footstep, the rustle of a woman's dress, disturbed him, and with a sudden flush of emotion he turned, half fancying that Lora herself had come to meet him at her favorite tryst.

But instead of the fair pale face, the golden hair, and spiritual blue eyes of his daughter, it was the joyous and brilliant face of Betty Alden, or as we now must learn to call her, Bettie Pabodie, subdued indeed by tenderest sympathy, but rich in color, in light, in abounding health, that met his gaze, and with a peevish exclamation he turned away, fixing his eyes again upon the water.

"Mayn't I come and sit with you a little minute, Captain?" asked Betty, seeing and hearing all, but noticing nothing, and without waiting for reply she sank down upon the other end of the bench, and for some minutes remained quite silent; then she said very softly,—

"I came here to find you, sir, for it seemed to me the fittest place."

"For what?" asked the father hoarsely, as his unwelcome companion paused.

"To speak of one I loved more than ever I loved mine own sisters." And the round firm voice grew very sweetly tender and tremulous, for it spoke no more than the truth.

"I cannot talk of her—I know you loved her, and she you—but"—

Again there was silence, for the great heart bled inwardly and made no sign. At last the girl ventured again:—

"Oh, forgive me, sir, if I seem to fail of respect to your wish, or of tenderness to your exceeding sorrow, but there's something she fain would have you know. God forgive me if I profanely touch his mysteries, but it seems to me that she who has gone straight to his presence has been sent to bring to mind words she spoke and I never yet have dared repeat. Will you say nay to her wish, dear and honored friend?"

"Words she said?" echoed the father, and, uncovering his face, he turned and fixed upon Betty such stern demanding eyes, that even her high courage almost quailed; but though her lips turned pale, she steadfastly replied,—

"Yes, words she said in the night before she went. Only I heard them."

"And God," suggested the captain as severely as if he were administering an oath.

"And God who hears me now," replied Betty, her eyes meeting his so bravely and so truthfully that his own softened as he said,—

"I marvel that you feared to tell me anything I ought to know."

"I did not exactly fear, sir, but I knew 'twould be unwelcome, and mayhap too soon to do good."

"Well. Leave skirmishing, and come out boldly with whatever it may be. I'll listen, at least."

And folding his arms and setting his lips, the soldier faced her with just the mien he would have worn in submitting to an amputation upon the field of battle. An answering courage lighted the face of the young woman, and although Standish did not then consciously notice how beautiful she was, doubtless that beauty made itself felt.

But brave as she was, Betty could not steadily endure the sombre flame of eyes that seemed to pierce the very core of her heart, and her own gaze, after a little wandering, fixed upon the thatched roof-tree in the plain below, where her baby girl lay asleep in its cradle, and her voice was calm and steady as she made reply.

"It was in the last night that our dear Lora was with us, and you had just gone somewhat hastily out of the room and out of the house"—

"Ay."

"And Lora looked after you a moment while her lips moved in prayer. Then she turned to me and said,—

"'Dear father! He'll miss me sore, and he'll grieve out of measure that he denied me my love,'"—

A bitter, bitter groan burst from the father's lips, and he buried his face in his hands for a moment, but uttered no word. Betty paused for a moment, and went on more softly,—

"'But tell him when he can bear it,' said she, 'that it made no difference and it did no harm. Before ever Wrestling spoke to me I had heard one say to my soul, The Master hath come and calleth for thee! and I have long been ready, ay, and fain to go.'"

"Said she so! Said my maid so! 'Ready, ay, and fain to go'?"

"They are her very words, her very, very words."

"I can believe it; I can believe my own lass would find some way to comfort me, even from the grave where she is laid."

"Nay, dear sir, from the heaven whither she has gone to live forever."

"I can believe that, too, from your lips, child, for you come to me as an angel. More, tell me more."

"I cannot tell all her words after those, for she grew faint and weak, and much was lost, but I gathered that her mind dwelt much upon some story Gillian Brewster had told her of a far away foreign convent, and she spoke of the leaves of a great tree that ever waved across an open door, and brought cool breezes to her head. I believe she wandered a little in her mind, and then she grew very still, and after a while she opened her eyes and smiled up into mine the while she whispered, ''Tis Mary and not Sally that will comfort him best. She'll be a daughter to him in a place next to mine. Tell him so.' Then she shut her eyes again, and we spoke no more alone."

"And it is all true truth?"

"All God's truth, sir. Oh, do you think I could say otherwise?"

"No. I know you could not. Wait." And with his head bowed upon his breast the captain took counsel with himself for many minutes. At last he looked at Betty, whose bright face now was pale with exhaustion, and said almost harshly,—

"I knew not that she cared overmuch for Mary Dingley; they were little enough alike."

"No; but don't you see, sir," replied Betty with a sort of sweet impatience, "that it was not her own likings or her own pleasure she was thinking of, but of you and your happiness? Even if she had misliked Mary and knew she would be a good daughter to you, she would have said the same."

"Yes, yes, you're right, girl, you're right, and I'm but a poor, blind, selfish old man. She'd have me think of others more than of myself. The mother getting old and no daughter to help her, no little children to cheer her,— yes, I see, my maid, I see, and I'll do your bidding—if I can."

"Oh, no, sir, not my bidding"—

"I know, I know, lass, and for all thy high spirit thou wert ever maiden meek and mild to thine elders. But it was not to thee I spoke just then. Yet now I will have thee to advise with me, for, truth to tell, I am a little fogged and stunned with all these matters, and since my sweet maid left me I've grown old and doddering—no, never mind naysaying me, I know what I know. What I will have thee tell me, Betty, is this. Shall I—would Lora have me bid Josiah bring his wife home—and let her sit in—Oh, my God! I cannot, I cannot"—

He covered his face again, and for some moments Betty sat in respectful silence, then, moving nearer, laid a light touch upon the shoulder heaving under its mighty struggle for self-control.

"Not in Lora's place, dear sir," said she softly. "No one can take that e'en if she would, and Mary Dingley would not an she could. I know her well, and a milder, gentler, sweeter maid no longer lives on earth. She is one who will ever bear your grief in mind, yet never speak of it; one who will give you a daughter's duty and tendance, yet never press for a daughter's freedom; one who will love you as much as you will let her, yet never be nettled at thought you do not love her as you might. She is as fond of Josiah as woman can be of man, yet modest and meek and shamefast as a maid should ever be. Oh, sir, she is a girl among a thousand, I do assure you, and if you will open house and heart to her you shall never, never repent of it."

"The maid must be worth something who can claim so leal a friend in you, Betty Alden."

And across that worn and haggard face gleamed a smile such as had not been seen there since Lora died. The certainty of success shot like a sharp pain through Betty's heart, and for a moment broke down the courage which failure would only have stimulated. Turning suddenly away, and leaning her head against a tree-trunk, she drew a long, gasping breath and burst into tears.

Was not Priscilla's intuition justified, and her theory proven? Had it been she herself, or any woman of her age and strong character, she would have learned self-control and so lost her best weapon; or if she had fallen into tears, the man would have simply felt that the weakness of age had overtaken her, and would have doubted the soundness of her advice. But when sweet-and-twenty weeps honestly and fervidly, and from a loving, honest heart, no man between thirty and seventy looks unmoved upon those tears; nor did Myles Standish, as hastily rising he hovered over the girl, not touching her, for no Spaniard ever treated his Infanta with more respect than this true gentleman showed to every woman, but pulling out a great handkerchief and making little futile efforts to apply it, while he incoherently exclaimed in almost the voice he might have used to Lora,—

"Why, there now, there, dear heart,—nay, child, for pity's sake—why, my little lass, don't 'ee take on so. Nay, what shall I say to pleasure thee? Come, now, Betty, come, now, dry up thine eyes like a good girl, and I'll give thee—what shall I give thee? If thou wert mine own lass I'd give thee a kiss"—

"And I'll give you one as it is, sir," cried Betty, and turning like a flash, she threw her arms around the old man's neck and pressed upon his cheek two lips so soft, so warm, so sweet, that a streak of dark red mounted to his temples, and taking the girl's head between his hands he kissed her forehead with a strange stir of reverent tenderness at his heart.

"Betty, my lass, thou'st done a good work to-day," said he simply, and she, with a smile and a, sob struggling for preëminence, murmured,—

"Thank God!"

CHAPTER XXXVII.

"MARY STANDISH, MY DEAR DAUGHTER-IN-LAW."

The lime-trees have shed not only flowers but fruit, and the bees are adding to their clover and clethra honey a last deposit from latest hollyhocks and goldenrod. The apples lie in fragrant piles beneath the orchard trees, or in a less worthy heap beside the cider mill; the maize and the pumpkins gleam in merry gold, exulting over the withered foliage that in their non-age flaunted above their heads; the barns are bursting, and the cattle sleek with plenteous corn; it is the jocund time of year when Mother Earth spreads an abundant board, and calls her children to eat and give thanks to their Creator and hers.

The waters of Duxbury Bay, placid and gleaming with the hazy sunlight of the Indian summer, reflect the sails of a dozen or more boats lazily gliding in from Plymouth, from Marshfield, from Scituate, and even from Barnstable and Sandwich, for the children of the Pilgrims have not yet outgrown the family love and interest that bound their fathers in so close a tie, and the Robinsons, children of the good pastor who so loved and so cruelly misjudged our captain, have come from the Cape to the wedding of his son, bringing with them little Marcy, to whom Standish left "£3 to her whom I tenderly love for her grandfather's sake."

Yes, this is the wedding day of Josiah Standish and Mary Dingley, whose parents have generously consented to bring their daughter to Duxbury and let the marriage take place in her future home, as the captain has requested; and now that he has given his consent, the old man gives his heart to the plan, and sends his own boat with John Haward or Hobomok laden with invitations to the old friends whom in these latter days he has almost churlishly avoided.

"Our maid would have us show true and hearty welcome to the new sister," he says rather wistfully to Betty, upon whom he leans pathetically for companionship and appreciation, and she confidently replies, "Yes, indeed, she would have it so."

"The governor's boat is coming in, father," announces Josiah, his honest face aglow with love and pride, and the captain rather heavily descends the path, and as the boat grazes the wharf extends his hand to the stately white-haired and benignant man, who grasps it affectionately and says,—

"So here we all are once more, Captain. 'Tis a great compliment these young folk pay me, when so many other magistrates are nigh hand to them."

"So many, ay," replies the captain heartily. "But shake us all up in a bag, and we'll not make one of Will Bradford, let alone that you're governor of the Colony and my boy's so cock-a-hoop that no less than the governor will serve his turn."

"Says your father sooth, Josiah?" demands Bradford, turning to give his hand to the bridegroom, who presents himself with bashful manliness, or if you please with manly bashfulness, to welcome his father's guests and receive their jocose congratulations.

"And now to business, that we may the sooner come to pleasure, for I shrewdly guess the housewife hath a crust and a cup ready for us somewhere, and so soon as we've settled these two young folk, we'll look for our reward."

So cried the captain, striving piteously after his old jocular air, as he led the way up the hill to the house, which, with doors standing hospitably open, white curtains waving from swinging casements, and groups of smiling matrons and maids standing around, presented a very festive appearance.

"You have added to your house since I was here, Captain," remarked Bradford, pausing at the top of the bluff to regard the scene before him.

"Yes. We had to make room for the young couple, and while we were about it, I pleased myself with shaping a sort of fortalice that's long been in my mind, and the rather that I forebode trouble with the Indians before many years. Hobomok is uneasy, and if the Dutch hanker too greedily for our roasted chestnuts they'll like enough thrust in a red man's paw to scratch them out."

"Why, what hath Hobomok learned? We should know as soon as you, Captain."

"Oh, there's no cut-and-dried story to tell, or I would surely have carried it to you, and as it is, I shall offer some good advice to you at Plymouth; but one thing at a time, Will, and to-night we're at a wedding and not at a council. Think you not 't is a pretty notion of a fortified cottage?"

"Why, yes"—began the governor, but the soldier eagerly interrupted him, pointing out, with the professional pride of an engineer, how the two parallelograms of the building, so placed as to form two sides of an irregular triangle, inclosed a court or corral closed on the third side by a high stockade. Into this the livestock could be driven, and the farm utensils and other outdoor property secured, at very brief notice, while portholes, cunningly masked, commanded not only the approach to this corral, but to the only outside door of the house, placed at the junction of the two parallelograms, one of which slightly overlapped the other. Three substantial chimneys, two in the southern and one in the northern wing of the house, promised domestic comfort amid all this warlike defense, and beneath the white-curtained casements cottage flowers bravely bloomed, and tossed their heads in saucy security.

"We keep the southern front for ourselves," remarked Myles with his grim smile. "Old folks need the sun to warm their sluggish blood, but these youngsters can make their own summer, for a while at least."

"Nay, you've lent them some sunshine at the east end of their wing, and well do I hope they'll lend you some of the summer of their joy, Myles." So spoke the governor, looking shrewdly into the face of his old friend; but he, avoiding the glance, slightly shrugged his shoulders, muttering,—

"He who lives will see," and led the way into the house.

The brief and bald civil service soon was said, the hearty salutes bestowed, and the sturdy handshaking over; then Governor Bradford, with an air at once paternal and courtly, led the bride to the head of the principal table, and the feast, upon which the skill of a select committee of our old friends had expended itself, began. But too many feasts have been described, and I dare not tell of the glories of this, save only of the great wedding-cake, with its choice frostwork of flowers and foliage, shaped by Betty Pabodie's nimble fingers,—a cake to be carved with much ceremony, and amid much mirth and jubilation, by the bride's own hand, with the gold ring hidden somewhere amid its sweets for the next bride, and the toy half of a scissors for the man doomed to be an old bachelor.

But at last all was over; the hunter's moon, whose culmination had fixed the date of the wedding, hung glorious in heaven, shedding almost the light of day; the neighbors' horses were saddled and pillioned, and the boats of those who came from farther afield were manned and ready; Alice Bradford, muffling herself in cloak and hood for the voyage, was changing a last word with Priscilla and Barbara, while sweet Alice Richards, her daughter-in-law, was deep in baby lore with Betty Pabodie, and the governor and the captain outside the door were by chance left for a moment quite alone. Turning by a common impulse—one of those impulses we all have felt compelling us to undreamed-of action,—they faced each other and grasped hands.

"I'm glad you came, Will," said the captain.

"Ay, and so am I. 'Tis many a year since first we clasped hands in old Amsterdam, Myles."

"More years than there are months between this and our last hand clasp, friend."

"God knows—God alone knows."

"Mind you of that other moonlight night, Will, when you and I stood by my girl's new-made grave, and you moved me to bury my revenge with her?"

"I've thought of it more than once to-night, more than once."

"He's dead."

"What, your cousin?"

"Yes. The man that slighted my maid. He's dead and buried."

"And revenge of thought as well as deed is buried with him, Myles, is it not?"

"H—m! Now, that's a fight where I'm willing to cry craven. See you here, Will, the Lord that made me fashioned me out of mere mortal clay, and his work stands fast in spite of my good will or yours to change it. While I was a young fellow, I fought the Spaniards and the Turks; in my lustyhood, I fought the Indians and the wilderness; and now, in mine age, I fight Myles Standish and the devil; and though I've as good a stomach for hard knocks as most men, I feel betimes 'twill not be a sorry thing to undo harness, hang up Gideon, and lay me down to rest and sleep."

"Not yet, old friend, not yet! We came on pilgrimage together, and we'll march shoulder to shoulder into the holy city,—that is, if God will."

"If God will," echoed Standish, and as the merry throng poured out, they found the elders standing hand in hand and face to face, with the moonlight gleaming softly over them and glistening in their eyes.